The Analytics Process
Strategic and Tactical Steps

T0141294

The Analytics Process
Strategic and Tactical Steps

Edited by
Eduardo Rodriguez

CRC Press
Taylor & Francis Group
Boca Raton London New York

CRC Press is an imprint of the
Taylor & Francis Group, an **informa** business

AN AUERBACH BOOK

CRC Press
Taylor & Francis Group
6000 Broken Sound Parkway NW, Suite 300
Boca Raton, FL 33487-2742

First issued in paperback 2021

© 2017 by Taylor & Francis Group, LLC
CRC Press is an imprint of Taylor & Francis Group, an Informa business

No claim to original U.S. Government works

ISBN-13: 978-1-4987-8464-1 (hbk)
ISBN-13: 978-1-03-209714-5 (pbk)

Visit the Taylor & Francis Web site at
http://www.taylorandfrancis.com

and the CRC Press Web site at
http://www.crcpress.com

Contents

v

Editor

Eduardo Rodriguez, PhD, is principal of IQAnalytics Inc. Canada, an analytics adjunct professor at Telfer School of Management at Ottawa University, graduate corporate faculty in analytics at Harrisburg University of Science and Technology US, creator of the analytics program at the University of Fredericton, Canada, senior associate faculty of the Centre for Dynamic Leadership Models in Global Business at The Leadership Alliance Inc., and principal–owner at IQAnalytics Inc. Research Centre and Consulting Firm in Ottawa, Canada.

Eduardo has extensive experience in analytics, knowledge, and risk management mainly in the insurance and banking industries. He has been knowledge management advisor at EDC Export Development Canada in Ottawa and regional director of the Professional Risk Managers International Association (PRMIA) in Ottawa. In Colombia, he has been Executive VP Health Care Colmena, Planning VP Insurance Colmena, corporate marketing director Fundacion Social Holding, and member of the Board of Directors of local organizations. He has been a professor at Andes University and CESA in Colombia, quantitative analyst for EDC, the author of four books in analytics, reviewer of four academic journals, and author of several publications in peer-reviewed journals and conferences. Currently, he is the chair of the permanent Think Tank in Analytics in Ottawa, chair of the International Conference in Analytics ICAS, member of academic committees for conferences in knowledge management, and international lecturer in the analytics field. Eduardo earned a bachelor's degree in mathematics, and an MBA from Los Andes University, Colombia; an MSc in mathematics from Concordia University, Montreal, Canada; Certification of the Advanced Management Program, McGill University; and a PhD from Aston Business School, Aston University in the UK. His main research interests are in the fields of knowledge management applied to enterprise risk management, risk analytics, and strategic risk.

Contributors

Katerina Andronis
Deloitte Consulting
Melbourne, Australia

Axel Benjamins
Management of Support Systems
    Department
University of Osnabrück
Germany

Stephen Burgess
Victoria University
Melbourne, Australia

Russell J. Butson
Educational Technology Group Higher
    Education Development Centre
University of Otago
Dunedin, New Zealand

Ben K. Daniel
Educational Technology Group Higher
    Education Development Centre
University of Otago
Dunedin, New Zealand

John S. Edwards
Aston University
Birmingham, United Kingdom

G. Scott Erickson
Ithaca College
School of Business
Ithaca, New York

Avi Herbon
Bar-Ilan University
Ramat Gan, Israel

Sharon Hovav
Bar-Ilan University
Ramat Gan, Israel

and

Clalit Health Services
Tel Aviv, Israel

Eugene Levner
Ashkelon Academic College
Ashkelon, Israel

Marcin Lora
Asseco Poland S.A.
Katowice, Poland

Monika Mačiulienė
Mykolas Romeris University
Vilnius, Lithuania

Tomasz Oziębło
Department of Informatics
Faculty of Informatics and
    Communication
University of Economics in Katowice
Katowice, Poland

Joanna Palonka
Department of Informatics
Faculty of Informatics and
    Communication
University of Economics in Katowice
Katowice, Poland

Gintarė Paražinskaitė
Mykolas Romeris University
Vilnius, Lithuania

Alexander Ptuskin
Bauman Moscow Technical University
    (Kaluga Branch)
Kaluga, Russia

Eduardo Rodriguez
IQAnalytics, Inc.
Telfer School of Management
University of Ottawa
Ottawa, Canada

Helen N. Rothberg
Marist College
School of Management
Hudson River in Poughkeepsie,
    New York

Aelita Skaržauskienė
Mykolas Romeris University
Vilnius, Lithuania

Arthur Tatnall
Victoria University
Melbourne, Australia

Hanan Tell
Bar-Ilan University
Ramat Gan, Israel

and

Ashkelon Academic College
Ashkelon, Israel

Agnė Tvaronavičienė
Mykolas Romeris University
Vilnius, Lithuania

Chandana Unnithan
Charles Darwin University
Melbourne, Australia

Introduction

This book is about the process of using analytic capabilities in today's organizations. This book is not about the techniques and methods used in analytics work per se. Although the term *analytics* has become a buzzword loaded with expectations for both results and the nature of those results, the aim of this book is to demystify the concept and ground it back within its operations research and management science context. Analytics as a set of tools and processes is both only as good as the nature of the data with which it is working and as good as the quality of human judgment applying the processes and understanding the outputs of said processes. That is the reason for the emphasis on analytics process in the title of this work. It is because analytics as such, as a set of tools, and data as a set of latent information are extraneous to the real outcomes with real organizational impact that are required in order to make both analytics and data concepts, such as Big Data, worth their while. What is intrinsic to real organizational impact is the considered application of these tools and the considered application of their outcomes. This work wants to emphasize analytics as part of the process of thinking that can support decision making within organizations. It wants to deemphasize the expectations by management that somehow analytics outputs or analytics as applied to other hot buzz concepts, such as Big Data, can be the end all and be all of the analytics process. They are, instead, only a step within a holistic and critical approach to management thinking that can then create real value for an organization.

For this purpose, the book has been divided into two main sections. The first section is dedicated to a discussion and clarification of concepts that will make the case for a holistic approach to management through the use of analytics and drawing from the rich operations research and management science context within which analytics tools get applied. As such, there is a strong emphasis on knowledge management concepts and techniques as well as risk management and enterprise risk management concepts and techniques and the different intersections between these literatures. The second section is a collection of articles selected for their emphasis on both the use of the analytics process within organizational contexts as well as the intersection of other organizational aspects outside of analytics that need to be brought to bear in order to make the work of analytics relevant to those organizations.

Section I, presented by Eduardo Rodriguez, has been organized into three chapters based on the following topics:

The first chapter is about the analytics process and it includes the following topics:

- The roots and pillars of analytics process
- Use of analytics in management
- Data and analytics
- Analytics professionals
- First steps in the analytics process

Chapter 2 is about the presentation of the risk modeling process as an example of the analytics process. This chapter emphasizes the combination of risk and knowledge management.

Chapter 3 is concentrated on reviewing management aspects of analytics, strategy, and management control systems. The presentation is based on the concept of analytics as a means for creating the measurements and management control systems.

Section II is written by several authors and presents a group of examples of the analytics process. These examples are represented though applications to various areas of knowledge and organizations. Each chapter is the contribution of the authors to analytics process development in the following order:

- Data, Information, and Intelligence by G. Scott Erickson from Ithaca College and Helen N. Rothberg from Marist College
- The Rise of Big Data and Analytics in Higher Education by Ben K. Daniel and Russell J. Butson
- Google Analytics as a Prosumption Tool for Web Analytics by Joanna Palonka and Tomasz Oziębło from the Department of Informatics, Faculty of Informatics and Communication, University of Economics in Katowice, Katowice, Poland, and Marcin Lora from Asseco Poland S.A., Katowice, Poland
- Knowledge-Based Cause–Effect Analysis Enriched by Generating Multilayered DSS Models by Axel Benjamins from the University of Osnabrück
- Online Community Projects in Lithuania: Cyber Security Perspective by Aelita Skaržauskienė, Gintarė Paražinskaitė, Agnė Tvaronavičienė, and Monika Mačiulienė from Mykolas Romeris University, Vilnius, Lithuania
- Exploring Analytics in Health Information Delivery to Acute Health Care in Australia by Dr. Chandana Unnithan from Charles Darwin University, Melbourne, Australia, and Ms. Katerina Andronis, Director—Life Sciences and Healthcare, Deloitte Consulting, Melbourne, Australia

- Information Visualization and Knowledge Reconstruction of RFID Technology Translation in Australian Hospitals by Dr. Chandana Unnithan from Charles Darwin University, Melbourne, Australia; Dr. Arthur Tatnall and Dr. Stephen Burgess from Victoria University, Melbourne, Australia
- Health Care Analytics and Big Data Management in Influenza Vaccination Programs: Use of Information–Entropy Approach by Sharon Hovav from Bar-Ilan University and Clalit Health Services, Tel Aviv, Israel; Hanan Tell from Bar-Ilan University and Ashkelon Academic College, Ashkelon, Israel; Eugene Levner from Ashkelon Academic College, Ashkelon, Israel; Alexander Ptuskin from Bauman Moscow Technical University (Kaluga Branch), Kaluga, Russia; and Avi Herbon from Bar-Ilan University, Ramat Gan, Israel
- Sharing Knowledge or Just Sharing Data? by John S. Edwards from Aston Business School, Aston University, Birmingham, UK

ANALYTICS PROCESS CONCEPTS

Chapter 1

About the Analytics Process

Eduardo Rodriguez

Contents

Everything has changed except our way of thinking.

Albert Einstein

You can analyze the past, but you need to design the future.

Edward de Bono

This chapter is focused on presenting the basics of the analytics process. The core of the book concerns presenting the analytics process in management and how to develop a capacity for using analytics resources in order to improve corporate performance. With that purpose in mind, five sections are included to connect the analytics process with the setting in which it will be used. In our current setting of analytics processes, we relate these thoughts as part of the inductive and deductive work, the same as dealing with intuition, and quantitative and qualitative analysis of data. All of them are necessary in analytics-based solutions.

The chapter structure is based on starting with the main concepts that are coming from multiple disciplines and presenting the adaptation of these concepts to the management world. It is the case that we need to talk about analytics in general in the same way as knowledge and to put these concepts in the setting of organizations in which analytics are more business analytics and knowledge is more in the area of knowledge management.

In this chapter, we look for the way to connect the analytics process to knowledge creation, risk management, problem solving, and decision-making processes. We consider analytics as a way to create knowledge and knowledge as a means to control risk. Analytics provides a better level of organizational intelligence, and analytics is converted into the neuroplasticity of the organizational brain connecting the dots of strategy design and strategy implementation. Analytics is the way to use intellectual capital—data, relationships, and processes—to compete and keep sustainable competitive advantages.

Section 1.1 refers to the roots and pillars of analytics. Based on the history of management sciences, we give a broad background to the field of analytics. Section 1.2 develops around the concepts of analytics and management. We discuss the relationship between analytics and the knowledge that can be derived from it and how it can inform decision making, especially within its organizational context. Two main points are presented for that purpose: first, how analytics knowledge has opportunities and barriers in a management environment and, second, the recognition that there is a kind of threat and weakness in developing analytics knowledge that is conducive to reducing the impact of analytics work.

In Section 1.3 of this chapter, the emphasis is on data and the need for data for the good development of measurement processes that are fed by analytics. Section 1.4 is related to people who work in analytics—that is, it identifies the attributes and skills that are expected from people working in analytics. Finally, in Section 1.5, the purpose is to indicate the first steps of using the analytics process in the organizational setting.

1.1 The Roots and Pillars of Analytics Work

Three topics are developed in the following sections: first, a general view of some of the background concepts of management science, data mining, and decision sciences. We use concepts that are in line with what analytics is looking toward in development of today's organizational environment. Second, this section reviews aspects of the relationship between intellectual capital, knowledge, and analytics supporting the decision-making process. The importance of reviewing these relationships is that the backbone of this book is in showing how the analytics process and its application can create knowledge that will be used to improve the decision-making and problem-solving processes in organizations. Better analytics can contribute to better knowledge, and knowledge can control the variability of the organization's results. Third, we examine ideas about how it is that people make decisions. This section describes in broad terms the concepts and assumptions that underlie our discussion of analytics as well as the scope and lens through which we propose to undertake a look at the analytics process in management.

The point to begin with is that it is important not to get bogged down by terminology. The word *analytics* is a loaded buzzword in management that can mean many different things across several disciplines. For our purposes, we want to stress the thinking and solving background of the word. The word *analytics* comes from the Greek word *analutos* meaning solvable and the Greek verb *analuein* meaning to solve. However, in management, there are multiple answers for the question of the meaning of analytics, and some of them are presented in the following paragraphs. Merriam-Webster (2012) defines analytics as "the method of logical analysis." The Oxford Dictionary (2012) points out "the term was adopted in the late 16th century as a noun denoting the branch of logic dealing with analysis, with specific reference to Aristotle's treatises on logic."

Analytics is a concept that has been used in management in the last years, but in reality, the term encompasses concepts and activities that have been developed for more than 50 years in support of management. There are multiple definitions of analytics, including factors that are key in the analytics process. Davenport and Harris (2007) define analytics as "the extensive use of data, statistical and quantitative analysis, exploratory and predictive models, and fact-based management to drive decisions and actions." And Davenport (2010) continues, "The goal for analytics is to make better decisions. However, while many organizations collect data and some organizations engage in analytics, few organizations link their analytics activities to their decision making." Furthermore, some authors concentrate analytics on the concept of rationality such as. Saxena and Srinivasan (2013) point out, "In our view, analytics is the rational way to get from ideas to execution."

In addition, Eckerson's book (2012), which covers the expertise of leading analytics, defines analytics as everything involved in turning data into insights into action. Some authors present analytics from conception to implementation as in the case of Sheikh (2013), who says, "We will use two different perspectives to lay out the characteristics of analytics: one is related to how business value is achieved and the other regards how it is implemented." Sheikh (2013) continues, saying that a business perspective deals with actions and the technical implementation is related to the techniques to implement solutions.

Nevertheless, analytics is related to the concept of creating intelligence in organizations. The word *intelligence* is part of the artificial intelligence development in the 1950s—the same as in the 1990s we referred to *business intelligence. Business analytics* and *Big Data analytics* were introduced in the 2000s (Chen et al. 2012). The idea of these concepts has been to describe the emerging need to deal with data in many different formats with high volume and created very quickly in order to develop intelligence in organizations.

Likewise, there are multiple concepts associated with analytics that are part of management science and related disciplines. One of these concepts is data mining as Baesens et al. (2009) define it: "Data mining involves extracting interesting patterns from data and can be found at the heart of operational research [or], as its aim is to create and enhance decision support systems."

These previous definitions are summarized by Holsapple et al. (2014) who presented how analytics has been defined through time. They express a taxonomy of categories: movement of management practice, collection of practices and technologies, the transformation process, capability set, specific activities to examine and manipulate data, and a decisional data-driven paradigm. All these categories interact in three dimensions of the domain of application, the type of work that is required, and the way to use methods and techniques—and at the end with the purpose of developing means to manage a data-driven, decision-making process.

Based on these analytics concepts, in this book we are concentrated on the way to use and apply analytics concepts, tools, methods, technology, and resources in general. We call the analytics process the application and use of the analytics arsenal to problem-solving and decision-making process improvement. We start by saying that the analytics process includes both deductive and inductive processes of creating actionable knowledge in organizations. These two concepts of deduction and induction capture what the analytics process is about. In every way, the analytics process requires the definition of assumptions and their validation to build conceptual and logic models that can be used to deduce conclusions. At the same time, based on data, it is possible to identify patterns and propose hypotheses that can be validated by statistical methods. The paradox is that, in some cases, analytics need to be strong enough to avoid the errors related to bad induction—generalizations that can be inferred by the review of nonrepresentative population samples.

When people in analytics are creating knowledge from theory to extend results, they are working deductively, and when knowledge is being created from data, people are working inductively in analytics. For instance, mathematics lies at the basis of analytics, and any development of thought is based on those required tasks that mathematics can support. In analytics, the purpose is not only how to use deduction and induction, but how to know and how to identify what it is possible to know. Depending on the way that the knowing process is defined and how what is achievable is identified, the analytics process can be tuned to produce better solutions in management.

Tools and concepts have evolved. There is a better understanding of how information systems, statistics, applied mathematics, computer science, and other disciplines are connected and complemented by one another. However, there are issues yet to be solved that are not just related to the development of the discipline. They are issues related to management engagement, adoption of techniques, and ways of thinking as well as the capacity to detect and create solutions to problems in organizations.

With this brief review of the basic concepts associated with the term *analytics*, the next step is to introduce the analytics process in the context of management. The following sections present the main points considered in analytics that are required to add value to organizational improvement. Analytics, in order to be effective and to provide value to organizations through the improvement of the decision-making process, need to use both rationality and intuition. Analytics needs the context and the knowledge domain at the same time as the process to build conceptual, logical, and mathematical models to provide possible solutions in the decision-making and problem-solving processes.

1.2 Using Analytics in Management

Using the ideas brought up in the previous section, we will now seek to tie them together through a discussion of the use of analytics in management. Ideally, we want to focus not simply on the application and use of particular analytics techniques. Instead, we want to focus on a holistic understanding of the processes underlying analytics techniques that can inform management decisions. This means a focus on the analytics process. Thus, the analytics process in this book is presented based on knowledge management processes. Knowledge management processes are the framework to develop actions in analytics. In general, analytics is considered to be based on a blend of rationality and intuition. Intuition is considered as a result of knowledge processes. This is more related to the development of analytics knowledge in order to use it in developing more analytics knowledge and more answers to problems and decisions. The next section introduces the basics of analytics knowledge management.

1.2.1 Managing Analytics Knowledge

This section introduces concepts related to analytics and the capacity to develop knowledge as an organization's asset that provides the appropriate actions for the organization using internal enterprise expertise systematically.

Analytics include the concept of knowledge as a concept that can be presented as a combination of information processed by individual minds with a purpose. In an organizational setting, this means developing meaningful patterns for when a person reads, understands, interprets, and applies the information to a work function.

For example, risk classification in an organization is knowledge that comes from raw data. Using analytics is a means to create knowledge—knowledge that needs to be stored, accessed, transferred, and applied.

There are different perspectives through which the definition of analytics knowledge can be studied (Table 1.1). The process of knowing can be described as a set of steps to know and subprocesses to organize the knowledge that has been developed. Knowledge meaning needs, at the organizational level in management,

Table 1.1 Perspectives of Knowledge

Perspective	Meaning	KM View	KMS View
After data and information	Personalized information	Expose to useful information	KMS is very similar to Information System (IS)
State of mind	State of knowing and understanding	Enhance individual learning and understanding, providing information	IT provides access to sources of knowledge rather than knowledge itself
Object	Object to be stored and manipulated	Building and managing knowledge stocks	IT involves gathering, storing, and transferring knowledge
Process	Process of applying expertise	Focus on knowledge flows and process of creation, sharing, and distributing	IT provides link among sources of knowledge to increase knowledge flows
Access to information	Access to information	Organized access to and retrieval of content	IT provides effective search and retrieval for locating relevant information
Capability	Potential to influence action	Building core competences and understanding strategic know-how	IT enhances intellectual capital by supporting development of individuals and organizational competencies

Source: Adapted from Alavi, M., and Leidner, D., *MIS Quarterly*, 25, 1, 107–136, 2001.

Note: KM, knowledge management; KMS, knowledge management system.

to be connected to the ways that this knowledge can be used and supported for the benefit of the stakeholder.

In addition to identifying the kind of knowledge that analytics is, there is a question about the scope of analytics and our capacity to know. Table 1.2 refers to the possibility of knowing and the difference between having the ability to know and defining what it is not possible to know based on the current and future conditions of the organization.

Based on Table 1.2, the main point that we maintain in this book is that analytics contributes to create the map of known, unknown, and unknowables. There are many things that can be known using analytics, but at the same time, there are many things that cannot be known either based on the development of analytics or because they simply are unknowable. A good example is in the application of analytics in risk management (see Chapter 2). Knowledge is a way to mitigate risk (Rodriguez and Edwards 2014), and what is key is the development of better measurement systems, better conditions to protect organizations, and better theory to develop more knowledge. "Knowledge is both measurement and theory" (Diebold et al. 2010).

In risk management, in some cases, it is not possible to measure or to assign probability values to events; they fall in the land of pure uncertainty. This means, through analytics, we can identify patterns, maintain a theoretical paradigm, discover knowledge, assign probabilities, and measure events in organizations and in nature. When it is possible to identify the events and assign a measure of occurrence, we are in the land of known things. Meanwhile, in some cases, there is not a paradigm or an event that can be identified, but the occurrence is unable to be calculated; in that case, we are in the land of unknown things. The most complex situation is when it is not possible to identify the events themselves or to measure events or if there is not a theory behind the event. In that case, we are confronted with an unknowable situation. In an unknowable situation, analytics work will be devoted to the definition of the problem or event potential. Thus, analytics will represent a means to know and to develop knowledge management (KM) processes.

Even though it is not possible to know everything, we are looking to use analytics in order to create knowledge. On the one hand, important areas must be

Table 1.2 The Possibility of Knowing

What Can We Know?	We Can Know	We Cannot Know
We know	We are able to develop means to know	We can use the time in discovering knowledge in a feasible area
We do not know	In some cases, the process of discovering knowledge from raw data	Uncertainty and potential inefficiency and ineffectiveness

considered when knowledge discovery is the priority in the analytics processes. In Figure 1.1, there is an example using a book selection process. We would like to identify a reader's potential selection. We could use different sources, from sales data to tweets or other social media. Several theories and hypotheses about preferences can be tested in order to perform the hypothesis test. The requirements of good taxonomy or analytics subprocesses are needed.

On the other hand, we are accumulating knowledge from the analytics process in order to reuse it in similar problems or decisions. The reuse of knowledge requires the definition of methods in order to store and provide access for the organization's stakeholders. What is highly important, in a system involving people and technology, which is a socio-technical system, is the identification of the manner in which people share or transfer knowledge in the search for multiple applications.

Analytics KM includes the concept of analytics knowledge creation presented by Nonaka and Takeuchi (1995), who concentrate on the interaction between two knowledge types: tacit and explicit knowledge. Tacit knowledge is represented by experience, beliefs, and technical skills accumulated in the people's minds. Explicit knowledge is the knowledge expressed in documents, data, and other codified forms.

The interactions and movements from tacit and explicit knowledge to tacit and explicit knowledge on the individual and organizational level generate knowledge creation within an organization. The dynamic is expressed through the processes shown in Table 1.3.

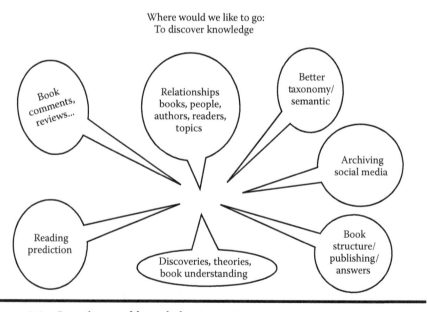

Figure 1.1 Questions and knowledge to create.

Table 1.3   Dynamic Stages of Explicit and Tacit Knowledge

From\To	Explicit	Tacit
Explicit	Combination	Internalization
Tacit	Externalization	Socialization

Source: Nonaka, I. and Takeuchi, H., *The Knowledge-Creating Company: How Japanese Companies Creates the Dynamics of Innovation*, Oxford University Press, New York, 1995.

In addition, Davenport and Prusak (1998) identified components of knowledge that can be incorporated into analytics knowledge in particular: First, the sources of knowledge are experience, values, context, and information. Second, people are considered the original repository of knowledge from information and experience. Third, processes and procedures act as means to retrieve knowledge and the way to describe and apply knowledge. Fourth, the organization is the place where the knowledge is offered and processed.

Moreover, Alavi and Leidner (2001) complemented the previous definition's components, describing the subject of interest for KM and summarizing knowledge as "a process of applying expertise." In addition, managing analytics knowledge requires the fundamentals of KM as Burstein et al. (2002) presented "a management technique to maximize the co-ordination and organization of knowledge." At the same time, analytics KM needs to identify the processes that are required by itself. Regarding that, Alavi and Leidner (2001) identified the KM processes as creation, storage and retrieval, and transfer and application of knowledge. These processes are looking to create value from intangible assets: human capital, structural capital, intellectual capital, and customer or relationship capital. To achieve the goal of creating value, the KM processes are described as follows:

- Analytics knowledge creation: Generation and discovery of new knowledge. Acquisition, synthesis, fusion, and adaptation of existing knowledge.
- Analytics knowledge storage and retrieval: Codification, organization, and representation of knowledge. It includes the activities of preserving, maintaining, and indexing knowledge.
- Analytics knowledge transfer: Knowledge dissemination and distribution within a community using different channels. Individuals, groups, organizations, and interorganizations.
- Analytics knowledge application: It is here where the competitive advantage is. This is the clear relationship with business processes.

Furthermore, analytics and KM require information systems designed to perform the required tasks. Information systems have influence in KM process development as a means to provide support to analysis and solutions in the decision-making process and as a step in transformation in organizations. The reason is that a system is an interaction of components that together search to accomplish a purpose (Alter 1999)—in particular, the business processes that people follow in order to add value to internal and external users. Organizations have followed two approaches (Laudon and Laudon 2004) to design information systems: the technical and the behavioral, which include social sciences, operations research, and computing. Both approaches can consider the following as main phases for building a system (Alter 1999): initiation, development, implementation, operation, and maintenance.

Analytics development requires the design of information systems. In our current situation, Big Data is a problem of information systems, and we need analytics to get the value of the data resources. The purpose in the design of an information system is supporting the decision-making process, feeding analytics capabilities, and taking actions. From the results of these decisions, it is possible to accumulate knowledge in order to use it later. However, the literature currently is full of new concepts that are defined enterprise-wide as an evolution of the search for enterprise-wide answers with principles of integration and consolidation, searching for the way to develop capacity in order to manage multiple business units, gaining synergies and sharing experience in order to provide better answers, services, and products to the customers: for instance, enterprise resource planning (Stevens 2003), enterprise risk management (Dickinson 2001), enterprise architecture (Zachman 1997), and enterprise content management (Smith and McKeen 2003). However, systems are more for operation and less for interpretation, workflow, and collaboration.

From this evolution of information systems and enterprise integration systems comes the knowledge management system (KMS). The KMS design requires an understanding of the five stages of the organization of KM processes: identification of knowledge areas, knowledge mapping or knowledge identification, championship and organizational support, performance evaluation, and implementation (Lehaney et al. 2004).

These stages have to be supported by a KMS, which, according to Alavi and Leidner (2001), is composed of two subsystems: technology and organization. The KMS is an information system that can help in many tasks of knowledge recovery, networking, and knowledge access. However, the KMS is not just technology oriented; it also has to include the social and cultural components of KM (Davenport and Prusak 1998; Malhotra 1999), or as has been expressed by Edwards et al. (2003), the KMS technology and people are important factors for the KMS design and implementation. Finally, Lehaney et al. (2004) summarized that the KMS is the ensemble of three subsystems:

- People interactions, KM, and knowledge acquisition are subject to perceptions and agreement.
- Technology acting as support and the way to enable the KM function.
- Organizational structures.

Analytics work requires socio-technical systems. Analytics cannot be developed without a KMS. Analytics knowledge requires collaboration for creation and application. Analytics knowledge requires people with the capacity to develop models and provide interpretation of outcomes, people with a permanent learning and teaching dynamic, and at the same time, a powerful technological structure is required.

With this view of the concepts of analytics KM and development of KMS, the next point is to identify how to develop meaning from data. The value of analytics work is based on meaning for stakeholders. The following section provides some ideas regarding the concept of meaning in analytics work.

1.2.2 Analytics Knowledge: Intelligence, Decisions, and Meaning

As mentioned in Section 1.1, Holsapple et al. (2014) reviewed the foundations of business analytics and identified three dimensions for business analytics: domain, orientation, and technique. This means application field, type of work to perform (predicting, describing, prescription), and using several tools and methods. These dimensions indicate that we need to present analytics knowledge as a combination of knowledge sources and knowledge domains. We refer to knowledge sources because knowledge comes from statistics, mathematics, computer sciences, and social sciences. It is a combination of knowledge that uses several tools and a means to provide meaning to data. Meaning appears when the outcome of the analytics process is framed by the knowledge domain. For instance, predictive analytics in the health care system and in the police department can be used with the same purpose and with similar models, but the meaning will appear when the results are interpreted and developed in each sector under the settings and conditions of the organizations. Once the meaning is clear, proper actions will come up.

Analytics is not just interested in how to use tools, but also in how analytics actions require the analytics processes and capabilities in order to provide value to organizations. Analytics can use a set of tools and abilities that can generate value added to the organization through their proper use. Moreover, analytics processes and thinking properly about analytics means applying judgment in order both to understand what tools and systems need to be applied at a given time (such as whether it is even relevant to engage in analytics activities at a given time or to what extent) and also what to do with the information output that the analytics process can provide in order that it becomes useful and offers tangible gains at the organizational level.

In summary, we develop the concept of the analytics process as the search for answers and meaning using analytics. There are many important conditions that have to be developed in order to create knowledge that can be converted into valuable actions for organizations. This book is focused precisely on the intelligent use of the important intangible assets and the outcomes provided by analytics, such that they can become actionable information products of benefit to the organization. This is by and large the focus of the case studies and chapters that are included in the Part II of the book.

1.2.2.1 Intelligence

One of the aims of the analytics process is to develop a smarter organization—that is, to develop strategic intelligence inside organizations. This means organizations with continuous learning, knowledge creation, innovation, and development of solutions for stakeholders, using it in the best way given the resources available. Strategic intelligence in this book is understood as a combination of knowledge and risk management to develop and implement appropriate strategies in organizations. Strategic intelligence is permanently evolving, and analytics is providing the means to positively consolidate that evolution. To improve getting answers and developing the analytics process and analytics knowledge means to understand what an organization is trying to do from the beginning. In this book, we summarize this by saying that organizations are trying to improve their capacity to make better decisions (Figure 1.2), to solve more problems in a proper manner (Figure 1.3), and to reduce the risk of falling into strategic and tactical traps (Figure 1.4).

Moreover, improvement in strategic intelligence is based on a decision-making process supported through analytics. This support means the contribution to the search for the improvement of human and machine decision-making processes. We need to deal not only with robots, circuits, agents, and decision software but also

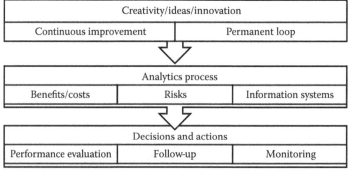

Figure 1.2 Problem solving.

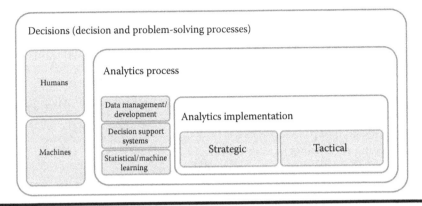

Figure 1.3 Decision making.

What are organizations trying to solve?
Avoiding falling in decision-making traps

- Bias of last information
- Keeping the status quo
- Justifying past choices
- Supporting instinct
- Problem-solving methods affecting decisions
- Lacking forecast feedback

Figure 1.4 Potential decision-making traps. (From Hammond, J., Keeney, R., and Raiffa, H., *Harvard Business Review*, 84, 1, 118–126, 2006.)

with the human creation of means to develop normative support tools and descriptive means for better decisions.

1.2.2.2 Decision-Making Process

One of the most intriguing points in management is identifying how people make decisions. There is not a consensus about the answer. There are approaches considering only components or factors associated with rational and logic steps or only based on intuition or some based in a blend of intuition, instinct, and rationality. In this book, the approach is based on a blend between rationality and intuition in specific contexts. The identification of possible barriers for good decisions is a starting point to improve analytics work for supporting the decision-making process. A reason is that the decision-making process entails dealing with the way people perceive and act in the world. Different factors are involved in decision making.

Decisions are not all of the same type. Organizations are dealing with rational and nonrational decision-making processes. Analytics move in the direction of avoiding falling into decision-making traps (Hammond et al. 2006). These traps refer to the following:

1. Giving the last information too high a weight in the decision-making process
2. Keeping the status quo
3. Justification of past decisions
4. Keeping the instinct as king
5. Managing the problem-solving capabilities
6. Not finishing the whole cycle with the understanding of what happened with prediction

The analytics process is in search of the factors influencing decisions and how to use them in a proper way to overcome barriers and decision traps. Some factors do not follow logical steps using the best tools or data to understand problems, solve problems, and make decisions. In this book, we want to use the concept of rationality as the systematic approach to solve problems and make decisions based on the use of logical thinking based on evidence. For our purposes, intuition is a level of knowledge that appears in our mind not necessarily as a direct result of perceptions without immediate evidence and a systematic way of arriving at a conclusion. This is well described by Peter Senge (1990), who points out, "People with high levels of personal mastery ... cannot afford to choose between reason and intuition, or head and heart, any more than they would choose to walk on one leg or see with one eye." This useful quote can be interpreted here as kind of synthesis of the analytics process, in which rational and intuitive thinking are permanently leading the way to approach solutions to organizational problems.

However, for many authors, analytics is concentrated on the quantitative and rational aspects of problem solving and understanding of the decision-making process. In addition, analytics needs a highly developed understanding of what is happening within the knowledge domain and the behavioral settings in order to interpret and to provide meaning to methods and results. Analytics needs to deal with the challenges of a decision-making process that is not only rational. Recent advances in the understanding of the decision-making process show the importance of considering not only ideas such as the utility theory, but also ideas around satisfaction. The following are issues that can affect the analytics process's capabilities to deal with a nonrational decision-making process: issues of considering only utility theory. Kahneman and Tversky (1979), in their article "Prospect theory: an analysis of decision under risk," identify factors that cannot be explained only through utility theory and require additional approaches to study the influence of underweighting outcomes and balance the probabilities of these outcomes with the assignment of value for gains and losses.

Moreover, Simon (1987) and Tversky and Kahneman (1986) open a window to considering in the analytics process a combination of rational capacity and intuition. This is part of the concept of behavioral economics or the understanding of how behavioral factors affect rational choices: "Of course the gut/brain dichotomy is largely false. Few decision makers ignore good information when they can get it. And most accept that there will be times they can't get it and so will have to rely on instinct" (Buchanan and O'Connell 2006). Issues involve managing a systematic process to get and use evidence. Another aspect is the use of the knowledge that has been acquired for the decision-making process. Cascio (2007) points out, "Why don't practitioners know about research that academics think is very important? Managers need not be exposed to scientific knowledge about management to practice their craft."

Several examples of the misuse of evidence appear in the practice of multiple disciplines. For example, in investment, *The Economist* (2013) had these comments about investors and irrational decisions: "Academics accept there will always be irrational, or foolish, investors but argue that these will be driven out of business by arbitrageurs who can profit from mispricings."

There are also issues with practical and theoretical reasoning. Evans et al. (1993) say about rationality, "It is argued that reasoning in the real world supports decision making and is aimed at the achievement of goals. A distinction is developed between two notions of rationality: rationality which is reasoning in such a way as to achieve one's goals—within cognitive constraints—and rationality which is reasoning by a process of logic."

As we can see, rationality is a contested concept under continuous review that requires deep study. As Shafir and LeBoeuf (2002) express, "Human rationality has been celebrated as one of the species' greatest achievements and is often considered a trait that distinguishes humans from other animals."

In some cases, a model and the analytics process do not need to be complex. It can be an organized way to develop a systematic way to infer and identify potential results based on the available data. A good example of the support to logic–conceptual models is this, which appeared in *The Guardian*, Thursday July 20, 2006: Gavyn Davies said, "The statisticians had one key piece of information, which was the serial numbers on captured mark V tanks. The statisticians believed that the Germans, being Germans, had logically numbered their tanks in the order in which they were produced. And this deduction turned out to be right." The Allies could estimate the number of tanks produced per month.

Overall, the decision-making process involves resources and people. In particular, computers, information, and minds are connected in order to develop solutions to decision problems. Creation of knowledge through operations research, decision analysis tools, data structures, and methods of sharing knowledge and collaboration are part of the support system to the decision-making process. In some cases, the machines are designed with the means to make some decisions, and at the same time, some systems are designed to make decisions based on algorithms, rules, and predefined models. The limitation of the machines, as Turing (1950) presented, in relation to their capacity to think, identifies that the human knowledge used in the creation of models can contribute to the reduction of uncertainty. With the support of machines, it is possible to develop the capacity for better modeling processes and risk management. In particular, the risk modeling process requires risk knowledge and management of the structure in order to coordinate the knowledge required in the modeling process in a decision-making process under uncertainty.

1.2.2.3 Meaning

In the end, people in organizations are looking for meaning. There is an expectation about insights and options to see reality or approach the future. The question in any approach to supporting organizations in their strategies, tactics, and control is what the value that new approach brings to the organization is. Analytics needs to demonstrate its value. Analytics work cannot be just a token aspect of the organization shown in order to pretend leading-edge advancement in how management is conducting business.

Understanding and meaning are associated with two relevant thoughts by Viktor Frankl (1984):

■ "An abnormal reaction to an abnormal situation is normal behavior."
■ "It is not freedom from conditions, but it is freedom to take a stand toward the conditions."

Part of the art and science in analytics process is to discover patterns—this is a mathematical process—and to identify how to make decisions and to solve problems under constraints. This is to maintain the known and potential conditions that can affect what organizations would like to do. Another point is that communication does not mean understanding. Sull et al. (2015) indicate that in organizations people can receive the message about strategy orientation, but in many cases, the understanding of this message or strategy is not what management expected.

Cathy O'Neil (2013), a former quant, expressed her frustration at the preparedness of the users of analytics knowledge. Part of the work of analytics is the development of a learning process inside organizations. People in organizations require a better understanding of analytics and the way that everything done in analytics can affect their own results: "Then I got put on a job where I answered the phone to the clients. And that's when my eyes really opened, and I realized that the too-big-to-fail banks, the clients of our risk firm, were using us as a rubber stamp. They weren't even looking at the numbers" (O'Neil 2013).

We use this anecdote to stress that the value of analytics in organizations is the meaning that the analytics process and thinking provide for understanding what is not evident. For example, analytics knowledge is related to supporting the knowledge discovery process. This refers to creating systems that provide understanding; for example, in a human body, millions of cells carry information that needs to be connected and organized to create life and intelligence or to understand laws and relationships among components of the organization's system. Or, in another example, it is like understanding galaxies and the universe, which, in general, requires not only the observation of millions of stars, but also the identification and understanding of cosmic laws and their relationships.

The concept of meaning from data encloses knowledge discovery from different levels of processed data. For example, knowledge can be created from raw data, and then that knowledge is converted as the basis to develop new knowledge. This is a kind of meta-knowledge. An example is when explicit knowledge from different people is deposited in knowledge repositories (documents, concepts, judgments, and so on), and it is then necessary to find patterns in documents in order to discover knowledge that is common to many experts. Another situation is when we use expert input for estimating parameters in probability distribution functions when we do not have data. We need this input to generate simulations that will allow us to understand another phenomenon or to solve additional questions, for example, in operational risk when data is scarce but we need to predict events and to measure the impact of the events on the organization's performance. Figure 1.5 shows the increasing levels of complexity on what analytics can do within organizations—that is, for example, how to identify good candidate attributes for a role based on the reports that some interviewer prepared about the candidates. Another example is taking the qualitative analysis that credit rating

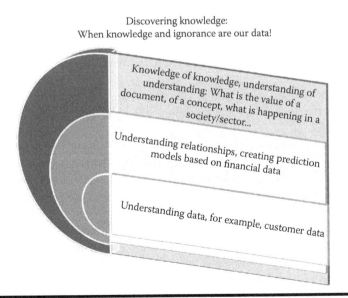

Discovering knowledge:
When knowledge and ignorance are our data!

Knowledge of knowledge, understanding, understanding of document, of a concept, what is the value of a society/sector...

Understanding relationships, creating prediction models based on financial data

Understanding data, for example, customer data

Figure 1.5   Growing in the knowledge discovery process.

agencies perform and searching for a description of patterns of the qualitative analysis that analysts develop.

However, to reach the desired level of meaning in analytics is not an easy task. There are many barriers to it that need to be considered. Therefore, analytics value demonstration requires overcoming difficulties, both technical and human, associated with areas of management, such as the following:

■ Mind sets and behaviors
■ Data management
■ Modeling process
■ Results interpretation
■ Follow-up and training
■ Control and maintenance

For example, a brief examination of what happens in organizations indicates that there are technical barriers, such as the following:

■ Data availability and its quality.
■ Model development process.
■ Syntax or semantics, words or sentences and paragraphs, documents.
■ Structuring documents, creating tags from the beginning based on user's questions.
■ Classifying, indexing, predicting, knowledge creation, categorizing, comparing …
■ Each problem can have different approaches or methods to be solved.
■ Part of knowledge discovery is in discerning what to use where.

The most prominent barriers can be human in origin, such as the following:

■ Lack of human capabilities to transform data into knowledge, understanding, and actions. "Any fool can know. The point is to understand." —Albert Einstein.
■ Following trends and fashions without a clear reason for doing it. In some cases, organizations spend precious resources paying for technologies or innovations that they do not even need and missing out on investments in technology that are required or that the organization is not prepared for.
■ Acceptance of ignorance and taking no action to reduce it. These two examples illustrate a reality in organizations associated with analytics:
  – The F-laws (Ackoff and Addison 2007): "The lower the rank of managers, the more they know about fewer things. The higher the rank of managers, the less they know about many things."
  – Dilbert (Adams 2000): "When did ignorance become a point of view?"

■ Not knowing the purpose of data. What is it for? This includes accumulating data for its own sake, having unnecessary data, or not having the necessary data.
  – Adams and Le Verrier in 1845 had a problem (Planetarium Berlin). Neptune was predicted but not observed.
■ Reduction in the awareness of potential dangers. Warning—we have weapons of mass confusion! There are many tools, models, and technologies that if not well used will create chaos. In some cases, success comes in converting these tools and models into means of mass construction!
■ Short time expectations and scope are not well defined. The path of going from "this is clear as mud" to "this is crystal clear" is a tough one. This involves bias and registration of nonrepresentative data and lack of identification of behind-the-scenes actions in the analytics process.
  – Big is not always better for analytics work and purposes. "The problem is that most companies are not succeeding in turning data into knowledge and then results. Even those that do are doing so only temporarily or in a limited area" (Davenport et al. 2001). Or the do not concentrate on improving techniques, design, and problem definition. Big Data for small-scale problems is possible, but do you really need it? More data does not necessarily mean better results.
■ Organization's planning traps can be on the way, and management is not aware of them—that is, "Bounded awareness can occur at various points in the decision-making process. First, executives may fail to see or seek out key information needed to make a sound decision. Second, they may fail to use the information that they do see because they aren't aware of its relevance" (Bazerman and Chugh 2006). They conclude saying that executives are not sharing information and limiting organization awareness.
■ It is possible to fall into traps related to maintaining the status quo or the acceptance of everything because it is not clear that in the process the organization is looking to confirm what it wants to see or expect. This is what is called "the confirming-evidence trap: This bias leads us to seek out information that supports our existing instinct or point of view while avoiding information that contradicts it" (Hammond et al. 2006). This trap is complemented by estimation and forecasting traps—that is, "estimation and forecasting: While managers continually make such estimates and forecasts, they rarely get clear feedback about their accuracy" (Hammond et al. 2006).

Thus, on the one hand, the analytics process is in search of creating a more intelligent organization that makes better decisions and provides more solutions to organizations. On the other hand, the analytics process requires a motive to act in order to provide value—value that is possible only if we provide meaning for data. And the search for meaning requires overcoming several organizational barriers.

This means answering different kinds of problems and tasks in the organization's plans and their implementation. The next section addresses this topic.

1.2.3 What Are the Types of Questions, Problems, and Tasks in Analytics?

The analytics process is an approach to answer many questions in management. Diverse fields of activity by sectors or type of processes require solutions using multiple approaches based on analytics work. In this book, we can identify three situations for the use of the analytics process: first, the search for answers that are related to general and practical analytics areas and development of logic–conceptual models in the problem-solving process; second, development of the theory that analytics requires; and third, control of the analytics process such that it provides correction to errors.

The first situation requiring the search for answers related to general and practical analytics areas are represented by the cells in Table 1.4. This table shows a kind of SWOT connection of areas in which analytics theory and conceptualization is required and needs development. In each cell, the idea is that analytics needs to contribute to supporting organizations in being better at reaching opportunities and managing risks. This is possible through the following:

1. Predictive analytics: This is not only about forecast, it is about classification and identification of behaviors.
2. Descriptive analytics.
3. Soft analytics: Problem-solving methods, decision-making processes, and the capacity to develop conceptual models. This is part of documents and

Table 1.4 Analytics as a Way to Support Multiple Areas

	Strengths (Internal)	*Weaknesses (Internal)*
Opportunities (external)	Strengths/opportunities, probably justifying immediate action planning or feasibility study	Weaknesses/opportunities, likely to produce good returns if capability and implementation are viable
Threats (external)	Strengths/threats, only basic awareness, planning, and implementation required to meet these challenges	Weaknesses/threats, assessment of risk crucial; when risk is low, then we must ignore these issues and not be distracted by them

includes input for forward and backward analysis, cause–effect analysis, and many others in management.

4. Searching for the best analytics and optimization: prescriptive analytics.

A second situation is the development of the theory that analytics requires: This is based on the application of the source theory. Figure 1.6 shows areas in which the application of analytics is contributing to developing theory and practice in management areas—areas such as human resources need analytics when the project is designing a benefits plan for all employees or special executive packages. The benefits plan is associated with the strong and solid use of actuarial science in combination with performance measurement systems. The request of analytics could be

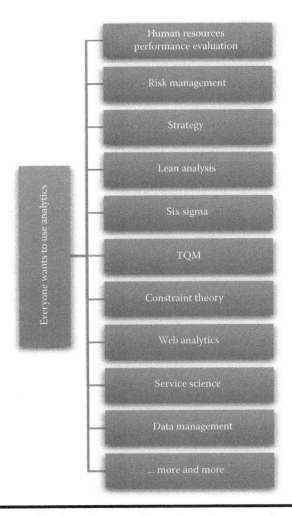

Figure 1.6   Areas of application of analytics knowledge.

the same as the web channels needed to measure its use. In the end, application is a problem that comes across any process and organizational area because everyone needs to measure. Analytics is a way to measure and to find the way to achieve the metrics that the organization has defined.

Theory development comes from a variety of knowledge domains, for example, from actuarial science to semantic web, but common sources of analytics knowledge. Some examples of these sources of analytics are shown in Figure 1.7, and include the following:

1. Statistical multivariate analysis
2. Decision support systems
3. KM systems
4. Operations research
5. Information and communication technology
6. Computer science
7. Machine learning
8. Risk management

Finally, the third aspect of analytics work is related to control of the application of the analytics process. It can be involved in operational risk management from the point of view of the solution. This means searching for the correction

Figure 1.7   Examples of analytics knowledge sources.

of errors. There are interesting examples that illustrate the need for analytics in this field. There is a kind of risk that emerges in organizations when more analytics are involved. There is a need to audit, stress test, back test, or in general apply methodologies to ensure good modeling processes. This means form data up to the possibility of using analytics. A good example appeared when on April 16, 2013, Mike Konczal wrote, "In 2010, economists Carmen Reinhart and Kenneth Rogoff released a paper, 'Growth in a Time of Debt.' Their 'main result is that … median growth rates for countries with public debt over 90 percent of GDP are roughly one percent lower than otherwise; average (mean) growth rates are several percent lower.'" A critique of the Reinhart and Rogoff paper came from Thomas Herndon, Michael Ash, and Robert Pollin of the University of Massachusetts, Amherst (2013), in which they, pointed out, "… three main issues stand out. First, Reinhart and Rogoff selectively exclude years of high debt and average growth. Second, they use a debatable method to weight the countries. Third, there also appears to be a coding error that excludes high-debt and average-growth countries. All three bias in favor of their result, and without them you don't get their controversial result." Examples such as this illustrate the capacity of analytics to correct errors and even uncover infractions when dealing with data.

This section has shown three main pieces to connect the analytics process and management. First is the basis of analytics KM, a second aspect related to the search for meaning and value in the analytics process and thinking, and the last section connected the search for meaning and value with three big tasks of analytics regarding the answer to problems in organizations, theory development, and the control of the analytics process itself. From the previous example, there are some takeaways: First, data needs to be reviewed, tested, validated, probably shared, and open; second, the models need to be validated from different angles and include a complete assumptions validation; third, develop a means to permanently and systematically document the analytics process and bring inputs to practical results before getting the final result without enough validation. This analytics process needs to demonstrate the value for the organization when performing some tasks and solving specific problems, and the analytics process and thinking are based on data and its management. The next section refers to aspects associated with data and its use in analytics.

1.3 Thinking about Data and Analytics

To create knowledge from data, we need to develop the analytics process and improve the organization's actions based on analytics. However, data is the source material of the whole analytics process. As we mentioned in this book, the concept of analytics is associated with the measurement process, and based on this, the analytics process is a set of actions in measurement, and conversely, when the measurement process is performed, the process has to create metrics or outcomes based on analytics. Measurement is based on data. Data is not only important for model development. Data is also the basis of the analytics process and requires that it be clearly defined from the beginning as to in what way the data will be used in the analytics process. There is a clear and important premise: Data will have value if data use is defined. In most cases, data is gathered and created for a reason: because of a particular goal identified by the organization that needs to be measured or because there is a need to control and develop some actions in processes.

In some cases, accumulation can be important even when the data use is not clear. (A lot of Big Data is accumulated, and analytics has not been performed, which is short of the search for meaning.) But, in principle, for business analytics, it is important to think from the beginning about the use of data. If the use of data is not clear from the beginning, potentially data will be available, but it may not have the proper attributes when it is required to create knowledge and improvement of the measurement processes.

Moreover, issues about data are not just due to availability; they are also related to the willingness to use or to improve raw data in order to create new and more valuable data. Pfeffer and Sutton (2006) note, "Evidence-based medicine and evidence-based management require a mind-set with two critical components: first, willingness to put aside belief and conventional wisdom …; second, an unrelenting commitment to gather the facts and information necessary to make more informed and intelligent decisions, and to keep pace with new evidence and use the new facts to update practices."

The weak attitude toward developing data as an asset and facts use are presented as potential disconnects between the environment of the current and future organization in which data will be available everywhere with much value and quality. However, the organization needs to develop capabilities in order to put the opportunity to good use. In addition, there are human issues related to managing data-driven decisions and actions based on and dealing with facts. Below are some related quotes that illustrate the point:

- "Get your facts first, and then you can distort them as much as you please." —Mark Twain
- "Wisdom is merely knowing what to do next." —Anonymous
- "A beautiful theory, murdered by a gang of brutal facts." —Thomas Huxley

Data used as an asset and as part of the intellectual capital of the organization are concepts that need to be prepared for the waves of data that have influence on the way that we do things in the present and the future:

- Semantic web: When data on the web is available, or better, when the web is a data source.
- Standardization of reports: When all public companies have the same type of report for their results that are directly written in XML.

- Open source and research: This is when data can be analyzed using R, Python, and many other great tools, languages, and means that require a low investment on the hard side but place importance on the human side of analytics.
- Data available everywhere and anytime: Examples in which counties, cities, and organizations are making data available to everyone.
- Maturity of models: For many years, most analytics models have been in the knowledge market; now the maturity of the models is good, and all they need is their application.

These concepts promote the observation of the analytics process as the connection between data and meaning. However, the connection requires the development of data management capabilities, the same as dealing with the use of data and the results from data in management.

1.3.1 The Concepts of Small Data, Big Data, and Great Data

The next subsections indicate a transition from small data or regular data, Big Data, and meaningful Big Data, which we will call Great Data in this book. It includes the measurement process as the basis for analytics endeavors.

There are different types of data. Or, rather, data can be classified in multiple ways, according to its size, measurement scales, and some other attributes, such as structure, access speed, and so on. There are data that can be considered continuous, discrete, and that can be represented by categories—that is, static, deterministic, or random; there are data that are structured, data that are unstructured, and data that come from multiple sources and with various formats. Analytics needs to deal with all of these types of data.

Currently, people are talking a lot about Big Data potentially converting the concept into another management fashion. Analytics has to be understood as the way of studying the proper use of data that has been created. Given the presentation of Big Data within the organizational environment we use here, the term *small data* is used to refer to regular data that is structured and that is related to databases or data warehouses that are predictable and certain.

Big Data refers to massive data that can be created based on attributes of the 4 Vs: variety, velocity, veracity, and volume. In the end, however, Big Data is a problem in information systems: Although Big Data can exist, the point in this book is that analytics is required in order to use the data and create meaning. There is no value in just having a huge volume of data or many sources. What is conceptually important is to understand how this Big Data will be analyzed and will create value. Accumulation, volume, and variety are not worth it as such. Thus, Big Data is not analytics, and it is not Big Data analytics. Big Data is, in the end, a potential source of knowledge that needs analytics for it to be used. As I mentioned, Big Data is a problem in information systems and computer science. Analytics of Big Data is the use of the methods and techniques to analyze Big Data. In the end, the purpose is to provide meaning to Big Data—that is, Big Data can be a source for solving a problem that requires analytics for its solution.

Analytics is related to the means for managing and getting meaning from data: cloud computing, parallel computing, machine learning tools, statistical learning, and other technologies. The use of these methods and technologies for discovering knowledge from data requires enough people who are sufficiently trained—people capable of analytics processes not limited to knowledge of some tools or means to manipulate data. The work cannot be performed only by technical people. Analytics work is a combination of collaboration and individual input for problem solutions and meaning identification. Many areas in management can be updated to utilize current advances. People cannot continue using only the basic tools they need to do more (improve, create, solve) with what they have at hand (scope economies). In many cases, people do not know what to do with what they have in their hands in order to solve more problems in organizations. Computation and analytics go together, but it is the user and modeler who will take advantage of the resources available.

Many Big Data concepts are not for organizations in the Stone Age of analytics. For the most advanced, if there is not a clear analytics process, probably it has applied Big Data approaches when they are not required. For example, an organization can perform a good market analysis or auditing study using a correct sampling process, and it does not require Big Data. The same happens if the experiment or the problem is not well defined: The Big Data source is not a solution. Or the worst can be when the data is available but can have a lot of bias. For example, some types of studies related to sentiment analysis through social media. However, the principles needed to manage Big Data can contribute to using data in a more productive way in organizations even though the data is not *big* enough yet. Just think about the issues related to data governance for documents. Once you have a lot of data deposited in repositories of documents, what is this resource for? There are many different problems associated with documents in an organization. An example is related to guidelines, manuals, and working documents. In the documents, there are not only raw data, there is also knowledge. In many cases, it is not possible to access and to use it. For instance, finding what people need can be a difficult issue to solve. Likewise, keeping documents in good shape, updated, and organized in a proper manner is also hard, and many people might lose trust in using the data inside documents if they do not believe they will be up to date. Instead, people will prefer to ask other people or the source or creator.

The priority in dealing with data and data analytics, no matter the size, is related to the development of the following:

■ People competencies for performing analytics work
■ Trust and alignment in the performance and strategy definitions
■ Accessibility for many stakeholders with clear and consistent definition of data components
■ Usability of data, models, and technology

- Learning and knowledge discovery as a continuous process
- Identification of the problem–tools–people relationships

Based on that, we propose to leave size as an attribute that can affect the information system's design and use. However, the main point for the analytics process is the capacity in development for creating a smarter organization and from data to provide meaning. Thus, it is required to develop the transition from Big Data concepts to the Great Data™ practice. Great Data is Big Data that has meaning (Figure 1.8).

This transition is based on these principles:

- The value of Big Data is in being insightful.
- The pillar is the design of a process for providing meaning.
- Problem-solving orientation.
- Knowledge-creating structures.
- Connection of analytic tools and problem solution.

In big data analytics, it is appropriate to use the VIBO model. The VIBO model is a conceptual model to frame what the analytics process requires to be implemented in using Big Data. The model is compose of four pieces:

V is the Vs of Big Data
I is the Is related to impact
B is the Bs related to business
O is the Os related to the organization or operation

The Vs are all these attributes that we give to Big Data: velocity, variety, veracity, volume, and many others. The Is represent some aspects to consider in order to reduce the risk of being involved in a Big Data project with low preparation or when it is not required. We need to remember that having more data is not the solution

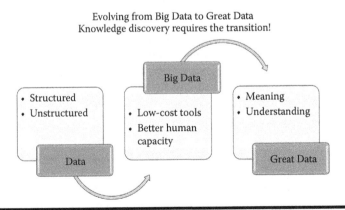

Evolving from Big Data to Great Data
Knowledge discovery requires the transition!

Big Data

- Structured
- Unstructured

- Low-cost tools
- Better human capacity

- Meaning
- Understanding

Data

Great Data

Figure 1.8 Transition from Big Data to Great Data.

to the organization's problem. Big Data is a problem of information systems that provide an opportunity to solve more problems with the proper use of analytics. The Is can be summarized as follows:

1. Identification as a management of scale
2. Intelligence as a formal process of searching for solutions
3. Interpretation as data in a context and application
4. Importance as the reduction of the bias analysis, good sampling
5. Interest as the clear expected value search
6. Integrity as a permanent data cleaning–organization process
7. Integration as accommodating data properly
8. Improvement as ensuring continued results
9. Inherent as guided by organizational processes
10. Impact as the creation of value, application, and usability in the organization

The VIBO model involves the Bs related to business development and bringing to attention what in any Big Data analytics process should be considered:

- Business: All work in analytics and Big Data needs a link with the organization's business risk control.
- Benefit: In search of benefit not necessarily profit-related or economic but with a clear purpose.
- Barriers: Clearly defining limitations and gaps in the analytics process.
- Boundaries: There is a problem of scope—working or building by blocks.
- Background: Developing and building based on previous understanding or feedback.
- Bridging: Creating the spaces for connecting areas and disciplines in order to provide better solutions.
- Building: Generating the actions with the support of what the model's outcome is and a permanent review of the results.
- Benchmark: Keep the process up to date with the best resources available.
- Boards of directors: The hope is everyone is connected and understanding.
- Behavior: Managing the learning and teaching process, reviewing the way to gain good attitude or willingness to solve the problem in a good or correct way.

Finally, the VIBO models consider as key in any Big Data analytics project the Os represented by embedding all steps in the following:

1. The organization's systems that are supporting the business process and data governance
2. Operations and production in any way to add value
3. Opportunities for improvement and developing sustainable competitive advantages for the organization

The application of the VIBO model can be done in any setting. Let us first look briefly at an example related to risk management in which knowledge discovery is indispensable. In risk management, there are many opportunities to apply Great Data based on the VIBO model, such as in citizen risk management. The following three examples could be an open reflection of if there are possibilities to derive patterns from Big Data in a field such as risk management and to think if analytics is required. In 2014, there was in Canada a tragedy described by the infliction of damage; it was registered: "… has several anti-police and pro-gun posts on his Facebook account" reported the *Epoch Times* and comments such as "make a person disappear, and no one will ever miss you." The idea is if this type of data can guide one to describe any potential behavior. That is part of a trash metal band's song and reported by the *Epoch Times*.

Another example was a case in Calgary in which a pattern was identified because of the music and lyrics. "Dread and the fugitive—the world needs a hero," which refers to a song and album from a thrash metal band and reported by the *Montreal Gazette*. A similar data situation is present in a Mexico tragedy where a text read, "It may seem that I am very calm, but in my head I have killed you at least three times," and was sent through Twitter. In these three examples, text can be related to profiles that can identify some behavior that can affect the integrity of people. Possibly, Big Data analytics could identify traces or patterns. This does not mean that it can be an easy task, but with some tools and good work on gathering appropriate data, possible patterns can be used for early warning systems to control risk and, in some cases, avoid negative events.

Another application of the principles of Great Data is when there is in the marketing field a search for a better understanding of customer behavior. Issues can arise if the work is not correct in its interpretation and use of the data. For example, when McDonald's in 2012 used Twitter as a means to promote new products, the reaction was not the expected one. The communication strategy created a negative impact on the brand because of the negative sentiments that were expressed by consumers using Twitter. For example, this is a comment that was part of the McDonald's experience: "It was hoping that the hashtag would inspire heart-warming stories about Happy Meals. Instead, it attracted snarky tweets and McDonald's detractors who turned it into a #bashtag to share their #McDHorrorStories" (*Forbes*). As well, in information science, there are many opportunities for developing markets for books, for organizing contents, etc., using Great Data principles the same as in other organizations. Here are some examples:

■ Using explicit knowledge as data. Our way to think about text (potentially explicit knowledge) has changed since we converted text into vectors and matrices.

■ Understanding the black box further. Converting into mathematics the problem of dealing with language, text, or explicit knowledge.

The question continues: How does Great Data™ work? We have in mind the following steps: Problem definition and methodological considerations should come first and then the tools to solve the problem. Second, prioritize understanding and the creation of meaning. Third, develop the awareness of a correct use of technology. Technology is often not the main issue in managing Big Data but rather the whole of our capabilities to deal with the data in analytics steps. The analytics steps are where the value is created. To have access to tools is not a difficult or costly part in the analytics process. Hadoop and friends are free. Hadoop is a group of tools, but the important part is to define if we need them and how we are going to use additional subsystems and tools to generate value from the Big Data. For example, focus on understanding the process that leads to solutions. This is what will create value, or put in another way, knowledge discovery is a product of a well-defined problem-solving process.

This transition toward data with meaning requires a measurement process as the guide in order to develop any action and solution. The next section describes the measurement process.

1.3.2 Measurement Process

A measurement process is a set of steps all connected in order to create, control, and put in practice measures and metrics within the organization. The measurement process is the support of a whole set of other processes in the organization. Planning, strategy, control, operations, and in general all the areas in any organization require measurement systems. From them, analytics is part of the method to better make the measurement system. The process can be described through these steps:

- Start from the goals of the organization.
- Review the business processes and the way that they are related to the goals.
- Make it part of the management control systems.
- Keeping understanding of the relationship between analytics and the business processes along the organization is key.
- Maintaining data alignment and availability is crucial.
- Review business process steps with partial results that contribute to the final one.
- Organize final values of metrics as part of the cause–effect relationships of business process steps.

Analytics and metrics are tools of the performance evaluation system in organizations. There are relationships among data and measurement processes as a way to create knowledge and actions. These relationships are all in the analytics process. With analytics, the measurement process is in action, and the measures and metrics are part of the outcomes—outcomes that can be scores, parameters, indicators, etc. Metrics require a good definition on the one hand and attributes such as the following:

■ Metrics are based on goals, and they have dimensions, such as time, geographical areas, or products. Dimension means, for example, that we can measure sales, but how often? Every second, every year …?

■ This means a metric cannot be just a number; it is a piece of business knowledge with potential for creating additional knowledge.

■ The same goal can have different metrics. Metrics, planning, and reporting are connected.

■ Metrics can work for expressing the same kind of event, activity, or phenomena in different and equivalent ways. For example, a ratio can have as numerator income, and you can express income in many ways keeping the same denominator.

■ Information and KMS start from what we want in order to be measured. Metrics can be very good in theory but not feasible or understandable in practice.

■ Metrics can have assumptions that are key to the correct problem understanding, problem scope, and problem definition. For example VAR—a phenomenon can be described by many metrics or it can be possible to split metrics into pieces, factors, or terms.

■ Metrics could be considered in groups: deterministic, currents and facts, forecasts, and random. The treatment in the analytics process will be different because of the models that are deterministic or stochastic. The results will be considered in different ways as well. In the deterministic area, the result will be a fact, and in the stochastic, the result will be associated with statistical metrics, such as expected values, variance confidence intervals, or more elaborated such as risk adjusted return on capital (RAROC).

On the other hand, in measurement systems, we need to create time series. This means the analytics for forecast, for example, is not only studying probability distributions, but also considering time as a factor affecting the results of the studied variable. The time series by themselves will be analyzed, and analytics methods will be used in order to identify patterns and behaviors in the metrics—metrics that are representing a phenomenon. Metrics have to be kept and organized as new data that constitutes the time series, this means the analysis will be the same as other data, and the interpretation in many cases will be related to variability—variability that can be an expression of risk.

A measurement system needs some elements of control and standards, for example, a clear description or understanding of the concepts and data required as well as correct use (consistency) of label names of the variables or metrics and alignment of the reports—that is, for instance, in order to avoid referring to office turnover with different denominators or numerators or both. Another element would be connecting everything to the business process steps more than specific areas of the organization (the organization's chart) that are continuously changing. In addition, a metric should, in principle, be general in nature and a variant specific for functional areas. For example, productivity—we need to use the same concept at the aggregated level for the organization or for areas or business units or control units. This means productivity according to the resources and outcomes of the processes related to functional areas.

The final point to keep in mind in a measurement system regarding analytics is the need for reviewing metrics, models, and outcomes against reality and the plans that the organization had. The system as it should be needs permanent feedback. A metric can be modified or improved permanently given better knowledge reached through analytics. In order to design and perform the measurement system, the organization needs people, and those people have some particular attributes, which are described in the following section.

1.4 Who Are Analytics Professionals?

As we have seen, good thinking about analytics must consider different aspects and concepts in order to apply good processes to good decisions. But just who is carrying out these processes? Who are the people that must think and apply analytics in order to offer value to the organization? In this section, we will attempt to examine and assess some of the expectations placed on analytics professionals and offer some thoughts on what we consider positive ways to view the work of people working in the field.

Many people have been working in management science, analytics, and related fields for years. In this section, we talk about the skill set of people in analytics and the need for organizations to adapt in order to maintain these valuable assets in ongoing development for the good of the organization. The current difference with what happened with people in analytics some years ago versus what is happening now is mainly along two lines: First, there is a new and abundant valuable asset that is not very expensive called *data*. Second, more clarity has been incorporated in management areas about the value that people with analytic skills bring to organizations—people who have been involved in many projects and processes in organizations, such as statisticians, applied mathematicians, computer scientists, and all STEM professionals.

The current point in human resources is that there is a belief that searching for analytics people can open a path for advancing the organization's intelligence. There are excellent opportunities not only for participating in projects and supporting more decisions, but also promoting risk control and management of expectations.

However, a company cannot hire analytics people thinking about them as magicians who will solve all problems or who can have a perfect solution for every problem in the organization. Barton and Court (2012) comment on the three capabilities that companies should have, and all of them will be part of the analytics expert work: "First, companies must be able to identify, combine, and manage multiple sources of data. Second, they need the capability to build advanced analytics models for predicting and optimizing outcomes. Third, and most critical, management must possess the muscle to transform the organization so that the data and models actually yield better decisions."

In organizations, and given the buzzword status of *analytics* and *Big Data*, people supporting analytics work are being considered data scientists (DSs). The question is if organizations are presenting DSs as super humans (see Figure 1.9)—mainly in a management setting. DSs are people who can belong to the z-generation and thinking in p-dimensions of the data that they use in their work and in the ways models need to deal with multiple dimensions even to reduce many dimensions to two or three for analysis and creating visualization methods. This means they have been involved in a world with technology that carries data everywhere, and data are no longer of one type or representing only few things. This is then related to the dimensions of the way that people can perceive reality, depending on how many dimensions they are observing and whether they find value in understanding that reality.

A DS is a blend of many valuable skills and capacities. A DS is a person who combines technical skills and people skills. The reason is that a KMS requires knowledge creation at the same time as knowledge sharing and application. People are interacting with technology and processes, and in the end, the analytics process and thinking is a complete symbiotic development through people interactions and the support systems that are created (Figure 1.10).

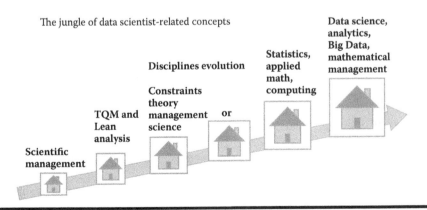

The jungle of data scientist-related concepts

Data science, analytics, Big Data, mathematical management

Statistics, applied math, computing

Disciplines evolution

Constraints theory management science   or

TQM and Lean analysis

Scientific management

Figure 1.9   Evolution of quantitative disciplines in management.

What a data scientist is

A good blend of good things:
- Achiever and thinker
- Computer scientist
- Applied mathematician
- Statistician
- High EQ worker
- Organizations learner
- And more...

A surrealist human,
A super human,
A really great organizational
resource

Painter Oleg Shuplyak

Figure 1.10 A DS is a blend of good things.

DSs are looking to support what organizations are trying to do, which is based on enhancing processes to solve problems. These include better approaches through the following:

- A formal scientific method (not Taylor's vision) of thinking (Lean analysis is an example, systems thinking)
- Following systematic steps for the problem-solving process
- Developing means for supporting the decision-making process
- Creating and conserving management control systems
- Motivating actions based on evidence and an objective search of explanations and solutions to problems
- Looking forward to building supported, prospective views
- Consolidating the competencies required to add meaning to data
- Answering more complex questions every day (questions that, in many cases, have been there forever)
- Being better in the measurement of efficiency and effectiveness
- Developing methods for defining and achieving targets

Thus, DSs are at the end working using specific capabilities (Figure 1.11), such as the following:

- Programming: back-end programming, front-end programming, systems administration
- Stats: classical statistics, data manipulation, science, spatial statistics, surveys and marketing, temporal statistics, visualization
- Math: algorithms, Bayesian or Monte Carlo statistics, graphical models, math, optimization, simulation

A complex mix of skills:
How can a person fit in this profile?

- **Data businessperson:** businessperson, leader, entrepreneur
- **Data creative:** artist, jack-of-all-trades, hacker
- **Data researcher:** scientist, researcher, statistician
- **Data engineer:** engineer, developer

Figure 1.11 A complex mix of skills.

- Business: business, product development
- Machine learning/Big Data: big and distributed data, machine learning, structured data, unstructured data
- High EQ: in the sense of adaptation, collaboration
- Data business person: business person, leader, entrepreneur
- Data creative: artist, jack-of-all-trades, hacker
- Data researcher: scientist, researcher, statistician
- Data engineer: engineer, developer

All these above points are the bases to define the roles and tasks that I mentioned in the previous section. The support is converted into specific roles, such as the following:

- Data management
- Information science
- Data mining
- Text mining
- Business intelligence
- Strategic intelligence
- AI, robotic, machine learning
- Semantic web, converting the web into a web of data

These roles include users of the outcome of the activities that DSs perform. In most cases, users of DSs' work are not focused on the methods or tools used in problem solving. This means sometimes what is in the black box or behind the scenes is not a priority for the user to understand. Users are looking for answers or outcome interpretation and not just the method used for the solution. Nevertheless, there is a need in organizations for a better learning and teaching (analytics knowledge transfer) process to improve communication between technical people and users (Rodriguez and Edwards 2014) because gaps in knowledge sharing processes can affect the outcomes of decision-making and problem-solving processes. There is a need to understand and manage many concepts related to the DS's work from technical people and from users of their work.

On the one hand, there is a need to deal with tools to be used (Figure 1.12)—tools that are coming from many disciplines and that carry a wide set of assumptions for their application. These tools are created through the convergence of knowledge coming from mathematics, statistics, computer science, and some other areas, such as biology and social sciences. What is key is that the evolution of technology and its capacity to get better solutions is found on the way through which organizations adapt to these new developments. In organizations, the time to mature, use, and align resources or capabilities that are available and strategy design and implementation can be very long. In many cases, they happen only for a reduced knowledge transfer. Some examples are the following: First, some of the analytic tools are created because basic models are put in the knowledge domain or context in which the model could be applied, for example, stochastic processes, such as the Brownian process identified with biology and its relationship with risk management.

Second, the search for the explanation of some phenomena in specific fields has provided ideas in order to open new model creation. A good example is to go from research in neuroscience and to connect the neural networks creation model that can be used in many problems.

Third is using the understanding of what is not possible to do or to know in order to define the scope, constraints, and assumptions for developing models. A good example of tools in this area is when optimization and prediction models are used. The underlying relationship of the variables in their context allows a definition of a model from the mathematical structure to the final usable model.

Fourth, there is the understanding that tools are, in most cases, the structural or basic mathematical model. The models needed for answering what is happening in a given problem require the identification of parameters; for instance, in a multiple regression (the structural model), the final model to use is the one for which the variables have been selected and the parameters estimated. Another case is when, based on linear models, we learned to classify objects, and the machine learning algorithms connect these approaches, creating decision and classification trees.

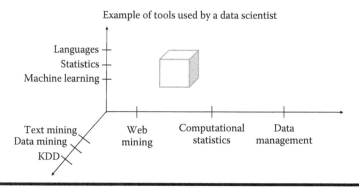

Figure 1.12   Intersection of skills.

On the other hand, the set of concepts that are related to analytics and DSs' work is composed of the design and creation of plans, blueprints, and structures for having what is required to perform the analytics process. In Figure 1.13, the representation is based on a cube that contains other cubes. The meaning is that each block is part of a bigger block, and the development of solutions in analytics needs the full ideal objective built, and in order to get there, it is required to build by blocks. The final goal of the analytics process can be related to a blend of management control systems, enterprise risk management, strategic development, etc. The concept starts from what the organization wants to do and works backward in order to build the data or text mining capabilities, reports, and measurement systems for corporate and individual performances.

Thus, a DS is in the practice of dealing with tools in order to understand data and processes to create the structures not only to manage data and tools, but also stakeholder relationships. The DS's work is based on the KM process because a DS is developing a KMS to put data of any kind into the service of building and keeping strong the sustainable competitive advantage of the organization. The value proposition of the organization is developed through the organizational design in which analytics is the nervous system that creates intelligence through the development of the analytics "brain."

In the end, a DS is not a super human; it is a person able to connect the dots for converting knowledge into actions: tactical and strategic. A DS can be defined based on Abell's model (1980) (Figure 1.14) in the way that the DS's work is like a business definition in terms of the functions that he or she can perform, the

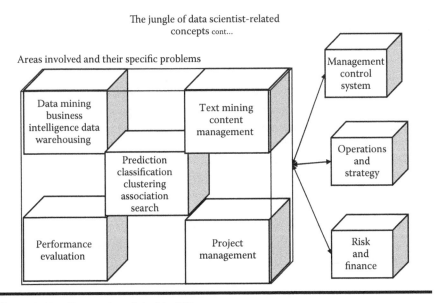

Figure 1.13 Concepts related to DS.

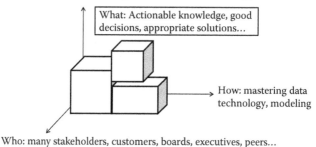

What a data scientist is cont...
And what is a good business definition for a DS?
Using Abell's (1980) business definition model:
To generate appropriate actionable knowledge for
stakeholders using data, minds, and technology

What: Actionable knowledge, good
decisions, appropriate solutions...

How: mastering data
technology, modeling

Who: many stakeholders, customers, boards, executives, peers...

Figure 1.14   Using Abell's model to represent DS roles.

technologies that he or she can use, and the customers or internal market that he or she can support. Depending on the kinds of problems that the DS needs to solve, the functions will be defined as marketing, risk, human resources, production or operations, etc.

There are multiple technologies, as I mentioned before, and there are several stakeholders to interact with. The point is that the product of a DS in the analytics process is in the end knowledge required in order to solve problems and support decision-making processes or to develop intelligence in organizations—intelligence that is going to provide the value of creating stronger competitive advantages and, at the same time, to work with the reality as Pfeffer and Sutton (2006) express, "Too much common management 'wisdom' isn't wise at all, but instead is based on flawed knowledge of best practices that are poor, incomplete, or outright wrong—not to mention hazardous to an organization's health."

In summary, what a DS is doing is finding the ways to match what organizations are trying to solve with the DS's methods, technology, and knowledge. This is a way of supporting organizations in risk control: "Most people fail to bring the right information into their conscious awareness at the right time" (Bazerman and Chugh 2006). In an analogy with the work in the medical field, a DS is working on creating the lab and the measurement system, gathering the data, performing lab analysis and medical analysis, providing diagnostics, and participating in the control of treatment—and, after that, inputting new data to learn to improve the system.

Organizations need roles, and skills are then converted into tasks to perform. The tasks associated with these purposes of the DS work require the following (Barton and Court 2012):

1. Choosing the right data and the right tools
2. Sourcing data creatively

3. Building models that predict and optimize business outcomes
4. Transforming the company's capabilities
5. Developing business-relevant analytics that can be put to use
6. Embedding analytics into simple tools for the front lines
7. Reducing one of the most aggressive strategic risks = blindness

These tasks are defining the future of the DSs in organizations. First, there is the need of a DS's proactivity to understand and maintain the following:

■ A closer understanding of the organization system, the problem, and where the problem emerges and acts within the system.
■ A better definition of the value of business actions in order to foster the DS's passion and motivation.
■ A powerful capacity for teaching, teaching, teaching … learning, learning, learning.
■ A good matching to what organizations are trying to solve (key problems) with DS attributes. A DS has an unprecedented mastery of many tools, skills, and understanding. The challenge is to create organizational support that fosters his or her creativity and neither stifles or overburdens his or her.

Second is improvements in the way a DS has to deal with potential and real organizational issues. This is represented, on the one hand, by dealing with management-related issues—that is, how to communicate and to influence management direction or guides based on analytics work. Regarding the analytics work, we can bring Ackoff's thoughts mentioned in his F-laws quoted in Section 1.2.2: There is an aspect of communication and development of a permanent learning and teaching process that is required to develop analytics work. On the other hand, understanding and meaning creation—this is work with scientific principles but not through magic; there needs to be a balance between speed and scope. Organizations can avoid frustration by better defining what organizations want, and a DS needs to be prepared to create real impact. This means reducing the risk of falling into a black hole in management investment on technology and specialized people when there is no good definition to create value (Gartner Inc. 2014). There is a consistent level of frustration due to multiple cases in which there is not the expected value added. For instance, BI does not meet expectations in several cases; however, "by 2015, enterprise buyers of BI platforms will predominantly purchase platforms that support both strong and broad business-user–accessible data discovery capabilities and IT-driven enterprise features for data reuse, governance, security and scalability" (Gartner Inc. 2014). The main reasons for the business frustration are the following:

■ No IT–business partnership
■ No link to corporate strategy
■ No connection to the processes

- Not enough governance or too much
- No skills

Finally, the DS needs to overcome the issues generated by hyperspecialization and work satisfaction. Malone et al. (2011) points out that there can exist some perils in the good management of specialized people, potentially not good and fair payment. And from the turnover and job satisfaction point of view, Miller and Miller (2012) point out, "Talented people are going independent because they can choose what to work on and with whom to work." And "they leave behind the endless internal meetings and corporate politics ..."

What is proposed in this book is that management and its control systems need to have a better approach to the problem of analytics KM and organizational learning—to develop means for reducing silos and islands of knowledge and operation and to generate organized collaboration with a possibly different performance evaluation of people that deals with management frustration and a different work environment. This is because there are many things that the traditional models of management are not developed to deal with, for example, experts who support and share their knowledge, organizations that learn, processes that foster collaboration, and technology that enables collaboration and measures impact. There is data for everyone and a permanent learning and teaching cycle. From the point of view of performance evaluation, we need to avoid falling into the trap and confusion of overly general evaluations that try and evaluate a boxer along with a tennis player or vice versa—that is, both are very good independently, but it is not common to have a great tennis player who is also a heavyweight boxer or a heavyweight boxer who is also a professional tennis player.

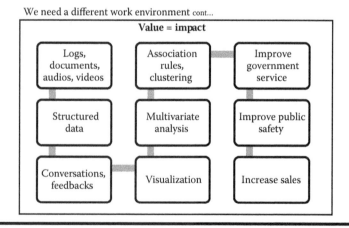

Figure 1.15 Value generation through a chain of activities in the analytics process. (Adapted from Chen, H., Chiang, R.H.L., and Storey, H.C., *MIS Quarterly*, 36, 4, 1165–1188, December 2012.)

In this section, we have introduced the skills and professional profile that a DS could have. The value generation of the person providing services in analytics process (Figure 1.15) is a chain that is connecting the decision-making and problem-solving processes, data, models, and technology. A main point is that analytics work requires plenty of skills and that the good use of them depends on an environment conducive to the transfer of analytics knowledge within the organization. If there is no collaborative work being done and development for working multiple areas with multiskilled people, then the analytics work cannot add the value that is expected of it.

The next section illustrates through data visualization some of the steps that analytics requires. Data visualization and exploratory data analysis are the pillars needed to start more complex processes for understanding and discovering analytics knowledge and meaning.

1.5 First Steps in Analytics Process Design

Before going into the practice of analytics, there are some steps we need to keep in mind in order to perform the tasks that are mentioned in the previous sections. This section focuses on how important it is to present things in a way that will allow people to understand ideas and feel comfortable with visual and easy-to-understand results. The three key steps in control of the analytics process will be validation of assumptions, testing models, and contextualizing the results (Figure 1.16). The first step is to decide on a methodology in order to work with data and to mine data in order to discover knowledge.

In general, we can find two main options for describing a data-mining process: The CRISP methodology and the SEMMA methodology. In this book, the analytics process is described as a process that contains the data-mining process and some other actions. In the analytics process, there is a combination of KM processes and data-mining ones. In the analytics process, we have, at the same time, data to mine and data to gather. We need to design experiments and to provide meaning to the knowledge discovery from data. The cross industrial standard process for data mining (CRISP-DM) methodology comprises six steps:

1. Business understanding
2. Data understanding
3. Data preparation

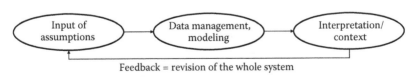

Figure 1.16 **Possible controls of an analytics process.**

4. Modeling
5. Evaluation
6. Deployment

The second methodology mentioned is SEMMA from SAS, which is defined by the search of the sample definition, exploration, modification, modeling, and assessment. This methodology is mainly derived from SAS, the statistics software. In general, the analytics process and the way to develop it in the direction of building an analytics KMS requires permanent feedback (Figure 1.16) and to design the appropriate methodologies, techniques, and tools to perform the process.

This means, at this level, it is important to clarify what we mean about these three concepts:

Methodology: This is the set of steps that, in a sequence, will connect techniques or methods and models or tools in the problem or system solution or design. This is the way to achieve the analytics KMS and to implement the analytics process.

We refer to methods and techniques as processes (subprocesses) that we need to follow and to apply to the analytics process in order to obtain answers and to generate actions.

At the same time, models and tools are the vehicles to create meaning from data. These models and tools will be mainly the systems, computing, mathematics, and statistics-based capabilities that we use for solving problems and supporting decisions.

In general, we could say that we need the analytics process defined in Figures 1.17 and 1.18. For following this process, we need methodologies to perform some of the

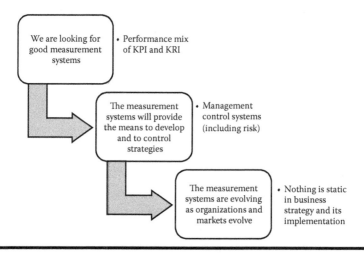

Proposed analytics process
• **Prediction – Description – Diagnosis – Prescription – Controlling – Embedding**

Figure 1.17 Basic actions that are performed in the analytics process.

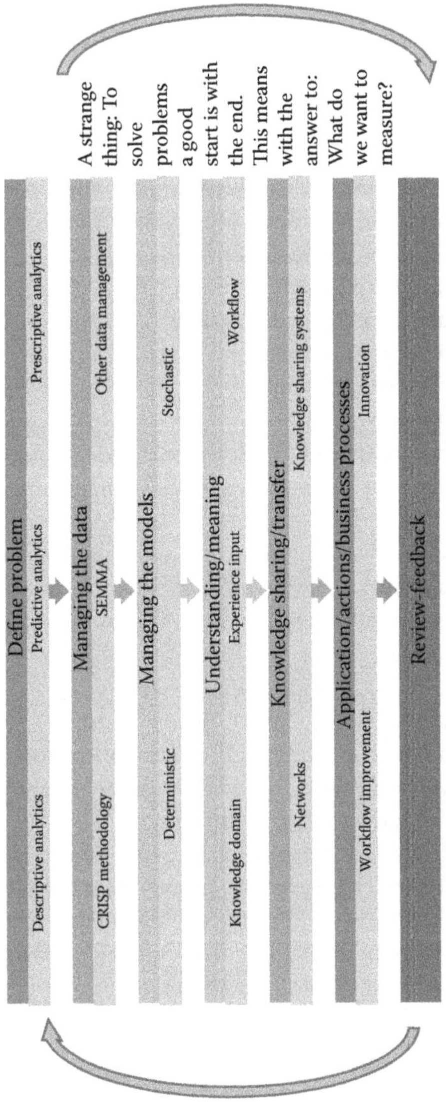

Figure 1.18 Analytics process summary.

actions; at the same time, we need some methods and techniques in each action and models and tools to create the solution.

In this book, the suggested analytics process requires the combination of problem solving, data management steps, and the KM process. The analytics process comprises the following (see Figure 1.18):

1. Problem definition, delimitation, definition of scope through the needs of the business. At this level, it is important to review some possible problem categories of description, visualization, forecasting, classification, optimization, and simulation. This will be part of the connection with Step 3. It is common that, from the beginning, the possible models to solve have not been considered, and later, when data has been gathered and organized, some data issues emerge. This stage has the following aspects to work on:
   a. Answer the questions: What is the company trying to accomplish? How is the corporate performance measured? What are the needs of data to support the measurement system? What are the analytics steps, and how can the analytics projects support the planning and control of strategy design and implementation?
   b. Develop a conceptual model to describe the ideal solution and the blocks that are required for getting to that solution. Identify the blueprint to build the solution by blocks.
   c. Start from the possible solutions of the problem to solve—that is, assuming a potential solution and identifying the relationships to the organization's strategic and tactical metrics. Review the measurement process (in case the metrics are not well defined), identify the metrics that are a priority, and go backward to identify the data that is required for the intermediate steps.
   d. Build the first model starting with exploratory data analysis (EDA) and Visualization. Review what is needed in order to have a good model and look at issues with data and with models.
2. Managing the data. Participate in the data-fixing process, data gathering, and data architecture design. However, the methods are not straightforward, and they need to consider extra actions, such as the following:
   a. Data transformation. In many cases, continuous data has to be transformed into categorical data. The transformation can be based on statistics or based on the understanding of the problem or variable.
   b. Variable creation. Many variables can be created from the raw data (original data). For example, there can be the case of a metric or the relationship of two raw data variables. If, for instance, we want to measure driving behaviors, and we have data about pushing a brake or acceleration pedal, we can define a variable that could say something about driving behaviors.
3. Managing the models: This process is based on thinking the approach deterministic or stochastic and using models of multiple shapes, algebraic,

statistical, machine learning-based, etc. The steps cover not only the creation, but also the testing of the models and their assumptions. In particular,

    a. Assumption validation. The analytics process has to be connected to the context, and the *assumptions* of the modeling process need to be well managed. We have to keep in mind the creation of models that are under the principle of simpler and understandable better than extremely complex and not easy to digest.

    b. Modeling, testing, revising the risk model, prototyping.

    c. Delivery of partial and final results in each step.

    d. Validation and feedback of results. Permanent feedback from each step; this is a back-and-forth process. The agile approach is highly recommended in the analytics process.

    e. Creation of a time series of the metrics in order to perform further analysis when the same experiment or business problem solution is repeated.

4. Developing understanding and meaning. Review of the context and knowledge domain. This refers to the work of creating meaning that is not only based on the results interpretation side, but also on the initiation of the data selected and the model construction.

5. Knowledge sharing and transfer. Analytics work is, in most of the cases, multidisciplinary and in multiple areas of organizations. The analytics process cannot finish when the results are obtained. The results need to create actions. The results need to be embedded in the organization through the adoption of them in business processes. Frame the work of the analytics process under the view of creating an analytics KMS. In principle, we should start, if the time allows it, the same as in the systems analysis and design, prototyping and showing partial or functional results.

6. Application, actions, and business processes under a permanent plan and act. The analytics process requires a very strong and permanent back-and-forth flow of teaching and learning. Contextualization of the results is crucial. The workflow improvement and innovation are part of the objectives in analytics knowledge creation.

The analytics process should be considered as ongoing innovation. Analytics creates new connections—like new neural pathways between previously unconnected dots in the organizational setting—permanently reconnecting data and people's minds with the organization's problems. Innovation based on analytics means many things:

■ From self-driven cars to an automated system for customer service
■ From crime prevention to the development of better quality of life

The analytics process is part of developing more analytics thinking than analytics operations only. The reason is that analytics is not only a set of tools, but also and mainly a way to think about and develop solutions in organizations. This analytics thinking within organizations has the creation of solutions as the priority—the study of problems in the whole spectrum. No problem is the same—different conditions, settings, data, challenges, and tools. But analytics thinking keeps the same approach:

- Systematic
- Rigorous
- Inductive–deductive
- Testing and prototyping

The analytics process needs the KM processes because we need to develop permanent analytics learning and teaching processes in organizations—not only to learn and solve, but also to be part of the solution implementation, helping others to understand what we do, our methods, and our tools. We do not need to reinvent the wheel every time. There is no sense if other people cannot understand what we do. The principle will be to be good at managing economies of scope. The problem is to do more with what we have. We don't need more people with access to Excel's powerful features still using it like Visicalc from 30+ years ago. In many cases, we do not need, for now, more models or more computational capacity or frameworks. We need more people exploiting the great analytics arsenal that we already have.

The implementation of the analytics process has some difficulty in design and implementation. Possibly, one is the management of expectations. The reason is that when a management movement is in place, a "magic" touch is expected for solving various problems. Most difficulties are human in origin, for instance, identification of problems and intelligence to solve them.

They arise from the lack of human capabilities to transform data into knowledge, understanding, and action. It is appropriate to think about this quote: "Any fool can know. The point is to understand" —Albert Einstein. The difficulties come as a result of trends and, putting it in simple terms, fashions, which, because of wrong understanding, are converted into paying more for what you do not need.

At the same time, difficulties arise as a result of ignorance. This concept is highly interesting. Ignorance is a lack of knowledge, keeping the organization under uncertainty in many areas. This is different from risk management practice, in which variation of results is a focus to develop better management practices and to control risk based on knowledge creation. Ignorance comes not only because of lack of knowledge in dealing with problems to solve data and models, but also because of interpretation. The danger is when the organization is not doing something to improve and reduce ignorance or worse as Dilbert (Adams 2000) points out: "When did ignorance become a point of view?"

Another way to observe the issues in the analytics process adaptation is because of bias and use of no representative data, lack of appropriate steps to improve integration of data, plus reduced alignment among the data-problem-model-understanding of context. This reduced alignment could lead to thinking about Big Data as always better for solving problems or, in particular, some problems for which solutions are not related to the volume of data but in the understanding of the problem itself and possible solutions in the knowledge domain.

In summary, possibly it is a good practice to start the analytics process correctly through the development of the art of visualizing data. The main reason for this is that from this visualization process many hypotheses can be formulated and ideas about potential needs in the analytics process can be identified. Visual and report-related activities need to be analyzed within a bigger context or under the influence of more variables. This means there is a need to start with bivariate analysis and to move to multivariate analysis.

In this chapter, the presentation has been based on the analytics process: the roots and how data and knowledge are related to the analytics process. I have presented some illustration of the type of analytics work and people performing this work as well as the first steps in analytics: plan and data visualization that can move to present the analytics process structure based on the modeling process in risk management in order to prepare us for the second part of the case reviews. In the following chapter, the discussion is about the commonalities of the analytics process and mathematical thinking using the illustration of problems and solutions in risk management.

References

Abell, D.F., 1980, *Defining the Business: The Starting Point of Strategic Planning*, Prentice Hall, Englewood Cliffs, NJ.

Ackoff, R., and Addison, H., 2007, *Management F-Laws: How Organizations Really Work*, Triarchy Press, Axminster.

Adams, J.C., and Le Verrier, U., 1845, "A Brief History of Astronomy in Berlin and the Wilhelm-Foerster-Observatory," Planetarium Berlin, Germany, Available at http://www.planetarium-berlin.de/pages/hist/WFS-History.html, accessed September 23, 2010.

Adams, S., 2000, *When Did Ignorance Become a Point of View*, Andrews McMeel Publishing, Kansas City.

Alavi, M. and Leidner, D., 2001, Review: Knowledge management and knowledge management systems: Conceptual foundations and research issues, *MIS Quarterly*, 25(1), pp. 107–136.

Alter, S., 1999, *Information Systems: A Management Perspective*, Addison Wesley, Reading, MA.

Baesens, T.B., Mues, C., Martens, D., and Vanthienen, J., 2009, 50 years of data mining and OR: Upcoming trends and challenges, *The Journal of the Operational Research Society*, 60(Supplement 1: Milestones in OR), pp. 16–23.

Barton, D. and Court, D., 2012, Making advanced analytics work for you a practical guide to capitalizing on big data, *Harvard Business Review*, October, 90(10), pp. 78–83.

Bazerman, M.H. and Chugh D., 2006, Decisions without blinders, *Harvard Business Review*, January, 83(1), pp. 88–97.

Buchanan, L. and O'Connell, A., 2006, A brief history of decision making, *Harvard Business Review*, 84(1), pp. 33–41.

Burstein, F., Zyngier, S., and Rateb, Z., 2002, Knowledge management in the financial services sector: Understandings and trends in Australia, in *Proceedings of the 3rd European Conference on Knowledge Management*, September, pp. 113–125.

Cascio, W., 2007, Evidence-based management and the marketplace for ideas, *Academy of Management Journal*, 50(5), pp. 1009–1012.

Chen, H., Chiang, R.H.L., and Storey, V.C., 2012, Business intelligence and analytics: From big data to big impact, *MIS Quarterly*, 36(4), pp. 1165–1188.

Davenport, T., 2010, Analytics at work: How to make better decisions and get better results, Harvard Business Review Webinar. Available at: https://www.scribd.com /document/74996956/Analytics-at-Work-how-to-make-better-decision-and-get -better-results.

Davenport, T. and Harris, J., 2007, *Competing on Analytics*, Harvard Business School Press, Boston, MA.

Davenport, T. and Prusak, L., 1998, *Working Knowledge*, Harvard Business School Press, Boston, MA.

Davenport, T., Harris, J.G., De Long, D.W., and Jacobson, A., 2001, Data to knowledge to results: Building an analytic capability, *California Management Review*, 43(2), pp. 117–138.

Dickinson, G., 2001, Enterprise risk management: Its origins and conceptual foundation, *The Geneva Papers on Risk and Insurance*, 26(3), pp. 360–366.

Diebold, F.X., Doherty, N.A., and Herring, R.J., 2010, *The Known, the Unknown, and the Unknowable in Financial Risk Management: Measurement and Theory Advancing Practice*. Princeton University Press, Princeton, NJ.

Eckerson, W., 2012, *Secrets of Analytical Leaders: Insights from Information Insiders*, Technics Publications, LLC, Westfield, NJ.

Edwards, J.S., Handzic, M., Carlsson, S., and Nissen, M., 2003, Knowledge management research and practice: Vision and directions, *Knowledge Management Research and Practice*, 1(1), pp. 49–60.

Evans, J.S., Over, D.E., and Manktelow, K.I., 1993, Reasoning, decision making and rationality, *Cognition*, 49(1–2), pp. 165–187.

Frankl, V.E., 1984, *Man's Search for Meaning: An Introduction to Logotherapy*. Simon & Schuster, New York.

Gartner Inc. 2014, Gartner's Hype Cycle Special Report for 2014.

Hammond, J., Keeney, R., and Raiffa, H., 2006, The hidden traps in decision making, *Harvard Business Review*, 84(1), pp. 118–126.

Herndon, T., Ash, M., and Pollin, R., 2013, Does *High Public Debt Consistently Stifle Economic Growth? A Critique of Reinhart and Rogoff*, Working Paper Series, Number 322, Political Economy Research Institute University of Massachusetts Amherst.

Holsapple, C., Lee-Post, A., and Pakath, R., 2014, A unified foundation for business analytics, *Decision Support Systems Archive*, 64(3), pp. 130–141.

Kahneman, D., and Tversky, A., 1979, Prospect theory: An analysis of decision under risk, *Econometrica*, 47(2), pp. 263–291.

Laudon, K. and Laudon, J., 2004, *Management Information Systems: Managing the Digital Firm*, Prentice Hall, New York.

Lehaney, B., Clarke, S., Coakes, E., and Jack, G., 2004, *Beyond Knowledge Management*. Idea Group Publishing, Hershey, PA.

Malhotra, Y., 1999, Beyond hi-tech hidebound knowledge management: Strategic information system for the new world of business, Working Paper, Brint Research Institute.

Malone, T.W., Laubacher, R.J., and Johns, T., 2011, The big idea: The age of hyperspecialization, *Harvard Business Review*, 89(4), pp. 56–65.

Merriam-Webster, 2012, Merriam-Webster, Incorporated.

Miller, G. J., and Miller, M., 2012, The rise of the supertemp, *Harvard Business Review*, 90(5), pp. 51–62.

Nonaka, I. and Takeuchi, H., 1995, *The Knowledge-Creating Company: How Japanese Companies Creates the Dynamics of Innovation*, Oxford University Press, New York.

O'Neil, C., 2013, Cathy O'Neil on Wall St and Occupy Wall Street, Media New York.

Pfeffer, J. and Sutton, R., 2006, *Hard Facts, Dangerous Half-Truths and Total Nonsense: Profiting from Evidence-Based Management*, Harvard Business Press, Cambridge, MA.

Rodriguez, E. and Edwards, J.S., 2014, Knowledge management in support of enterprise risk management, *International Journal of Knowledge Management*, 10(2), pp. 43–61.

Saxena, R. and Srinivasan, A., 2013, *Business Analytics*, Springer, New York.

Senge, P., 1990, *The Fifth Discipline: The Art and Practice of the Learning Organization*, Doubleday/Currency, New York.

Shafir, E. and LeBoeuf, R., 2002, Rationality, *Annual Reviews of Psychology*, 53(1), pp. 491–517.

Sheikh, N., 2013, *Implementing Analytics: A Blueprint for Design, Development, and Adoption*, Elsevier Science, Waltham, MA.

Simon, H.A., 1987, Making management decisions: The role of intuition and emotion, *The Academy of Management Executive*, 1(1), pp. 57–64.

Smith, H. and McKeen, J., 2003, Developments in practice VIII: Enterprise content management, *Communications of the Association for Information Systems*, 11, pp. 647–659.

Stevens, C., 2003, Enterprise resource planning, *Information System Management*, 20(3), pp. 61–67.

Sull, D., Homkes, R., and Sull, C., 2015, Why strategy execution unravels and what to do about it, *Harvard Business Review*, 93(3), pp. 59–66.

The Economist, 2013, Buttonwood, Sound the retweet, *The Economist*, October 12.

The Oxford Dictionary, 2012, Oxford Dictionaries.

Turing, A.M., 1950, Computing machinery and intelligence, *Mind*, 59, pp. 433–460.

Tversky, A., and Kahneman, D., 1986, Rational choice and the framing of decisions, *The Journal of Business*, 59(4), pp. 251–278.

Zachman, J.A., 1997, Enterprise architecture: The issue of the century. *Database Programming and Design*, 10(3), pp. 44–53.

Chapter 2

Illustrating the Analytics Process through Risk Assessment and Modeling

Eduardo Rodriguez

Contents

The aim of this chapter is to present concepts that describe the analytics process applied to a specific situation in an organization. For this, we have chosen the application of risk management (RM). We will first review how to design a methodology to improve the risk-modeling process, which, in this book, we treat as risk analytics or the use of the analytics process and knowledge management concepts and tools in an RM setting.

The chapter is organized through three concepts: the risk-modeling process in a transformation process of the organization, the concept of Big Data in RM, and the way that an enterprise risk knowledge management system (ERKMAS) can be built in order to respond to the needs of converting data, small and big, into knowledge and actions within organizations.

The main steps in the analytics process in an RM setting considered in this chapter are the modeling process and the way to organize an ERKMAS. The risk-modeling process is considered a support structure of the decision-making process in order to pursue a strategic-planning process and strategy implementation. The chapter identifies different perspectives of the problem of risk modeling and proposes a methodological approach in order to understand analytics process through: the use of theory in enterprise risk management (ERM) and knowledge management (KM) using the context of a new view of organizational problems, a review of the historical episodes that created mathematical knowledge when groups shared knowledge, and the analysis of the modeling process of three risk analysis examples. The value of the methodological approach is in contributing to the improvement of the risk-modeling process for the decision-making process in an evolving organization.

Let us first broadly consider some of the issues related to ERM and its possible relationship to KM. The issues with ERM related to the risk-modeling process are the need to be more efficient and effective in order to get better solutions for risk issues; the need to extend the experience, results, and solutions to more problems; the need to use technology in a better way; the need to organize an integral risk information system; and the need to improve the decision-making process. All these challenges are associated with work across the organization done with similar tools, different types of risk, and similar modeling processes (mathematical and conceptual).

In 2000, Earl pointed out that the evolution of organizations is based on looking for how to adapt their capacities to doing business in the information age. The actual process of the transformation of the organization comes in last, only after passing from different levels, beginning with external communications and e-commerce, e-business, and e-enterprise. In the context of the analytics process, the concept of the transformation stage has a critical factor—that is, continuous learning and change under a dynamic model of workers' mind set that needs higher coordination, information consolidation, and strategic planning. New ways of management have emerged to deal with transformation, and many authors identify KM and ERM views as very important in competitiveness and strategy (Dickinson 2001; Nonaka and Toyama 2003; Dalkir 2005). Moreover, in both disciplines, the management view is holistic. Transformation affects the basis for management, including a view in two dimensions: horizontal or across the whole organization and vertical or functions or specific areas. The concept of two dimensions looks for a holistic view of RM problems and needs to prepare management in order to use new tools, technology, and methods, such as the analytics means to develop the analytics process.

This two-dimensional (horizontal, vertical) view of transformation means searching for the capacity to identify market opportunities, manage their risks, and identify what the organization requires in order to reach these opportunities. The search for this capacity pushes companies to develop solutions and tools in order to expand covertures and diversify actions, which creates new risks that need to be managed. In particular, information systems and risk-modeling processes have to be more efficient and effective in order to help people to make more complex decisions. Transformation and strategy require some kind of integration in order to develop new answers for new business models and the way to manage them.

In new business models, there is a need to create analytical models that reduce uncertainty that may be unknowable so as to move to a risk scenario that is knowable in the transformation of the organizations. This means to develop the capabilities to control what is possible to know as a priority. Or as Buchanan and O'Connell (2006) express, "Companies must be able to calculate and manage the attendant risks."

The transition from uncertainty to risk understanding is supported by models. A model in the RM world is defined as "a simplified mathematical description which is constructed based on the knowledge and the experience of the actuary combined with data from the past" (Klugman et al. 1998). In order to describe the modeling process, we must name the steps involved in modeling: model selection, model calibration, fit validation, new model selection, comparison of models, and identification of application for the future. Thus, in order to understand the mobilization of knowledge to risk modeling, the next section includes the conceptual basis for understanding modeling under the concept of risk KM.

In this book, risk is "the uncertainty about the world and uncertainty expressed by probabilities related to the observable quantities (Performance Measures)" (Aven 2003). This means studying the variance of the expected results conditioned to previous knowledge. RM should not be confused with risk measurement. The difference is that risk measurement "entails the quantification of risk exposures," and RM comprises "the overall process ... to define a business strategy to identify the risks to which it is exposed, to quantify those risks and to understand and control the nature of the risks it faces" (Cumming and Hirtle 2001).

The risk-modeling process is a mathematical and conceptual process. The mathematical model starts from the definition of problems and variables, introducing observations, data, description of the relationships among variables (generally equations and basic data models), and assumptions (experience, knowledge) (Caldwell and Ram 1999). With people's knowledge, it produces solutions or outcomes (required knowledge for solving the model) that can be used for the solution of the specific problem or, with additional knowledge, can be applicable to several problems. Within the process, a loop of formulation and testing for different model options is always present, and at the same time, the question is always whether there are mathematical solutions that can be applied.

Thus, risk modeling is part of the risk measurement process or, better, of the analytics process of the organization, providing support for the role of RM in the development of strategic management (Meulbroek 2002; Sharman 2002;

Liebenberg and Hoyt 2003; Banham 2004). Risk modeling keeps the importance of RM with having the capacity of creating value from an integrated view of risk (Froot et al. 1994; Brown 2001; Banham 2004) in order to develop a competitive advantage (Galloway and Funston 2000).

However, the competitive advantage of an organization can be limited because of potential losses. Financial losses, according to Simmons (1999), have causes such as expansion, cultural pressures, reduced controls, miscommunication of business values, different learning systems, and high concentration on information, and some of them belong to KM processes. These causes are influenced by an increment in the complexity of business, creation of transactions, lack of control, information management, and in the use of cost as the only important factor to manage. The complexity of business and the cost of knowledge show the need for providing more meaning to the information available and better KM (Sutcliffe and Weber 2003) in order to build actionable answers to risk threats. Risk-modeling knowledge can provide meaning to information, create knowledge, and support actions, but it needs to find means for a better use of outcomes and their understanding.

Given the pressures of the business environment, organizations have transformed a reactive RM into a strategic discipline, which adds value through learning, risk analysis, and solutions as part of day-to-day business (Meulbroek 2002; Sharman 2002; Liebenberg and Hoyt 2003; Banham 2004). However, the exposure to more risk and the losses of previous years introduced doubts about the practice of RM (Smith and Dumasia 2011). These doubts are related to the influence of the coordination of work and the organizational capacity to transfer and use risk knowledge, in particular risk-modeling knowledge. Thus, in fact, the RM concept has evolved into ERM in order to gain an understanding of a holistic view of risk within an organization in "a systematic and integrated approach to the management of the total risks that a company faces" (Dickinson 2001).

The risk analysis tools and information structures supporting risk analysis and control are independent of the organizational areas. They have different views, specific objectives, and processes. In general, in the risk analytics process, it is expected to have an integrated view of the RM process across the organization. The main reason is that the independent treatment of risk has certain effects within an organization, such as the availability of a different language within the organization in order to talk about risk as well as the expertise of the analysts, which is not the same in different areas or applicable to different kinds of problems (Marshal and Prusak 1996; Daniell 2000; Dickinson 2001; Warren 2005; Shaw 2005). To overcome these issues in knowledge application and transfer, Shaw (2005) presented KM as a discipline that can contribute positively to the implementation of ERM with regard to data and information management, risk knowledge sharing, analysis consolidation, and reporting.

Thus, for our purposes in this book, the concept of risk knowledge management (RISKMAN) is used as the application of KM processes that support ERM. To get this support from KM to ERM (Shaw, 2005), it is necessary to use an ERKMAS in which the risk-modeling process is a component. Thus, the risk-modeling process is part of an ERKMAS as well as the risk measurement process. However, risk modeling is mainly a subset of mathematical modeling in which means are designed to access past experience, conceptualize it, put it into operation, develop it, and discover relationships between variables using risk knowledge.

Therefore, the development of RISKMAN needs the improvement of the capacity for risk-modeling knowledge for the following reasons:

First, risk-modeling knowledge can provide meaning to information: "Risk Management is frequently not a problem of a lack of information, but rather a lack of knowledge with which to interpret its meaning" (Marshal and Prusak 1996).

Second, risk-modeling knowledge is based on the measure of variability. RM is important (Oldfield and Santomero 1997) because of the search for the maximization of the expected profits that are exposed to potential variability, which can be transformed into losses. The causes of the variability can come from different sources: market, investments, operation, strategy, and so on. Organizations are looking for solutions to reduce, to control, and to mitigate risks in order to achieve their goals.

Third, risk-modeling knowledge can deal with different kinds of risk. Banks have a broader exposure to risk demands, requiring a better understanding and development of the risk-modeling capacity. These risks are classified as the following (Van Greuning and Brajovic-Bratanovic 2003):

- Financial: credit, currency, market, capital, etc.
- Business: legal, regulatory, country, etc.
- Operational: fraud, damage, information, products, etc.
- Event: political, contagion, etc.

Fourth, risk-modeling knowledge supports and helps to mitigate doubts about the integral view of risk and the capacity for managing the potential losses. Risk-modeling knowledge contributes to the main points or pillars considered in the Basel II and III accord: capital allocation, separation of the operation and credit risk, and alignment of regulatory and economic capital.

Fifth, Dickinson (2001) introduced knowledge as a factor used to reduce risk. Risk-modeling knowledge is one of the pieces of knowledge that can be used. Table 2.1 includes areas in which risk knowledge is associated with ERM and with risk-modeling knowledge. Risk knowledge contributes to control, business strategy, and underwriting processes because they depend on human actions. Moreover, the transfer of knowledge has value in those processes. Knowledge transfer can be influenced by the existence of knowledge silos as can happen within the risk-modeling processes, and the business units can require solutions for how to transfer experiences (Horton-Bentley 2006), taking into account the rate of change, which can reduce the value of experience in some specific fields (Hayward 2002).

Table 2.1   Four Areas in Which Risk Knowledge Is Associated with ERM

Strategy–risk–knowledge relationship	Noy and Ellis 2003; Alavi and Leidner 2001; Dickinson 2001	Risk is an important concept to deal with in strategy design, and KM and ERM are considered important pieces in the building of strategic competitive advantages for the company.
Information technology and risk	Oldfield and Santomero 1997; Cumming and Hirtle 2001; Smith and Dumasia 2011	Identification of the RM role in financial institutions showed areas in which KM might contribute to risk mitigation. This RM role in the financial institutions is clearly related to KM given the importance of information and technology in risk quantification and integral risk analysis across the organization.
Value and cost of information	Sutcliffe and Weber 2003	The cost of knowledge introduces the need of managing the understanding and use of the information rather than the information itself.
Opportunities for KM application to ERM	Ernst and Young 2001; Tillinghast-Tower Perrin 2000; CAS survey 2001; McKibben 2004	The ERM conceptualization can help to understand how to apply KM to ERM, and there are identified opportunities for designs of the knowledge management system in insurance and banking.

Sixth, risk-modeling knowledge as an RM process in banking, can facilitate knowledge transfer that is influenced by difficulties with the language spoken inside the organization related to risk and the application of expertise for solving different problems (Dickinson 2001; Warren 2002; Shaw 2005). Additionally, risk-modeling knowledge can provide organizations with knowledge, defining problems, variables and their relationships, and supporting search tools to facilitate the search task if there is a high volume of knowledge available (Alavi and Leidner 2001) or to organize the search tools that are crucial in RM (Simoneau 2006).

In summary, RISKMAN and risk-modeling knowledge can be developed through data analytics and information management (Shaw 2005), risk knowledge sharing, consolidation, and reporting. KM and information management are needed for actionable answers to risk threats (Sutcliffe and Weber 2003). In brief, the application of KM to ERM requires, on the one hand, the identification and development of knowledge processes and, on the other hand, the identification of the integrated knowledge that a knowledge worker requires, in particular the risk-modeling knowledge.

2.1 Observing Great Data in the Context of RM

This section introduces Great Data as a useful concept in order to underline the amorphous nature of Big Data and the need to turn its massive scope into something useful and digestible, hence Great Data. By way of illustration, for many years in the RM setting, mainly in insurance companies, Big Data has been accumulated through the use of pictures, in particular for automobile insurance. However, this data has not been used in a systematic and aggregated way in order to create knowledge, to predict events, and to provide insights to control risks. Instead, in most cases, it has been used to support decisions just for the one specific case. The search for the meaning of Big Data or Great Data requires not only the identification of data sources and filters, but also people who are responsible for risk analysis who use these pictures for inferring new knowledge usable in risk control. If people and data are not aligned with an analytics management perspective, the data that has been collected can be big but possibly not good for performing further analysis beyond the analysis at the time of the event. This means that potentially this Big Data can be converted into bad or unusable Big Data. Thus, it is possible that Big Data will be something other than an asset or a means to add value to the process of improving sustainable competitive advantages.

The concept of the ERKMAS introduced in the previous section is the basis for converting Big Data into Great Data for organizations. This is not only a problem of volume, variety, veracity, and velocity (the four Vs of Big Data), but also a problem of meaning, development, and the correct use of data that should add value to organizations. The reason is that there is a problem with creating and using data with the four Vs of Big Data in order to convert this data into more than a mediocre asset and a mediocre investment. Instead, it should be a highly valuable asset—value that is generated because of its attributes of being useful, worthwhile, and important to an organization's continuous improvement. This value appears when data is converted into knowledge that provides a sense of purpose and generates capabilities within organizations. Without the creation, access, storage, transfer, and application of knowledge, there is no de facto value being generated through the simple accumulation of Big Data for its own sake. This knowledge has to translate into actions that can be performed and developed and generate value added by performing what the organization's mission and value proposition have defined.

With this view, it is possible to describe in the next two sections the general attributes of the ERKMAS and the way in which the ERKMAS is part of the risk-modeling process.

2.2 Bases for Building an ERKMAS

This section presents the ERKMAS oriented to create the connection between the KM and ERM processes. The connection is based on using different types of data to manage risk knowledge. The ERKMAS abilities of managing the four Vs of Big Data are the same as standard (small) data with a view to creating knowledge through analytics capabilities. This is in order to identify means for converting Big Data and standard data into risk knowledge or, better, to create risk knowledge that is usable and potentially can generate actions.

The ERKMAS design needs to manage big and standard data through the manner in which those activities are potentially performed:

- Reduce, select, filter tons of data that are not required for organizations and do not add value.
- Goal congruency with people and the organization: This means identifying how processes are affected by data and how people are affecting data.
- Pattern identification and risk classification.
- Ongoing revision of financial transactions.
- Ongoing comparison of products, prices, and sales offers in order to avoid customer loss and to improve customer retention.
- Updating data, which is an issue with some tools that can be used with data already in place but which are not good for updating data, such as Hadoop.
- Management of appropriate models according to data. Continuous data models have a different complexity.
- The previous point is linked to the modeling process. It has to be organized and, more precisely, to avoid inefficiencies because of the data.
- Creation and development of the business model and computing architecture, computing policies, tools design, data government (for instance, document management), and analytics capabilities.

The challenge of Great Data is to build the ERKMAS in order to deal with big and standard data. The ERKMAS is a set of blocks that connects the following:

1. Risk knowledge experts
2. Knowledge system engineering
3. Risk knowledge users
4. Risk knowledge developers
5. Risk data managers
6. Artifacts, models, computers, and interfaces

For example, data in social media can be a kind of knowledge that will be the input for another layer of risk knowledge creation. Social media provides a kind of input for the risk analytics process, and we also use market data that is a kind of continuous data that, in the analytics process, is converted into knowledge. This is the case for stock prices, interest rates, currency exchange rates, energy prices, and so on.

We can also discover knowledge from one of the most important sources—that is, data from structured reports in credit risk where knowledge moves from tacit to explicit. Everything that is the outcome of an analysis is, at the same time, the input for further analytics work. For example, the use of credit analysis reports that are in documents or in text inside data repositories. In published data, there is data, such as Table 2.2 shows.

With these points, we have illustrated that the ERKMAS is one of the components for the analytics process in risk management. The ERKMAS is highly demanding because not only does it require the design of how to manage structured data, but also nonstructured data along with the need for involving risk analytics capabilities and providing support to the risk management processes as the modeling process itself. The modeling process is studied in the following section.

Table 2.2   Use of a Variety of Data in the Credit Risk Assessment Process

Company Overview	Financial Statement Analysis
• Business qualitative–general data knowledge • Company history • What, how, who (Abell's model, Porter's laws, value chain, supplier chain) • Product lines or services • Major markets • Seasonality • Terms given to customers • Customer base if there are large concentrations • Multiple locations • Major suppliers • Buying terms • Seasonal requirements • Fixed asset requirements • Labor relations	• Data review from financial statements, projections, and documents that are providing information of financial performance • Performance analysis: operation, processes • Profitability, variance analysis, leverage, operational marketing, financial, production • Benchmarking analysis • Key performance indicators and key risk indicators, variances and time series changes sales revenue • Gross profit margin • COGS • Operating profit margin

(Continued)

Table 2.2 (Continued) Use of a Variety of Data in the Credit Risk Assessment Process

Company Overview	Financial Statement Analysis
• Organizational control • The present legal form (proprietorship, partnership, corporation, LLC) • Principal owners and their percentage of ownership • Tax structure if not apparent from legal form (S-corp status vs. C-corp) • Major organizational units (divisions, subsidiaries, etc.)	• Other revenues • Net income **Qualitative analysis of financial statements** • Looking for cause and effect of results in terms of liquidity, capital position, and quality of assets. Policies affecting goal congruency, responsibility centers, service practice, employees, etc.
Management control systems • Name, title, and functional position of key players • Management background, education, experience, competence, years with company, legal issues, other commitments (side businesses) • Evaluation of the adequacy of management succession, goal congruency and loyalty, stability	**Marketing and strategy analysis** related to capital budgeting and revenue generation. Relationship between liquidity and profit generation. For cash provided by operations, discuss the historical cash flows of the company, identifying major sources and uses of cash. Based on historical information and your assumptions about the future, predict whether cash from operations will be adequate. Current conditions of operation, contracts, legal issues, etc.
Industry and economic outlook • Potential use of Porter's model and BCG model plus matrices of industrial attractive and company's growth • SWOT analysis has to be linked here	**Financing experience** • How the history of the organization has been and payment experience. The management of operations, logistics, and cost control is key in this part of the review. Cost assignment and transfer prices

2.3 Developing Risk-Modeling Knowledge: The Analytics Approach

This section presents the components of a method that can be used to support risk-modeling knowledge. The proposed method requires the implementation of an ERKMAS. This system supports the interdependent dynamic among the movements between tacit and explicit risk-modeling knowledge in the development of a RISKMAN:

- Socialization: social interaction among the RM employees and shared risk-modeling experience
- Combination: merging, categorizing, reclassifying, and synthesizing the risk-modeling process
- Externalization: articulation of best practices and lessons learned in the risk-modeling process
- Internalization: learning and understanding from discussions and mathematical modeling review

Figure 2.1 shows risk-modeling knowledge as a common area among RM processes in the organization. All these RM processes create models to describe the phenomenon. There is the possibility of using similar knowledge, techniques, and tools to solve different risk problems. Figure 2.2 shows that in three main components of ERM there are links among data, the search for problem solutions, and

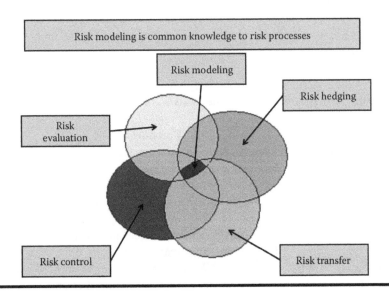

Figure 2.1 Different ERM processes have risk-modeling knowledge as a common process.

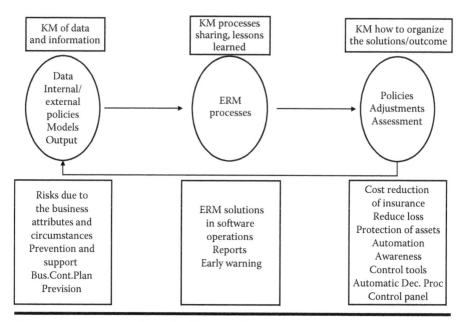

Figure 2.2 KM acts through risk modeling in different components of ERM processes.

policies, and the organization of outcomes such as risk-modeling knowledge has been conceived. Based on these previous points, the proposed method looks to use the context and experience to improve the risk-modeling process. Thus, the methodology proposed for developing risk-modeling knowledge is composed of the following seven steps:

1. Answering questions related to strategy and strategic planning in the organization
2. Identifying the enablers for the transfer of risk knowledge from tacit to explicit knowledge and vice versa
3. Understanding flows of information to produce knowledge
4. Understanding risk knowledge organization
5. Searching for KM technologies and techniques
6. Designing the ERKMAS to support risk modeling
7. Connecting organizational performance metrics and the risk-modeling process

The first step in the method is to get answers to questions such as what resources does the organization need? What does the organization want? What does the organization measure? What is the impact? What has been the experience? What are the errors? Where is the failure based on lack of knowledge management?

This step is based on the needs of the stakeholders, their value definition, and the strategy planning process. The risk-modeling process is in agreement with the "design approach to planning" introduced by Ackoff (1981) following his five proposed phases: formulating the systems of problems; identifying ideals, objectives, and goals; means planning; resource planning; and design of implementation and control. In summary, the risk-modeling process starts with the recognition of the strategic context and the contribution that it will make to the strategic process.

Based on this strategic orientation, the second, third, and fourth steps are associated with the understanding that individual minds and knowledge creation require three elements in order to discover KM and ERM process relationships: identification of the ways to transfer tacit to explicit knowledge and vice versa (Nonaka and Takeuchi 1995); clarity about the flows of information and how they produce knowledge (Choo 1998; Weick 2001); and understanding of the way that the risk knowledge is organized (Wiig 1993).

The second step refers to enabler analysis of risk knowledge transfer, studying traps, errors, and constraints of the process. Transferring risk knowledge in both directions, tacit to explicit and vice versa, starts with the identification of traps in the decision-making process (Hammond et al. 2006) affected by the modeling process. The risk-modeling process needs the understanding of risk knowledge transfer to tune up people's efforts and to reduce the wrong application and interpretation of concepts, relationships, and results. These traps are the following (Hammond et al. 2006):

- "The mind gives disproportionate weight to the first information it receives."
- "Decision makers display, for example, a strong bias toward alternatives that perpetuate the status quo."
- " ... is to make choices in a way that justifies past choices ..."
- "The bias leads us to seek out information that supports our existing instinct or point of view while avoiding information that contradicts it."
- "The way a problem is framed can profoundly influence the choices you make."
- "While managers continually make such estimates and forecasts, they rarely get clear feedback about their accuracy."

At the same time, it is necessary to clarify whether the models will be used for decision automation or for getting insight to problems only. For example, the automation of quantitative solutions in a trading operation can produce issues in a market if everyone is using the same strategy. For instance, "the report suggests that many of the quantitative portfolio construction techniques are based on the same historical data, such as value premium, size premium, earnings surprise, etc., and that there is a widespread use of standardized factor risk models that would explain why quant funds act in unison" (Avery 2007).

Additionally, the risk-modeling process can be affected by the process of transferring knowledge that produces risky exposure. The reason is that a lack of coordination of knowledge processes, according to some examples from financial practice, can influence losses:

- Expansion: Growth affected the operations at American Express. Expansion ran faster than growth of capacity. The knowledge support was minimal (Simmons 1999).
- Culture: The Banker Trust expansion reduced the quality of the product presentation to the clients. The reason was cultural pressures. There was a lack of information flow, and the products were not well understood. The culture of avoiding bad news reduced the possibility of finding solutions to errors (Simmons 1999).
- Controls: Barings Bank's failure is related to the creation of early warning systems and the relationship to a work environment of rewards and recognition. A short-term performance view and internal competition contributed to the bad results (Simmons 1999).
- Lack of understanding: What is happening, the complexity increment, transaction creation, lack of control, information management, and cost as the only important factors to manage, reducing the ability to react in difficult or good opportunity times. This complexity and the cost of knowledge show the need for managing the understanding and use of information rather than the information itself (Sutcliffe and Weber 2003).
- Lack of communication of business values in an understandable way, which people can embrace. Possibly the identification of off-limits actions was not clear (Simmons 1999).
- Reduced stimulation of a learning system in order to review processes and to discuss the results and adequate diagnostic control systems (Simmons 1999).

Finally, it is important to take into consideration that there are additional factors to add to the above list affecting the coordination of knowledge: new and different worker mentalities open to new technology and with different means of communication, the existence of a culture of knowledge silos, and a greater desire for understanding and resolving doubts. There are new problems with a higher degree of complexity and demanding the transformation of organizations in order to achieve solutions that require enterprise-wide answers with the appropriate technological support.

The third step relates to the understanding of flows of information to produce knowledge and how to use these flows in risk modeling. This means analyzing experiences of KM processes, methods, and technologies used in RM problems in order to develop risk knowledge management capacity. Some examples of the search for KM support in order to improve risk-modeling knowledge are the following:

- Application of prediction and classification models (Burstein et al. 2002), such as financial service technology and knowledge development of the organization

- Data mining practice as a means to support the customer focus; risk classification and loss estimation (Hormozi and Giles 2004; Dzinkowski 2002); the emphasis put on cost of integrating risk analyses, control, and risk policy creation, deployment, and application (Cumming and Hirtle 2001)
- The emphasis on acquiring knowledge and problem solving or on increasing the orientation to people and processes (Edwards et al. 2003)
- The search for a solution of sliced risk management data (McKibben 2004), the development of solutions to control risk exposure, and data structures to share them with different areas in the problem-solving process
- Orientation to new technology for data and information management and for the modeling process (Shaw 2005)

The assumptions behind decisions in hedging or investment can be different; the lack of sharing can create issues in RM processes, and the controls may not be enough. It is important to search for the truth outside the silo generated by risk analysis in order to get better answers. Lack of knowledge access can create failures. Weak means for transferring knowledge can provide insufficient knowledge of the operation, poor assessments of the lessons learned, and poor understanding of the present and the forecasts made through risk knowledge.

This lack of knowledge can happen because of an interruption in the flow of information, which is a component of the modeling work that is complemented and used properly by the expert. Goovaerts et al. (1984) wrote that only incomplete information is available, and it is the actuary who decides the principles and distributions that are to be used. Information use, with interpretation and context content or, in other words, knowledge is part of the risk-modeling process as a common area of the RM processes for the analysis of market risk, operational risk, strategic risk, credit risk, and actions of risk mitigation, risk transfer, and risk capacity evaluation.

On the whole, the flow of information for risk-modeling knowledge in ERM processes is related to KM processes associated with risk assessment and risk knowledge creation. This flow of information uses data, and information follows as a method for storing and retrieving raw and created data and transferring results for knowledge applications. Figure 2.3 shows some of the examples of RM activities classified by KM processes.

The fourth step consists of understanding the organization of risk-modeling knowledge. Risk modeling requires following the mathematical modeling process. Knowledge within the risk-modeling process can be organized as a collaborative effort and as the application of knowledge from different sources and disciplines.

The organization of risk-modeling knowledge means the identification of KM processes of the mathematical modeling experience. This refers to getting clarity about what to do and what to know and what the process to build a mathematical model is. Mathematics (Aleksandrov et al. 1969) has as its characteristics abstraction, demonstration, and applications under precision and logical rigor. Abstraction

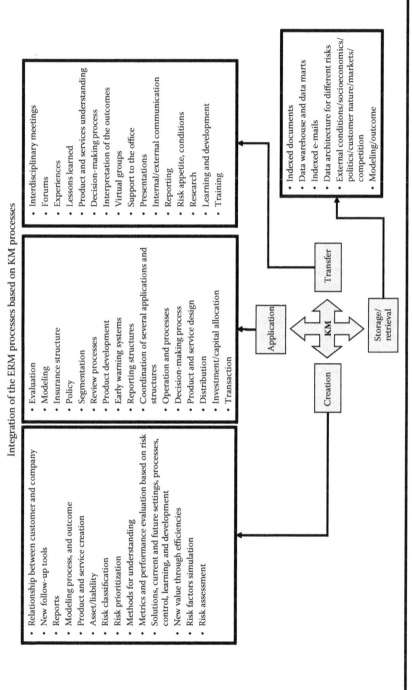

Integration of the ERM processes based on KM processes

- Relationship between customer and company
- New follow-up tools
- Reports
- Modeling process, and outcome
- Product and service creation
- Asset/liability
- Risk classification
- Risk prioritization
- Methods for understanding
- Metrics and performance evaluation based on risk
- Solutions, current and future settings, processes, control, learning, and development
- New value through efficiencies
- Risk factors simulation
- Risk assessment

- Evaluation
- Modeling
- Insurance structure
- Policy
- Segmentation
- Review processes
- Product development
- Early warning systems
- Reporting structures
- Coordination of several applications and structures
- Operation and processes
- Decision-making process
- Product and service design
- Distribution
- Investment/capital allocation
- Transaction

- Interdisciplinary meetings
- Forums
- Experiences
- Lessons learned
- Product and services understanding
- Decision-making process
- Interpretation of the outcomes
- Virtual groups
- Support to the office
- Presentations
- Internal/external communication
- Reporting
- Risk appetite, conditions
- Research
- Learning and development
- Training

- Indexed documents
- Data warehouse and data marts
- Indexed e-mails
- Data architecture for different risks
- External conditions/socioeconomics/politics/customer nature/markets/competition
- Modeling/outcome

Creation   Application   Transfer   Storage/retrieval   KM

Figure 2.3   Some information flows and relationships that KM processes have with ERM processes.

is the search for quantitative relationships; demonstration is part of the human knowledge needed in order to get generalizations about the quantitative relationships of the members of a group.

The organization needs to develop the capacity to solve problems and to provide support for the modeling process under the following premises (Mladenic et al. 2003):

- Decisions come from humans and machines. Machines use predefined decision systems and humans use some theory frameworks and decision support systems.

- People as the core of all processes: Management is about knowledge, and KM is about people, processes, technology, and organizational structure.

- Old computing is about what computers can do, and new computing is about what people can do. New computing is about reliability, comprehensibility, universality, and harmony with human needs.

- Power comes not from having knowledge. Power comes from sharing knowledge and using it to add value and to create a sustainable competitive advantage, which is similar to thinking in KM and business processes instead of business processes and information systems.

- Technology is more than software or hardware. It is the answer to the "how" for finding a solution. For example, modeling process capacity is competitive capacity (Davenport 2006).

The organization of risk-modeling knowledge can use experiences in KM practice in mathematical development, under the previous premises, with the development of communities of practice (Wenger 2000), such as the Bourbaki Group and the Cambridge Club of 1930. In both cases, the scientific work was based on common interest, and the organization was formed by volunteer members working for better development of the science. The Bourbaki Group was composed originally of Henri Cartan, Claude Chevalley, Jean Coulomb, Jean Delsarte, Jean Dieudonné, Charles Ehresmann, René de Possel, Szolem Mandelbrojt, and André Weil. The group was created in 1935 with the purpose of writing a comprehensive text on mathematics based on set theory and axiomatic foundation. There were meetings to review the content, to identify the production logic, and to decide the structures and mathematical development. The main point was to create forums for discussion and idea development based on formalism and axioms as proposed by Hilbert. The experience of communities of practice enhance RM process and, in particular, risk modeling because of the development and testing of modeling steps and result validations.

Another means of knowledge collaboration was the one described by Foster (1985), who wrote about what he called the Cambridge Club 1930: "These four men did not comprise a school since they did not appear to have a common objective, but they knew each other and influenced each other and so might be called a club." Foster referred to Sir Arthur Eddington, Sir James Jeans, Bertrand Russell, and A. N. Whitehead, all of whom were working at Cambridge at the end of 1930. The difference with the Bourbaki Group was the regularity of meetings and the specific objective. In both cases, the knowledge transfer was fundamental to contributing to the formalization of mathematics and to the new mathematical physics that emerged with the theory of relativity, quantum theory, and the uncertainty principle. These examples of the Bourbaki Group and Cambridge Club possess the attributes of the communities of practice presented by Wenger (2000) and are clear samples of collaborative work in knowledge creation.

Finally, a powerful example of modeling collaboration has been the development of open source in our society. Access to multiple tools is an example of what can be done with high levels of quality because of knowledge sharing for knowledge creation and knowledge application. Some examples of this modeling collaboration are R, Octave, Content Management Systems, and many other software solutions that are available for several problems.

A second point of view for using KM experience is to recognize learning processes in organizations (Senge 1990). Knowledge discovery and knowledge transfer from other disciplines have been used to provide solutions for risk-modeling problems. There are examples of theories that come from general stochastic process analysis (Compound Poisson Process, Brownian Motion; Karlin and Taylor 1998) or from other observations, abstraction, and reference theories, such as fractal geometry, or symmetry analysis of nature, which represent knowledge transfer from other disciplines into risk management. The Brownian theory of motion that comes from physics is one of the bases for financial mathematics or as the application of the general stochastic process, martingales, and compound Poisson processes are also the basis for the financial models and loss distribution modeling. The symmetry study through group theory is an example of starting from the observation of geometric figures to apply concepts to many different mathematical branches and solutions to practical problems in many disciplines. In addition, discovery of risk-modeling knowledge can develop innovation and application of methods and outcomes to problem solving in other disciplines.

Additionally, learning in organizations emerges from the analysis of experience and the identification of subprocesses in a risk-modeling process; this means the recognition of steps in the building model process that facilitate the identification of tasks and subprocesses that are based on knowledge and can be oriented and used toward the solution of different problems. The identification of the subprocesses of three risk-modeling examples is based on the work of Carnap (1966), Raiffa (1968), and Leonard (1998). Carnap introduced the idea of a law in science as statements expressing regularities in the world. He identified that not all the laws are universal but are, as he called them, statistical laws. The risk-modeling process belongs to the search for statistical laws and, as Carnap said, the process starts with direct observations of facts that in RM are called claims, losses, and exposures. Additionally, these laws are used to "explain facts already known, and they are used to predict facts not yet known."

Now, Raiffa (1968) introduced decision analysis, and he identified the value of the outcome of the models based on the relevance to a real-world problem. He said, "In these lectures I have indicated how a decision maker's preferences for consequences, attitudes towards risk, and judgments about uncertain events can be scaled in terms of subjective utilities and probabilities and how these can be incorporated into formal analysis." This reflection supports the review and identification of the subprocesses of risk modeling that include understanding, interpretation, and the possible application to other problems.

In order to complement Carnap's (1966) and Raiffa's (1968) views, Leonard's model (1998) is used. This model, called "knowledge creating and diffusing activities," considers a cycle in which core capabilities for shared problem solving in the present are connected to implementing and integrating, experimenting, prototyping, importing, and absorbing knowledge. The core capabilities have to reduce the core rigidity that comes from skills and knowledge, managerial systems, physical systems, and values. Subprocesses in risk-modeling processes are looking for a better knowledge development in order to use knowledge with different problems.

Based on the above ideas, the next examples (Tables 2.3 through 2.5) provide an identification of the attributes of mathematical modeling that are used for risk analysis and that share common knowledge following the steps proposed by Klugman et al. (1998). These examples are the use of the compound Poisson model for loss distribution modeling, a modeling process for risk classification, and a modeling Markov process for credit risk evaluation and behavioral prediction. From the review of these three examples, it is possible to identify four main components in each modeling process: information management, mathematical work, experimenting and prototyping, and communicating. These four components of the modeling process are presented in Tables 2.3 through 2.5 and divided into subprocesses identified as common. These subprocesses go from data gathering up to the application of the theoretical concepts to different kinds of problems.

Tables 2.3 through 2.5 show the common steps in the analytics process to solve the problem in three different applications: risk classification, estimation of the loss distribution, and the Markov process. These common steps are described as part of knowledge process development. This means the application of the knowledge gained to get new solutions, possibly with different data and relationships.

Many steps have common knowledge that needs to be aligned and to produce capacity for risk modeling. For instance, describing groups (groups can be defined as the sets of customers according to or as examples of the due date or delinquency level) clustering, selecting variables from a linear approach, and the classification process profile of payment quality. One of the steps that is central in risk analysis is using loss distribution for other applications, such as percentile analysis (VAR) or probable maximum loss. The groups of debt quality can be organized in a different way, producing a sequence of the credit process from selection to control of credit portfolio.

Table 2.3 Analytics Process and Risk Classification

Analytics Process	*Risk Classification*
Problem definition: understanding the phenomenon	Meaning of customer classification, attributes available, timing, groups, etc.
Search for general models, theoretical support, and mathematics	New theory for parameter estimation, testing new model decision trees, regression trees, neural networks ... GLM
Reducing the core rigidity: People coordination and project development	Expert identification, blueprint, maps, plans. Blocks and steps definition, capacity, and roles identification
Data gathering	Data experience, profile variables, default definition, claims data, exposure set definition, clustering for outliers
Data storage	Data mart creation and access, record selection, variable field selection
Data selection and preparation	Learning set, out of time, out of sample
Data for control	Selection of the samples, out of time and out of sample
Programming and specialized software	Testing assumptions, normality ..., modeling, categorization, regression process, model identification, model preparation
Prototyping: Model/program Testing definition of structure and relationships/model structure selection	Input data to different models
Parameters estimation and solutions of relationships and equations	Testing different methods
Model performance evaluation	ROC, classification tests, Kolmogorov-Smirnov
Model improvements	Identification of a different set of variables, parsimonious metrics, testing more variables

(Continued)

Table 2.3 (Continued)   Analytics Process and Risk Classification

Analytics Process	*Risk Classification*
Reporting	Problem solved, scope, model specifications, results, interpretation, new challenges, and priorities
Reducing the judgment gap: Results interpretation	Meaning of classification
Communication	Presentations to different groups, taking feedback
Search for a statistical law: New generalizations and weak assumptions	Look for panel data, time series indicators
New applications, input new models	Developing variance metrics, identification new significant variables, benchmarking, development of segmented models (economic sectors, by different clusters)

Generalization of a risk model can depend on the assumptions, theory, time, and data available. For example, time is a factor affecting whether the model is discrete or continuous in time. This has a big impact in RM modeling. In all these steps, knowledge is a component to be organized and promoted in order to achieve answers and to identify how to improve assumptions and methods.

The capacity for risk-modeling development is grounded in how people learn to work both independently and simultaneously with others, coordinately and looking at the forest and not just the trees. The challenge is that organizations need to coordinate resources under the understanding that they have knowledge workers and problem solvers and not just workers and jobs. Furthermore, organizations have problems to solve and not just tasks to do, which implies that organizations have managers and analytics professionals coexisting, which requires the organization of risk-modeling knowledge and the ability to use common knowledge in mathematical modeling.

The fifth step refers to identifying the KM processes and how to support the use of common knowledge of RM processes in mathematical modeling. The risk-modeling process needs to be supported in order to mobilize information flows to produce risk knowledge through a clear role of KM processes as a means to consolidate, integrate, and organize the risk knowledge. This can happen in the following way: knowledge creation with which knowledge is represented by risk assessment, knowledge storage and retrieval through the data support for external and internal users, knowledge transfer using the experience of many people in known cases, and

Table 2.4   Analytics Process and Loss Distribution Fitting

Analytics Process	Loss Distribution Fitting: Compound Poisson Process
Problem definition: Understanding the phenomenon	Concept of loss, claim process, cost associated, income associated, reinsurance, recoveries
Search for general models, theoretical support, mathematics	New approaches for numerical and analytical solutions of the stochastic processes
Reducing the core rigidity: People coordination and project development	Expert identification, blueprint, maps, plans. Blocks and steps definition, capacity and roles identification
Data gathering	Claims data, recoveries, reinsurance, investment, clustering outliers identification
Data store	Data mart creation and access, record selection, variable field selection
Data selection and preparation	Different periods of time, simulation points, empirical distribution, descriptive statistics
Data for control	Different periods of time, simulation points, filters
Programming and specialized software	Histograms, ways to estimate parameters, distributions simple and mixed. Tail analysis
Prototyping: Model and program, testing definition of structure and relationships, model structure selection	Input data to different models
Parameters estimation and solutions of relationships and equations	Testing different methods
Model performance evaluation	Fit tests, Kolmogorov-Smirnov, chi-square
Model improvements	Identification of special cases
Reporting	Problem solved, scope, model specifications, results, interpretation, new challenges, and priorities

(*Continued*)

Table 2.4 (Continued)   Analytics Process and Loss Distribution Fitting

Analytics Process	Loss Distribution Fitting: Compound Poisson Process
Reducing the judgment gap: Results interpretation	Meaning of loss distribution and applications
Communication	Presentations to different groups, taking feedback, developing new options
Search for a statistical law: New generalizations and weak assumptions	Mixed distribution and special groups for managing claim. Relationships with marketing, pricing
New applications and input new models	Loss given default, behavioral models, preventive dashboards, risk indicators management

knowledge application to discover business process opportunities. These KM processes in a risk-modeling process are described in detail in the following sections.

2.3.1 Knowledge Creation

This means identifying assumptions, development of the conceptualization process, identification and selection of techniques to use, selection of processes, development of collaboration, discovering of methods of solution, prototyping models, and testing. Knowledge is to be found in developing new models, replacing existing models, promoting new solutions, participating in problem solving, organizing product development, and risk evaluation for innovation. From the technology side, knowledge is created for providing access to models and results for managing technological support through the intranet, developing external solutions or answer methodologies for problem solving, increasing the sophistication of solutions, managing data and quality, analyzing multiple risks, and selecting solution development and accessibility.

2.3.2 Knowledge Storage and Retrieval

There are many different components in risk modeling that need to be stored and retrieved, such as documents, raw data, data created, taxonomy, metadata, and structured and unstructured data. The action of storing and retrieving implies cleaning data, developing and implementing a documentation process, structuring information, and codifying human knowledge with comments about tacit knowledge from individuals and groups. Measures need to be developed for identifying the quality of the data repository; data volume; codified documents, indexed,

Table 2.5 Analytics Process and Markov Chain Analysis in Credit Risk

Analytics Process	Markov Process for Credit Analysis
Problem definition: Understanding the phenomenon	Classification procedure, identification of units and amounts of credit, differences, trends, sectors, markets
Search for general models, theoretical support, and mathematics	New approach for transition. Time series review, comparison, GLM, Markov chains discrete, continue, absorbent, etc.
Reducing the core rigidity: People coordination and project development	Expert identification, blueprint, maps, plans. Blocks and steps definition, capacity, and roles identification
Data gathering	Classification of loans, default definition, identification of age groups, clustering outliers identification
Data store	Data mart creation and access, record selection, variable field selection
Data selection and preparation	Data from different groups in a different period of time, comparison of results
Data for control	Using automated process, discretization, programming the portfolio
Programming and specialized software	Matrix definitions, develop test of absorbing states, properties of Markov matrices, discretization process
Prototyping: Model and program, testing definition of structure and relationships and model structure selection	Input data to different models, identification transition matrices multiple steps, absorption, properties of the matrix type
Parameters estimation and solutions of relationships and equations	Testing different methods
Model performance evaluation	Testing assumptions Markov property, normality…
Model improvements	Time forecast, continue and discrete
Reporting	Problem solved, scope, model specifications, results, interpretation, new challenges, and priorities

(Continued)

Table 2.5 (Continued)   Analytics Process and Markov Chain Analysis in Credit Risk

Analytics Process	Markov Process for Credit Analysis
Reducing the judgment gap: Results interpretation	Identification of states and probability movements
Communication	Presentations to different groups, taking feedback, developing new options
Search for a statistical law: New generalizations and weak assumptions	Description with different stochastic processes modifying some assumptions
New applications and input new models	New structure of portfolio classification, market segmentation

structured processes to update; metadata structure; comfort with data repositories; documentation incentives; technology used for repositories; processes to populate data; document standards; and processes to access and use data repositories.

2.3.3 Knowledge Transfer

Risk-modeling knowledge can be transferred through presentations, portals, meetings, discussions, collaboration activities, content management design, distribution of content, testing, and reporting. There are differences to consider when there is knowledge transfer between individuals, between individuals and groups, between groups, across groups, and from groups to the whole organization. All of these differences require actions among the participants to improve the communication processes and willingness to share by fostering the existence and richness of transmission channels, such as unscheduled meetings, informal seminars, coffee breaks, quality of knowledge transfer channels, taxonomies, metadata, forums, bulletins, searching for interdisciplinary solutions, feedback sessions, discussing forums, and so on.

2.3.4 Knowledge Application and Learning

The application of risk-modeling knowledge is represented by decisions, business processes, or models in other organizational areas, such as impact analysis, evaluation, new developments, and new solutions of strategic and tactical decisions. Application occurs through the process of organizational performance evaluation, testing results, defining and implementing directives, organizational routines, process and technology updating, accessibility, workflow automation, training, experience support, business understanding, results interpretation, speed of the application, and risk case access.

The sixth step is the ERKMAS design to support the risk-modeling process. Davenport et al. (2005) presented analytics as a strategic capacity that the organization can have and develop for competing. Analytics work requires information systems support. However, RM information is based on context; it requires interpretation, which means to design and develop an ERKMAS—that is, because information without knowledge of the context can be dangerous. RM does not just have a problem with information; it also has problems with interpretation and the communication of meaning.

Companies are competing to optimize their performance on analytical capabilities, which means getting access to quantitative expertise, a capable technology environment and appropriate data. This analytics capability of risk modeling requires the ERKMAS to support what Pfeffer and Sutton (2006) called the craft of managers, which needs to be learned by practice and experience and through the use of evidence as a means for constantly updating assumptions, knowledge, and skills.

The ERKMAS has to go further in managing data and information. As Apte et al. (2002) say, the problem is not just to describe what the organization needs or the request; it is to predict, to optimize, and to classify. This means knowledge production, improvement of its attributes, and overcoming the issues of the ERKMAS design. For example, in actuarial science, there is a process for building statistical models, which describes claims behavior, creating different policies and adjusting models according to contract clauses of the products and their potential claim development.

There are three attributes of ERM implementation that create challenges in process definition and technology use and adoption: the integral, comprehensive, and strategic views (Abrams et al. 2007). This complexity is observed when the modeling process is looking for aggregation analysis when each organizational section can have a different performance, set of problems, and resources from the whole organization. Thus, the ERKMAS required is a dynamic bridge (Figure 2.4) between KM processes and ERM processes passing through people, business processes, and technology.

This bridge is the connection between processes and, in particular, in risk, modeling the use of data with different shapes: structured and unstructured. The bridge is the support to the outcome of the models for interpretation using context, which is, in most cases, unstructured data. The risk-modeling process design, coordination, and understanding are parts of the knowledge used in the decision-making process. It is possible to use some KM technology and techniques (Ruikar et al. 2007) in different levels of the design, coordination, and understanding of the risk-modeling process. Thus, KM technology uses IT with a focus on explicit knowledge, and KM techniques use people learning with a focus on tacit knowledge. KM technologies require support for risk-modeling processes in tasks such as reading data, monitoring data quality, retrieving data, and supporting software structures for quantitative analysis. These technologies are associated with data mining, data warehousing, project management, intranets, extranets, portals, knowledge bases, taxonomies, and ontologies or in explicit technological solutions for learning, content management, collaboration, or management of workflow.

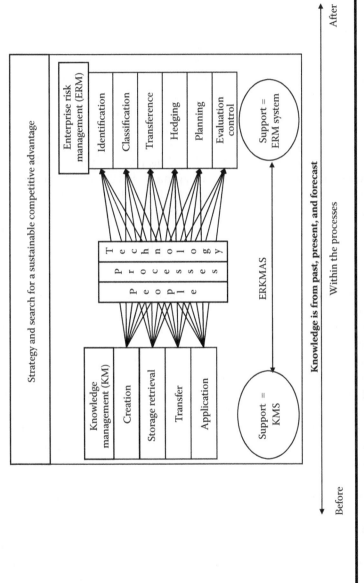

Figure 2.4 ERKMAS is the support for joining KM processes and ERM processes.

KM techniques supporting the risk-modeling knowledge process are associated with interdisciplinary work and interdepartmental work, controlling the whole process from problem definition to solution evaluation. Some of these techniques are communities of practice, forums, training, conferences, post-project reviews, mentoring, yellow pages, and so on. In summary, a goal is to build an ERKMAS in order to support decisions or, as Harris and Davenport (2005) say, to align the organization to the age of the automated decision systems, applying codified knowledge and providing decisions plus a knowledge-sharing environment. Human intervention is identified as a means to confirm decisions and to analyze particular cases, which means the use of knowledge for a risk solution.

In the seventh and final step, the ERKMAS design is complete when the performance evaluation subsystem is designed. This step means getting answers to questions such as how to measure, to interpret, and to discover the directions of the organizational performance connecting risk metrics with risk modeling. There is a search, in this step, for cause–effect indicators related to the risk-modeling process and other risk management processes. One of the points of the Basel II compliance is to build risk-adjusted performance management (RAPM). RAPM comprises risk model development and the construction of risk models requires the understanding of indicators used for enterprise performance evaluation.

KM relates to performance measures using the relationship between the four types of organizational capital (Fairchild 2002): intellectual, human, social, and structural. The BSC (Kaplan and Norton 2004) contributes to using strategy maps to provide a meaning for the intangibles and their influence in the risk-modeling process. The inclusion of risk factors and intellectual capital concepts in the balanced scorecard can be a step ahead in the performance evaluation processes relating KM and ERM. However, more than the metrics for organizational performance evaluation, the emphasis is in the process to build the metrics in a relevant way when risk is involved (Wu 2005). In addition, the KM metrics (Rao 2005) can be connected to the BSC in different fronts and settings.

The BSC can lead to the creation and formation of the strategy of intellectual capital and its fortification (Wu 2005). The integration of the internal perspective, learning and growth, and the strategic process of the intellectual capital are a direct consequence of the use of BSC. Measures of intellectual capital (Fairchild 2002) use metrics for financial processes, business processes, learning, and client and human development, combining components of intangible assets, growth, renovation efficiency, and stability. Fairchild (2002) explains that KM and BSC can be connected by the management of resources with a focus on the combination of the resources of intellectual capital with the processes of the organization.

In summary, the KM metrics can be included in the BSC, and some approaches are done relating risk factors, intellectual capital, and BSC but not the whole evaluation process of the organizational performance under risk. Barquin (2001) identified that managing and leveraging knowledge is crucial for improving organizational performance; however, risk was not included as a factor that needed to be evaluated. As a complement, Shaw (2005) presented the risk performance-adjusted measures and the process to calculate them. These processes are part of the KM processes in the sense of using data, creating models, and interpreting the results and, as Fairchild (2002) says, related to intellectual capital management. However, the integration of the risk measures with the BSC is not evident. There are two ways to develop risk-based performance measures. One is working directly from the definition of the indicators and the inclusion of the risk components in tangible and intangible assets. Another is to build special indicators (Albrecht 1998) as risk-adjusted return on capital (RAROC) and return on risk-adjusted capital (RORAC), for example, in order to relate return, expected losses, and exposure. In any case, the ERKMAS design requires data architecture and software to support combinations of cause–effect development when the risk-modeling processes are involved.

2.4 Conclusions

1. Analytics and KM are disciplines that are associated with ERM. The KMS needs to support ERM process development in common and different dimensions of the ERM processes. A better ERKMAS can provide support to the risk-modeling process as a common process in ERM. The ERKMAS includes the analytics process.
2. Assessment of risk organizational issues and the development of the analytics process are part of the creation of risk knowledge. The risk-modeling process is supported by the analytics process and follows similar steps for different problems to solve.
3. The management of the modeling process requires risk knowledge creation for effective and efficient development of solutions. There are tools to share knowledge and to produce results in the risk-modeling process that need identification, alignment and use of tools, methods, and technology from the analytics process.
4. The methodology summary for the development of risk-modeling knowledge is the following:
   - Answering the questions related to the strategy and strategic planning in the organization
   - Identifying the enablers to transfer risk knowledge from tacit to explicit knowledge and vice versa
   - Understanding of flows of information to produce knowledge
   - Understanding risk knowledge organization
   - Searching for KM technologies and techniques
   - Designing the ERKMAS to support risk modeling
   - Connecting organizational performance metrics and the risk-modeling process

This chapter has presented a view of the analytics process based on KM processes using three risk management activities. The analysis and design of the ERKMAS is a task to perform in order to implement the analytics process. In the following chapter, we are going to review how these steps are related to management control systems. In the past, management control systems were seen as part of cost control. In this book, we introduce the idea that management control systems are the systems to implement strategy at all dimensions of the expected value added from all stakeholders' points of view.

References

Abrams, C., Von Kanel, J., Muller, S., Pfitzmann, B., and Ruschka-Taylor, S., 2007, Optimized enterprise risk management, *IBM Systems Journal*, 46(2), pp. 219–2343.

Ackoff, R., 1981, On the use of models in corporate planning, *Strategic Management Journal*, 2, pp. 353–359.

Alavi, M. and Leidner, D., 2001, Review: Knowledge management and knowledge management systems: Conceptual foundations and research issues, *MIS Quarterly*, 25(1), pp. 107–136.

Albrecht, P., 1998, Risk Based Capital Allocation and Risk Adjusted Performance Management in Property/Liability-Insurance: A Risk Theoretical Framework, In *ASTIN/AFIR Colloquium 1997, Joint Day-Proceedings*, Cairns, Australia, pp. 57–80.

Aleksandrov, A., Kolmogorov, A.N., Lavrentiev, M.A., and Gould, S.H., 1969, *Mathematics: Its Content, Methods and Meaning*, MIT Press, Boston.

Apte, C.V., Natarajan, R., Pednault, E.P.D., and Tipu, F.A., 2002, A probabilistic estimation framework for predictive modeling analytics, *IBM Systems Journal*, 41(3), pp. 438–448.

Aven, T., 2003, *Foundation of Risk Analysis*, John Wiley, Chichester.

Avery, H., 2007, Don't shoot the quant guys!, *Euromoney*, 38(463), p. 42.

Banham, R., 2004, Enterprising views of risk management, *Journal of Accountancy*, 197(6), pp. 65–72.

Barquin, R., 2001, What is knowledge management? Knowledge and innovation, *Journal of the KMCI*, 1(2), pp. 127–143.

Brown, B., 2001, Step by step enterprise risk management, *Risk Management*, 48(9), pp. 43–50.

Buchanan, L. and O'Connell, A., 2006, A brief history of decision making, *Harvard Business Review*, 84(1), pp. 33–41.

Burstein, F., Zyngier, S., and Rateb, Z., 2002, Knowledge management in the financial services sector: Understandings and trends in Australia, In *Proceedings of the 3rd European Conference on Knowledge Management*, September, pp. 113–125.

Caldwell, J. and Ram, Y., 1999, *Mathematical Models Case Studies*, Springer, New York.

Carnap, R., 1966, *An Introduction to the Philosophy of Science*, Basic Books, New York.

Casualty Actuarial Society (CAS), 2001, Survey on Enterprise Risk Management. Available at http://www.casact.org/research/erm/survey.pdf.

Choo, C.W., 1998, *The Knowing Organization*, Oxford University Press, Oxford.

Cumming, C. and Hirtle, B., 2001, The challenges of risk management in diversified financial companies, *Federal Reserve Bank of New York*, March, pp. 1–17.

Dalkir, K., 2005, *Knowledge Management in Theory and Practice*, Elsevier, Boston.

Daniell, M., 2000, Strategy and volatility: Risk and global strategic challenge, *Balance Sheet*, 8(4), pp. 24–36.

Davenport, T., 2006, Competing on analytics, *Harvard Business Review*, 84(1), pp. 99–107.

Davenport, T., Cohen, D., and Jacobson, A., 2005, Competing on analytics, Working Knowledge Research Center Babson Executive Education.

Dickinson, G., 2001, Enterprise risk management: Its origins and conceptual foundation, *The Geneva Papers on Risk and Insurance*, 26(3), pp. 360–366.

Dzinkowski, R., 2002, Knowledge management in Financial Services, *FT Mastering Management*, http://www.ftmastering.com/mmo/mmo10_2.htm.

Edwards, J.S., Handzic, M., Carlsson, S., and Nissen, M., 2003, Knowledge management research and practice: Vision and directions, *Knowledge Management Research and Practice*, 1(1), pp. 49–60.

Ernst and Young, 2001, Risk management guide from theory to practice: Evolving your organization's risk management. *Insurance and Actuarial Advisory Services*.

Fairchild, A., 2002, Knowledge management metrics via a balanced scorecard methodology, *Proceedings of the 35th International Conference on System Sciences*.

Foster, D., 1985, *The Philosophical Scientists*, C. Hurst, New York.

Froot, K.A., Scharfstein, D., and Stein, J., 1994, A framework for risk management, *Harvard Business Review*, 72(6), pp. 91–102.

Galloway, D. and Funston, R., 2000, The challenges of enterprise risk management, *Balance Sheet*, 8(8), pp. 22–25.

Goovaerts, M.J., de Vylder, F., and Haezendonck, J., 1984, *Insurance Premiums. Theory and Applications*. North-Holland, Amsterdam.

Hammond, J.S., Keeney, R.L., and Raiffa, H., 2006, The hidden traps in decision making, *Harvard Business Review*, 84(1), pp. 118–126.

Harris, J. and Davenport, T., 2005, *Automated Decision Making Comes of Age*, Accenture Institute for High Performance Business.

Hayward, M.L.A., 2002, When do firms learn from their acquisition experience? Evidence from 1990–1995, *Strategic Management Journal*, 23(1), pp. 21–39.

Hormozi, A. and Giles, S., 2004, Data mining a competitive weapon for banking and retail industries, *Information Systems Management*, 21(2), pp. 62–71.

Horton-Bentley, A., 2006, The new best practice: Unifying banking across lines of business, *KMworld Best practices in Financial Services*, September.

Kaplan, R. and Norton, D., 2004, Measuring the strategic readiness of intangible assets, *Harvard Business Review*, 82(2), pp. 52–63.

Karlin, S. and Taylor, H., 1998, *An Introduction to Stochastic Modeling*, Harcourt Publishers, Orlando, FL.

Klugman, S., Panjer, H., and Willmot, G., 1998, *Loss Models from Data to Decisions*, John Wiley & Sons, New York.

Leonard, D., 1998, *Wellsprings of Knowledge*, Harvard Business School Press, Boston.

Liebenberg, A. and Hoyt, R., 2003, The determinants of enterprise risk management: Evidence from the appointment of Chief Risk Officers, *Risk Management and Insurance Review*, 6(1), pp. 37–51.

Marshal, C. and Prusak, L., 1996, Financial risk and need for superior knowledge management, *California Management Review*, 38(3), pp. 77–101.

McKibben, D., 2004, Banks evolve in their approach to enterprise risk management, *Gartner G2 Report*, pp. 1–10.

Meulbroek, L., 2002, The promise and challenge of integrated risk management, *Risk Management and Insurance Review*, 5(1), pp. 55–66.

Mladenic, D., Lavrac, N., Bohance, M., and Moyle, S., (Ed), 2003, *Data Mining and Decision Support and Integration*, Kluwer Academic Publishers, Boston.

Nonaka, I. and Takeuchi, H., 1995, *The Knowledge-Creating Company: How Japanese Companies Create the Dynamics of Innovation*, Oxford University Press, New York.

Nonaka, I. and Toyama, R., 2003, The knowledge-creating theory revisited: Knowledge creation as a synthesizing process, *Knowledge Management Research and Practice*, 1(1), pp. 2–10.

Noy, E. and Ellis, S., 2003, Corporate risk strategy: Does it vary across business activities?, *European Management Journal*, 21(1), pp. 119–128.

Oldfield, G. and Santomero, A., 1997, Risk management in financial institutions, *Sloan Management Review*, 39(1), pp. 33–47.

Pfeffer, J. and Sutton R., 2006, *Hard Facts, Dangerous Half-Truths and Total Nonsense: Profiting from Evidence-Based Management*, Harvard Business Press, Boston.

Raiffa, H., 1968, *Decision Analysis: Introductory Lectures on Choices under Uncertainty*, Addison-Wesley, Reading, MA.

Rao, M., 2005, *Knowledge Management Tools and Techniques*, Elsevier Butterworth-Heinemann, Burlington, VA.

Ruikar, K., Anumba, C.J., and Egbu, C., 2007, Integrated use of technologies and techniques for construction knowledge management, *Knowledge Management Research and Practice*, 5, pp. 297–311.

Senge, P., 1990, *The Fifth Discipline*, Doubleday, New York.

Sharman, R., 2002, Enterprise risk management—The KPMG approach, *British Journal of Administrative Management*, May/June, pp. 26–28.

Shaw, J., 2005, Managing all your enterprise's risks, *Risk Management*, 52(9), pp. 22–30.

Simmons, R., 1999, How risky is your company, *Harvard Business Review*, 77(3), pp. 85–94.

Simoneau, L., 2006, Enterprise search: The foundation for risk management, *KM World*, Nov. 1, 2006.

Smith A. and Dumasia N., 2011, Risk Management A Driver of Enterprise Value in the Emerging Environment, KPMG International. Available at https://www.in.kpmg.com/SecureData/aci/Files/RiskManagementADriverofEnterpriseValueintheEmerging Environment.pdf [accessed November 2016].

Sutcliffe, K. and Weber, K., 2003, The high cost of accurate knowledge, *Harvard Business Review*, 81(5), pp. 74–82.

Tillinghast-Towers Perrin, 2000, *Enterprise Risk Management in the Insurance Industry—2002 Benchmarking Survey Report*.

Van Greuning, H. and Brajovic-Bratanovic, S., 2003, *Analyzing and Managing Banking Risk: Framework for Assessing Corporate Governance and Financial Risk*, The World Bank, Washington, DC.

Warren, B., 2002, What is missing from the RMIS design? Why enterprise risk management is not working, *Risk Management Magazine*, 49(10), pp. 30–34.

Weick, K., 2001, *Making Sense of the Organization*, Basil Blackwell, Malden, MA.

Wenger, E., 2000, Communities of practice: The organizational frontier, *Harvard Business Review*, 78(1), pp. 139–145.

Wiig, K., 1993, *Knowledge Management Foundations: Thinking about Thinking. How People and Organizations Create, Represent and Use Knowledge*, Schema Press, Arlington, VA.

Wu, A., 2005, The integration between balanced scorecard and intellectual capital, *Journal of Intellectual Capital*, 6(5), pp. 267–284.

Chapter 3

Analytics, Strategy, and Management Control Systems

Eduardo Rodriguez

Contents

This chapter is about the relationship between analytics, strategy, and management control systems. Analytics is an input for a strategic process, for creating and defining strategies. Once the strategy has been built, the next step is to find the way to achieve a good implementation. Many strategies may be good, but the implementation may not be. Bad strategy and bad implementation increase strategic risk. Management control systems are the set of systematic activities used to implement the strategy to provide value to all stakeholders.

Analytics is part of the management control system. This is through the way in which it provides the insights that support any steps for implementation and in how using strategic intelligence can provide the structure for maintaining the competitive advantages of organizations.

This chapter has three sections: First, to present different kinds of organizations and encourage an open-minded and different way of looking at organizations; second, to connect organizations and management control systems; and third, to indicate how the measurement systems that analytics helps to create are based on key performance indicators and key risk indicators.

3.1 Breaking Paradigms and Organizations as Systems

There are not unique business models or organizational structures. The main principle is that first comes strategy design and then the organizational structure or design. This means that, depending on what the organization wants to do, it will decide how to use all its resources to work together to achieve the strategic goals. It is important to review the concept of organizational design according to the analytics process as it has been introduced in this book. Organizational design requires principles such as the following:

- Thinking strategically, involving risk management from the beginning of the strategic design process and review of the performance evaluation and the variation of the expected results.
- Thinking creatively in order to decide where to go and what to achieve with the business. This means defining the goals under the observation feasibility and ideal assumptions.
- Creating value in all dimensions of the business definition (who, what, how) and for all stakeholders. Evaluating what is or is not feasible.
- Keeping in mind that good implementation is the core of the functioning in the organization. Under the analytics process, the emphasis is on starting with the answer to what else can I do with the resources that I have today? This includes, for example, with data and analytics capabilities in organizations.
- Using an analytics view in the integration of information systems, operation management, customer care, and risk management.
- Getting a plan to manage strategic risk. This means learning from the beginning the strategic steps that need to be performed and the risk associated with those steps. Defining potential early warning systems about strategic risk, which will connect to many other risk control activities.
- Modifying the order of first compliance in risk management regulation and moving in the direction of thinking in risk management as a strategic opportunity. This means converting risk management into a means of strategic competency.

Strategic and organizational design for implementing strategy is not a task that is learned just through imitation or by considering the best practices that are seen in the market or economic sector. There are examples of organizations that have been very successful using structures outside of any paradigm, such as SEMCO Brazil Empowerment and the way to define management and employee relationships, developing a more open schema of working. This schema is based on the meaning and value of each employee in the joint achievement of goals and the control and decisions related to the use of resources. Fundacion Social Colombia decided to have two heads sharing power. This means two boards: one for social mandate and another for corporate mandate. The reason is that the model of Fundacion Social is a not-for-profit organization that has companies that produce the funds to achieve the final objective of intervening in society's improvement. Another example is Woodland (Hamel 2011) in which the flat organizational policy, modifying the structure of the hierarchical levels in organizations, allowed employees to share responsibility in the decision of what organizational resources could really provide value to the organization.

Moreover, according to the variety of business models, there are multiple strategies; they are not unique. As Mintzberg et al. (1998), in their book *The Strategy Safari*, present, there are various ways to develop strategies:

- Design: planned perspective, cerebral, simple and informal, judgmental, deliberate
- Planning: plans decomposed into substrategies and programs, formal, decomposed, deliberate
- Positioning: planned generic positions, analytical, systematic, deliberate
- Entrepreneurial: personal, unique perspective, as niche, visionary, intuitive, largely deliberate
- Cognitive: mental perspective, mental emergent, descriptive (main proponent Simon)
- Learning: patterns, unique, emergent, informal
- Power: political and cooperative patterns and positions, conflictive, aggressive
- Cultural: Collective perspective, ideological, constrained, collective
- Environmental: specific positions, generic, passive, imposed, hence emergent
- Configuration: any to the left, in context, integrative, episodic, sequenced

The variety of development of strategies and the options of business models affect directly all dimensions (who, what, how) of the organizational design and management control systems. These two aspects, the multiplicity of ways to develop strategy and business models, open the need to observe the support that the analytics process can provide. The analytics process needs to adapt to the selected strategies and, at the same time, to help in the definition of the strategies. This requires analytics to be a systematic approach of support for the following:

- Organizational structure definition
- Decision-making process and authority
- Management familiarity with industry
- Driver of operation on finance
- Culture building
- Strategic planning and budgeting
- Transfer pricing and resource allocation

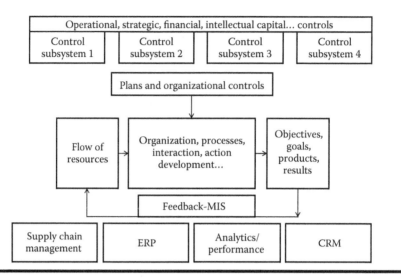

Figure 3.1 The general concept of a system.

- Balance among compensation, incentives, and HR mobility
- Improvement of resource management: synergies of scale and scope

In the organization's design, the analytics process can be considered as a flow that keeps awareness and helps the problem-solving process of the organizational system—the system that performs a process of planning, coordinating, communicating, evaluating, deciding, and influencing. An organization, as an open system, is permanently adapting the organization to the environment. The adaptation is part of strategy formulation and the organization's design. The organization as a system has a brain that processes information, learns, and creates knowledge to develop the organization itself. The organization's brain develops strategic intelligence to manage all the relationships of areas and business units (see Figure 3.1). Analytics knowledge management feeds and maintains the process of strategic intelligence improvement for a better system performance.

Based on the above points, the next sections present the relationship of the organization to management control systems.

3.2 Organizations and Management Control Systems

Management control requires a complete and clear definition of the goals that the organization would like to achieve. The definition requires the measurement system design, metrics, data, and the analytics process to measure. This means if we do not know where to go, any direction could be good or bad. This is, as Carroll expresses in *Alice's Adventures in Wonderland*: "If you don't know where you're going, any road will take you there."

How to get the answer to where we want to go? The answer can be addressed by the analytics process that provides insights to identify what is known, unknown, and unknowable: presenting in as clear a way as possible desirable and feasible futures and avoiding strategic traps, such as keeping the evidence out of the decision process just because it could be convenient to ignore it.

The definition of the goals will include the problems to solve and the process to define the problems in a clear way and to find the methods to get solutions. In the end, the management control system will be based on the following areas of development:

- People moving in a common direction to implement the strategy.
- Coordination, permanent search for solution of problems, search of the best.
- Problem-solving capacity. This is expected in most of the cases that are systematic, organized, and with attributes, such as efficiency and effectiveness.
- Review of strategic concepts, such as the bases of passing from a single industry to diversified (unrelated and related), sharing or no resources or core competencies, managing as a portfolio the business units.
- Use of tools that can be analytics in a qualitative or quantitative way. For instance,
  - Strategy and the four Ps (product, price, promotion, place)
  - Mapping market growth to relative market share
  - Attractiveness and strengths
  - Porter's forces
  - Generic competitive strategies (low cost – differentiation)
  - Value chain analysis
  - BSC Kaplan and Norton—structure of the BSC properly defined to support the BU portfolio.
- Start with a clarification to the whole organization of the mission, vision, and value proposition based on the mission to review the factors associated with the planning process, formalization of capital expenditure and evaluation, capital investment analysis, project development, compensation, and budgeting review.
- Design of detectors, assessors, effectors, and communication as Anthony and Govindarajan (2007) point out. We create early warning systems, control systems in the time of the action and post actions. Detectors are the ways to observe the information to be aware of what is happening. Assessors are a means to review similarities and differences between the current situation and the expected one. And effectors look for the reduction of the difference between the current and expected results. In our previous chapter, we view this comparison and observations as risk management-related tasks.

In general, the management control system is about supporting and developing capabilities for organization members to achieve goals and implementing

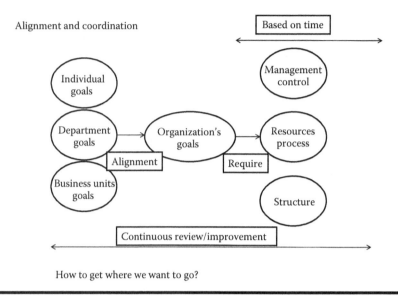

Figure 3.2 Implementing a strategy requires alignment.

the strategy. These actions are connected to improve alignment and coordination, deciding what to measure, creating the systems to measure, performing analytics, and generation of analytics knowledge for better business understanding. The development of the analytics knowledge process will cover defining the root causes of problems, solutions, and developing knowledge transfer methods to move the analytics knowledge across the organization, horizontally and vertically (see Figure 3.2).

Management control systems under the analytics process require a clear connection with measurement systems that include metrics with and without risk factors in their definitions. The next section presents some of the links between key performance indicators and key risk indicators related to the development of a management control system.

3.3 Key Performance Indicators and Key Risk Indicators

This section presents the analytics process as a way to develop the measurement system in the organization, which is the same as seeing the analytics process as the nervous system that activates the organization's intelligence in order to achieve its goals. The concept of connecting key performance indicators (KPIs) and key risk indicators (KRIs) is based on the theory and frameworks related to enterprise risk management and strategic risk (Figure 3.3).

Some of the key ideas in ERM

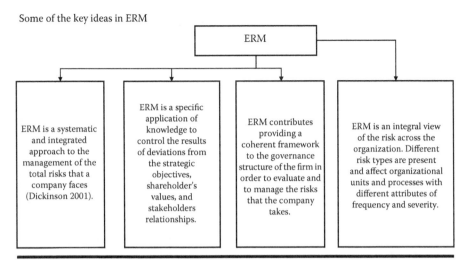

Figure 3.3   Foundations of ERM.

A business measurement system requires three components: goals, for example, related to sustainability, performance, and the components of a balanced scorecard—benefits, customers, processes, and employees. Next, metrics are the explicit identification of the methods of calculation of the factors to control and adequate values definition. There are metrics of several areas and types, such as quick ratio, and dimensions of the metrics, such as time, region, etc. A method to develop metrics is based on the following steps: connecting the desires of the organization and the structure of the management control system components

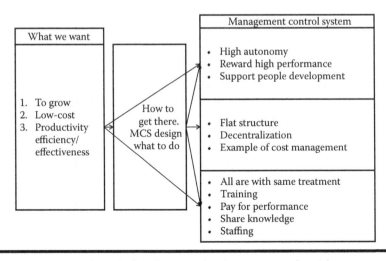

Figure 3.4   Connection of what the organization wants to do with a management control system.

(see Figure 3.4), embedding the concepts of efficiency and effectiveness in the definition of the metrics and the context of the strategy, and directing the general concepts of the organizations as a whole to the specific areas of the organization, manufacturing, marketing, and so on.

Once the areas are defined in terms of the measurement systems, at least two big tasks have to be performed:

a. Identification of costs associated with the measurement system
b. Identification of potential relationships of cause and effect of the results based on trees

The combination of KPI and KRI is based on the analysis of the possible events that can create variation of the KPIs. For example, the growth of market share can be part of the KPIs of the organization. The target is defined by a number, and the organization is prepared to achieve that target. In several cases, the targets are not exactly the final numbers from the results evaluation. The results of the market share are not exactly what the target was or better than the expected market share. In some periods, the target can be above or below the real value, creating variation through time that represents a measure of risk related to that KPI. The question for developing management control systems is how to improve the knowledge to reduce the uncertainty related to the market share. The actions that organizations take have risk associated with them, and the effects can be part of the causes for changes in the goal achievement. Table 3.1 shows the review of strategy goals; KPIs; expected results; circumstances or risks that can affect the achievement of the target, type of data, and possible steps in the analytics process that can be used.

The analytics process is related to the way to reduce risks related to that KPI and, at the same time, to the analytics knowledge creation to understand how the market share can be affected by market factors and competitive conditions of the organization.

With this section, the first part of the book has introduced the main concepts of the analytics process, and the second part will review the application of the analytics process to different sectors and several problems in various countries, using a variety of data and tools and following the steps to convert data into actions in organizations.

Chapter 4 introduces the value of the analytics process in the way that many other management tools are connected and required to keep alignment for better understanding of adding value in the organization. This presentation of the association of management concepts and the analytics process opens the description in the subsequent chapters about the way that analytics can be involved in several economic sectors.

Table 3.1 Finding the Relationship among Performance, Risk, and the Analytics Process

Review of the control and variation	The strategic goal is to improve the market share. The reason is it is assumed that better market share can bring benefits in profitability (this is not always the case).	As KPIs, it is possible to develop a metric that is just the ratio of value of revenues of the company to the total revenues of the sector. However, many other components can be required, for example, product definition, time, marginal changes, etc.	The targets or expected results will be achieved through the strategies. The analytics process can input into the target definition process the value of the metrics that can be expected.	Some conditions of the company, market, and business environment can affect the achievement of the goal, for example, cost increment, reduction of distribution channels, production capacity, mistakes, customer satisfaction, etc.
Data that can be required	Market indicators, company production capacity, economy expectations, etc.	Values of historical experience, values of other metrics, values of related financial indicators, values of related customer behavior, and engagement with the organization.	It can depend on the variables that are included in the metric development. It could be only numerator and denominator in the case of ratios, but these numerators and denominators can be deterministic or stochastic. They can be the results of additional model outcomes.	Each potential source of modification of expected results requires data. For example, changes in distribution channels can be related to costs, locations, etc. How can each event affect the achievement of the goal?
Analytics process steps	Descriptive visualization, exploratory data analysis, quantitative and qualitative analysis of the internal and external conditions of the organizations.	Review of the processes and data that each step uses and provides. There is a need for involving many variables and developing tables and statistical metrics to review relationships.	Performance models in the case that variables are used in combination. Identify if the probability distributions are possible.	Review the probability distributions of variables used, and identify approaches to describe variability.

References

Anthony, R.N., and Govindarajan, V., 2007, *Management Control Systems*, McGraw-Hill/ Irwin, Boston.

Dickinson, G., 2001, Enterprise Risk Management: Its Origins and Conceptual Foundation, *The Geneva Papers on Risk and Insurance*, 26(3), pp. 360–366.

Hamel, G., 2011, The Big Idea: First, Let's Fire All the Managers, *Harvard Business Review*, 89(12), pp. 4–13.

Mintzberg, H., Lampel, J., and Ahlstrand, B., 1998, *Strategy Safari: A Guided Tour through the Wilds of Strategic Management*, Free Press, New York.

ANALYTICS PROCESS APPLICATIONS

Chapter 4

Data, Information, and Intelligence

G. Scott Erickson and Helen N. Rothberg

Contents

Context

A substantial record of scholarly and practitioner work exists concerning intangible assets, from data to information, knowledge to intelligence. A better understanding of the interrelationships of such intangibles can enable more effective strategies.

Purpose

This chapter explores the relationship between different types of intangible assets, specifically Big Data and competitive intelligence. Are Big Data holdings likely to draw attention from competitive intelligence operations?

Design

Available data on Big Data holdings, by industry, is compared and contrasted with a proprietary database on competitive intelligence activity by industry.

Findings

A clear relationship appears to exist. Massive holdings of Big Data are associated with aggressive competitive intelligence activity. When little Big Data is applied, competitive intelligence activity is at a low level.

Research limitations or implications

This is an exploratory study. Although the results seem clear, they are not tested as hypotheses.

Practical implications

Readers should be able to discern the patterns in their own industry, providing insight into decisions about pursuing investments in Big Data systems, competitive intelligence operations, and/or counterintelligence.

Originality or value

The linkages between the diverse fields of Big Data and business analytics, knowledge management, and intellectual capital, competitive intelligence, and others involved with intangibles are not often explored. There are linkages apparent, and all the disciplines benefit from the cross-fertilization of ideas and techniques.

4.1 Introduction

4.1.1 Purpose of the Study

As Big Data and business analytics continue to grow and draw more attention, there is also an increasing recognition that existing theory and conceptual development in other areas studying intangible assets may have something of value to add. This study explores the potential of that relationship.

4.1.2 About the Background of This Work

The authors continue a research stream exploring the connections between knowledge management, competitive intelligence, and Big Data/business intelligence. This includes theory development, comparing the concepts of the different fields, and looking at where contrasting emphases can add value through cross-fertilization of ideas. The stream also includes comparison of methods and techniques, from Big Data platforms to knowledge management (information technology solutions, communities of practice, etc.) and on to competitive intelligence analysis tools (e.g., environmental scanning, war games).

4.1.3 What Is the Scope of This Work?

While further developing themes from some earlier work, such as the role of business analytics in recognizing the value of basic data and information and the similar contribution of knowledge management to encouraging and capturing insights from intangible assets, this chapter looks more specifically at the potential contribution of competitive intelligence to our understanding of all these fields. Data are available on the industry level concerning Big Data capabilities and knowledge management or intangible asset development. To these are added further data, specifically on competitive intelligence activity and threats in comparable industries.

Focusing on competitive intelligence (CI) can bring new insights to the conversation. CI has always valued the full range of intangible asset inputs (data, information, and knowledge) and actionable intelligence, something knowledge management can neglect (with its strict definitions of purportedly more valuable knowledge vs. mere data or information). CI can also be more directed, looking for additional data, information, or knowledge in a specific area in order to address a specific question. This chapter looks at data on CI activity in specific industries, identifying those with high intelligence commitment as opposed to those without.

These results will be compared and contrasted with data on Big Data potential, also by industry. As a consequence, the authors are able to prescribe directions for the development of all, some, or none of the disciplines in question while also providing recommendations for cross-field combinations for greater impact.

4.1.4 Definition of the Key Concepts

Data: accumulated observations
Information: organized data
Knowledge: data and information subjected to reflection and experience
Knowledge management: deliberate programs to leverage and grow knowledge assets, including learning, sharing, and discovery
Intellectual capital: knowledge assets, usually implying categorization and/or metrics
Intelligence: applied knowledge, often at the strategic level, usually implying action
Competitive intelligence: the process of gathering, analyzing, and acting upon data, information, and/or knowledge concerning a competitor, technology, or related subject

4.2 What Is the Work Performed in This Field?

Intangible assets and their role in obtaining and maintaining competitive advantage have a considerable history in the economics and business literatures albeit in different forms and with different definitions. But combining the different literature streams into a coherent whole can help us understand the opportunities presented by attention to these intangibles as well as develop a better grasp of the potential of the relatively new interest in Big Data and business analytics.

4.2.1 Knowledge-Based View of the Firm

The earliest interest in intangibles generally revolved around innovation. Given that context, it's not surprising that Schumpeter (1934) is often seen as an important source, especially his focus on knowledge combination, learning, and new insights. Nelson and Winter's (1982) evolutionary theory suggests that intangibles, such as skills and learning, might be the real drivers of competitive advantage in firms. This view fit nicely with the near-contemporary development of the resource-based view of the firm (Wernerfelt 1984) with organizational knowledge, in this case, as the key resource or differentiator. From there, a knowledge-based view of the firm with knowledge and similar intangibles at the heart of competitive advantage was a natural extension (Teece 1998; Grant 1996). Indeed, many in the field now argue that organizational knowledge may be the only source of unique, sustainable competitive advantage as other, more traditional assets and differentiators become commoditized.

4.2.2 Data, Information, Knowledge, and Wisdom or Intelligence (DIKW)

As may be discerned from the previous paragraph, it's very easy in this area to throw terms around loosely with somewhat ambiguous concepts such as learning, knowledge, know-how, and skills being used in precise applications. Fortunately, most of the disciplines have settled on definitions following Ackoff's (1989) DIKW hierarchy, positing that intangibles grow from basic data to ordered information, providing opportunities for users to obtain knowledge, which can then pass to wisdom. In more current applications, intelligence, or actionable knowledge, information, or data, is often used in place of wisdom at the highest level. These definitions recur in specific disciplines and have some importance in setting the boundaries and areas of study for fields. In knowledge management (KM), for example, data are simply observations, information is data in context, and knowledge itself is information subjected to experience and reflection (Zack 1999b). In this field, the data and information inputs are of interest as sources, but only the knowledge and insights created in employees' heads are really worth creating systems to manage. According to this viewpoint, data and information have little value on their own. And intelligence is left to other fields altogether. This leaves some gaps related to the more recent interest in Big Data business analytics, although other disciplines pay more attention. As we'll see, these differing perspectives create opportunities for cross-fertilization between disparate disciplines.

4.2.3 KM and Intellectual Capital

As just alluded to, KM as well as the related discipline of intellectual capital (IC) focus on the value of knowledge assets. IC is more about identifying, cataloging, and measuring knowledge assets (Bontis 1999; Edvinsson and Malone 1997; Stewart 1997). The field has generally settled on the areas of human capital (individual job-related knowledge), structural capital (organizational routines, culture, etc.), and relational capital (knowledge about external relationships) although we'll see some extensions shortly. KM, on the other hand, focuses on what to do with these intangible assets. In exploring ways to better manage knowledge, scholars and practitioners have explored differences in its nature that can make it more of a challenge to develop. In particular, the differences between tacit and explicit knowledge (Nonaka and Takeuchi 1996; Polanyi 1967) have been highlighted as well as characteristics such as complexity and stickiness (McEvily and Chakravarthy 2002; Zander and Kogut 1995; Kogut and Zander 1992). The nature of the organizations looking to manage knowledge have also been studied, focusing on absorptive capacity (Cohen and Levinthal 1990), social capital (Nahapiet and Ghoshal 1998), social networks (Liebowitz 2005), and related topics.

4.2.4 Leveraging Knowledge

With these types of circumstances in mind, KM practitioners can move to better managing their particular knowledge assets. KM is all about more effectively employing and growing knowledge by combination, sharing, socialization, and other such methods (Zack 1999a; Grant 1996). The appropriate tools for growth can be subject to the variables just mentioned, so theory and practice both emphasize assessing and reacting by using tacit tools for tacit knowledge, explicit tools for explicit knowledge, etc. (Choi and Lee 2003; Schulz and Jobe 2001; Boisot 1995). From this perspective, approaches ranging from communities of practice to IT solutions have been developed and employed (Brown and Duguid 1991; Matson, Patiath and Shavers 2003; Thomas, Kellogg and Erickson 2001).

But, as noted at the beginning of the section, KM and IC both focus largely on knowledge assets. Precursors, such as data and information, or extensions, such as intelligence, are rarely discussed. But that doesn't mean there isn't an emphasis elsewhere, in related fields.

4.2.5 Knowledge and Intelligence

Over the past decade, new views of intangible assets have resulted in new directions in strategic decision-making. Big Data and business analytics are only the latest step albeit a very important one. In one prominent example, Andreou, Green and Stankosky (2007) looked to make sense of a variety of related approaches by creating the list of operational knowledge assets (LOKA), including market capital (competitive intelligence, enterprise intelligence), human capital, decision effectiveness, organizational capital, and innovation and customer capital. Although many could be included in a standard human, structural, and relational capital taxonomy (as per intellectual capital theory, noted earlier), LOKA does explicitly recognize newer directions, such as CI and enterprise intelligence that don't fit neatly into those structures. A broader view of intangible assets also begs the question of whether data, information, and intelligence have more of a role to play in competitive advantage than is commonly thought in the traditional KM/IC disciplines.

One direction for exploring these questions in more depth is to look specifically at CI. CI has a more extensive history than some of the other "intelligences," growing in both practice and in academia over the past few decades. Basically, IC is about understanding and anticipating competitor actions by identifying, collecting, and analyzing relevant data, information, and knowledge (Prescott and Miller 2001; Gilad and Herring 1996; Fuld 1994). The result is actionable intelligence. CI has a number of distinctions from KM/IC as well as the readily apparent similarities (in particular, both focus on the value of intangible assets; Rothberg and Erickson 2002, 2005). Initially, CI tends to have a wider range of intangible inputs, including the data and information aspects already mentioned several times. Practice also combines these disparate inputs with specialized analysis techniques and applications (Fleisher and Bensoussan 2002; McGonagle and Vella 2002). CI is similar to KM/IC in that operations mature with added sources of inputs and increased analysis experience of the coordinating team (Wright, Picton and Callow 2002; Raouch and Santi 2001). Prior to and at the analysis stage, however, CI is much more likely to conduct targeted searches to fill specific information gaps and, of course, is also designed for action rather than reflection (Gilad 2003; Bernhardt 1993). KM/IC certainly encourages action, but the focus of activities is often more about building the knowledge base and the network for sharing it.

4.2.6 Big Data and Business Analytics

This contrast between KM/IC and CI provides a natural entry to a deeper discussion on Big Data and business analytics. A number of these topics should seem very familiar to anyone with experience with the latter. Big Data, by definition, is about massive amounts of data and information, the wider view of what intangible assets are valuable and the impact of Big Data comes through business analytics processes able to organize, analyze, and find higher level insights from these databases. Indeed, the Big Data, business analytics, and business intelligence area often references prior work in KM and these other areas (Bose 2009; Jourdan, Rainer and Marshall 2008).

For ease of reference, we'll refer to the whole area as either Big Data or business analytics from here on out. The seeds of current excitement about business analytics comes from rapid increases in the power of modern IT systems. Substantially decreased costs for storage and processing, including in the cloud, have enabled organizations to save more and more data while doing more and more analysis of the resulting massive databases (Bussey 2011; Vance 2011b). Much of the data or information collected revolves around operations, supply chain, and channel performance; transactional and customer information; and communications (including social media) (Vance 2011a). According to a much-cited McKinsey Global Services report, Big Data adds value with greater transparency and more immediate feedback on performance, an ability to experiment in real time, provide opportunities for more precise segmentation, rationalized decision making, and generating new product ideas (Manyika et al. 2011).

Scholarly development in this new field is limited. One does see repeated mention of the three Vs (and sometimes additional Vs), referencing data volume, velocity, and variety (Laney 2001). All have increased with the drop in IT costs, allowing for the increased storage and higher level analysis already mentioned, potentially leading to better decision making at all levels (Beyer and Laney 2012). Metrics to date have generally centered on data storage (Manyika et al. 2011) and case studies are used to good effect in explaining the details (Liebowitz 2013). As we know, however, it's not just the size of the databases that is important, it's what's done with them. Per KM/IC, CI, and related disciplines, the really valuable part of data and information comes from the higher level insights and the knowledge and intelligence derived from their analysis. A human element, through analytical techniques, is necessary to the process (Zhao 2013).

4.3 Description of the Problem

This synthesis of the human insight and the database is an important area in which previous research in KM/IC and related fields may have something to offer. KM perspectives would certainly be enhanced by attention to other intangible assets beyond knowledge as well as the added capabilities found in analysis and actionable intelligence. But the KM side does have its own contributions as there is deep scholarship and practice concerning growth in knowledge assets through combination and insight from users as well as how to engage humans to interact with KM initiatives, including IT systems (Matson, Patiath and Shavers 2003; Thomas, Kellogg and Erickson 2001). Person-to-person and person-to-system issues, such as perceived usefulness, motivation, trust, and other such matters, have been at the forefront of the field for more than 20 years.

Given our interest in finding connections between existing scholarship in KM/IC and CI, a comparison of how each field sees the world may be interesting. In previous work, we've looked at connections between KM/IC and Big Data (Erickson and Rothberg 2014). There were some connections, but the linkages were actually rather weak. In this study, we combine data specifically on competitive intelligence practice with that on Big Data capabilities.

4.3.1 Research Questions or Hypotheses

What is the level of data usage, by firm, in major industries?

What is the level of competitive intelligence activity, by firm, in the same major industries?

What comparison can we make between the two variables; what similarities and differences are apparent?

4.4 What Was the Methodology of the Problem Resolution?

In order to provide a framework for discussion, we created Table 4.1 cross-referenced from two sources. Initially, there is information concerning Big Data taken from the aforementioned McKinsey Global Institute (MGI) report (Manyika et al. 2011). This is combined with industry categorizations based on competitive intelligence activity (Erickson and Rothberg 2012, 2013). From this table, we can begin to suggest some ideas concerning the relationship between Big Data and

Table 4.1   Big Data and CI by Industry

Industry	Stored Data per Firm (terabytes)	Stored Data, U.S. Industry (petabytes)	SIC	CI Activity	Firm/CI Activity
Security and investment services	3,866	429	6211	13	8.74
Banking	1,931	619	6020	23	14.27
Communications and media	1,792	715	48	25	16.34
Utilities	1,507	194	49	19	6.94
Government	1,312	848			
Discrete manufacturing	967	966	36,37,38	40,29,45	8.97
Insurance	870	243	63	82	3.49
Process manufacturing	831	694	2834	78	10.96
Resource industries	825	116	13, 24	12,3	9.60
Transportation	801	227	40-45	7	41.46
Retail	697	364	53-59	23	23.25
Wholesale	536	202	50-51	27	14.29
Health care providers	370	434	80	4	300.28
Education	319	269	82	5	172.70
Professional service	278	411	731	6	252.32
Construction	231	51	16	2	113.04
Consumer and recreational services	150	105	79	4	179.20

knowledge as well as what underlying concepts may explain differences present in the information.

4.4.1 What Was the Data Used For?

The first three columns are taken straight from the MGI report, including the industry definitions, although sorted according to stored data per firm for our purposes. Stored data by U.S. industry was sourced by MGI from research firm IDC and is an estimate of the total data held by firms with more than 1,000 employees in each broadly defined industry. This number is then divided by the number of firms to get the per firm figure in the second column. Per firm obviously provides a much different assessment as the number of firms varies dramatically between concentrated industries such as those in financial services and dispersed industries, such as manufacturing. Figures are from 2008.

The last three columns come from our database via a Fuld & Company survey. Standard industrial classification (SIC) was used to sort the data by industry, breaking firms with similar products and operations into appropriate groups for comparison purposes. Sometimes this included SIC level one classification, and sometimes this included groupings down to the second, third, and fourth levels. Only groupings with at least 20 observations (firm and year, financial returns, at least $1 billion in annual revenue) were included in the database. We matched these SIC classifications as closely as possible with the more general industry categories of the MGI report.

Data from the Fuld & Company database includes self reports on the maturity and professionalism of each CI operation. These were weighted by level (four for the highest degree of proficiency, one for the lowest) and combined with the number of firms reporting, each to develop the index shown in the CI activity column. Typically, we use the total amount of CI activity within an industry or industry sector as a proxy for how aggressive the intelligence-gathering environment might be. Here, however, given that the industries and SIC categories between the two databases don't necessarily match up well and that the number of firms in the different industries vary so dramatically, we thought it best to also look at some per firm assessment of CI activity. This is presented in the final column (number of firms calculated from the two "stored data" columns and then divided by the CI metric). This figure ends up being the inverse of CI activity per firm, so a higher value indicates less relative CI emphasis.

4.4.2 What Were the Models and Concepts Used in This Study?

No specific models were employed in this research; it is still at the exploratory stage. What the data manipulation above enables us to do, however, is make some direct comparisons between some very different data sets. The end result is essentially an intensity comparison. The intensity of data storage or use by firms in each industry is compared to the intensity of competitive intelligence efforts conducted by the same firms. The results can eventually guide us in building a model of how these intangibles are used in different industry environments. The results can also be used to begin constructing a theory on how these and other intangibles are related to one another (e.g., is there a correlation between Big Data and competitive intelligence?).

4.4.3 About Validity and Reliability in This Work

As just noted, this is exploratory work and not necessarily meant to be statistically reliable or representative. The data, by their nature, are not amenable to hypothesis tests or other higher level analytical procedures. That being said, the data sets are large and likely to be very similar to the entire populations of both data users and competitive intelligence operations. In a sense, they are likely to be representative but are not yet testable. They are reliable, being good proxies for measuring the two variables in question (data usage and competitive intelligence activity).

4.5 What Were the Results and Their Meaning or Context?

4.5.1 How Are These Results Meaningful for Organizations and for Future Research?

The data are very revealing. On just the level of CI activity per industry sector, there is some evidence of more activity when higher levels of Big Data are present with double-digit CI activity scores. Essentially, there are more, and more professional, CI operations in data-heavy industries. But these metrics are also less than consistent with the highest levels of activity closer to the middle Big Data. There are likely explanations as we'll see, but these initial results are also a reason to look more carefully at the data.

Based on the additional adjustment, calculating the per firm CI metric to go with the per firm Big Data metric makes sense. The number of firms in the extremely broad MGI industry classifications don't necessarily match up well with the number in the SIC categories for IC. Indeed, if one closely examines the data, some industries with relatively high numbers of CI activity also have an abnormally large number of firms represented (retail, wholesale). Similarly, some of those with seemingly muted CI numbers have a relatively low number of resident firms (securities, utilities, natural resources). Consequently, the per firm CI score not only provides more information but is probably the truer representation.

And it does provide some very interesting results. Just as the stored data per firm column shows a clear progression from top to bottom, so does the CI activity per firm column. The level of CI activity for industries with a commitment to Big Data varies within a fairly small range but is of a magnitude difference from the level for industries with low commitment. Scores in the single digits and low double digits (showing aggressive CI operations) go along with a high degree of data storage per firm. Scores in the triple digits (muted CI operations) go along with a low degree of data storage per firm. The pattern is clear and convincing. High levels of CI activity appear to go along with high levels of investment in big data capabilities. Big Data has the potential to feed competitors' CI operations, and those pursuing Big Data strategies should probably be sure to invest in data protection, counterintelligence, and their own CI operations.

But there is even further depth to the data given what we know about KM/IC and CI in some of these industries. Those with the absolute lowest CI ratios—insurance, utilities, and securities—are all regulated industries generating a lot of operational and transactional data. Not all of that data is particularly interesting (movements of money, investments, power). Indeed, what we know from KM/IC is that these industries do not rate very highly for intangible assets, period (Erickson and Rothberg 2012). What is valuable is the rare tacit insight, the "eureka" moments that result in new directions in such industries (new portfolio ideas, new lending or investment strategies, whatever is new in today's old-line utilities). In such environments, the ability of CI operations to spot new ideas from competitors, based on changes in Big Data patterns or discovering the insight itself, can result in rapid copying. Consequently, CI can be both effective and profitable by cutting down periods of new product or new process exclusivity.

Similarly, the next lowest CI ratios are in manufacturing industries, both process (pharmaceuticals, plastics, chemicals) and discrete (machinery, transportation). Again, there is value in CI, not necessarily from the supply chain or operations data, but from what it tells observers is going on in terms of R&D and new products, process optimization, or other manufacturing improvements. Further, just as in the previous group, actual activities tend to be hidden from view, so CI operations of a certain maturity are needed to peek behind the veil.

At the other end of the spectrum, a very different pattern emerges. Those with very high scores on the metric (indicating low levels of CI activity) are invariably services. Services can employ Big Data as they have operations, transactions, and communications just as with other industries. Services, however, have unique characteristics that make them hard to manage, including intangibility, perishability, producer variability, and customer involvement. Consequently, optimizing and standardizing processes can be difficult, leaving a gap in terms of what Big Data is able to accomplish. Moreover, the services seen here are often right out in the open, making advanced CI operations something amounting to overkill. Much of what can be learned could come simply from walking through a public facility and observing the layout or operation. In such situations, fewer worries exist about CI, so there is less need for protection (or, as pointed out, important matters are so transparent as to be almost impossible to protect). There also appears to be less need for counterintelligence or heavy investment in a CI operation.

4.5.2 Where, How, and When to Use It?

Overall, there appears to be a link between a high level of data storage, indicative of industries and firms investing in a Big Data approach, and competitive intelligence interest in those Big Data stores. Even though the direct relationship between the two metrics is clear, there are also less obvious insights in the results. The type of data harvested in Big Data approaches is different, depending on the industry, and the insights or knowledge gained from such data also differ. The initial results show great promise, but there is additional potential apparent if further and deeper analysis is done.

Practitioners can use these results to review their own industries and their relative place in them. Is Big Data a capability necessary to compete in the industry? In some, as listed above, it is already apparently a major factor (financial services, communications) and in others, not yet, perhaps not ever (various services). Similarly, decision makers can ask whether they need a CI capability and/or counterintelligence to protect proprietary data, information, and knowledge. The results are again dependent on circumstances with some industries flush with CI operatives (financial services, utilities, manufacturing) and others not (various services). Strategists should consider the general industry environment, the reasons why data and/or CI may or may not be important, and how to respond—whether going with the flow or taking steps to invest and differentiate through something other than the standard industry intangibles strategy.

4.6 Conclusions and Recommendations

4.6.1 Are the Objectives of the Research Achieved?

Numerous fields look at intangible assets as a valuable corporate resource, ranging from traditional innovation studies to KM, IC, and CI. The newer entity of Big Data and business analytics has drawn great interest for its potential in helping firms craft contemporary competitive strategies and tactics. Big Data and business analytics hold tremendous promise, but these newer disciplines do not exist in a vacuum. There is a strong likelihood that similarities exist with the other fields and that cross-fertilization is possible, helping us to understand all disciplines better as we move forward.

This chapter looked specifically at competitive intelligence activities, at the intelligence or wisdom end of the DIKW hierarchy, opposite Big Data's data or information end. Results drawn from a study of Big Data by McKinsey and our own database on CI activity show a strong relationship between the fields. Higher investment in Big Data capabilities appears to go along with higher levels of competitive intelligence activity. Competitors would appear to be interested in Big Data holdings (and business analytics results). Further analysis of the relationship suggests that there are differences in the nature of the Big Data and related knowledge insights that can lead to further distinctions in the pattern of Big Data and CI activity.

4.6.2 Strategic

As just noted, the implications of this research are primarily at the strategic level. Generally, firms in industries with considerable Big Data holdings should expect an aggressive competitive intelligence response from other firms. As a result, counterintelligence efforts are probably appropriate as is a CI operation of one's own. But practitioners should work to understand their own competitive environment in terms of all intangible assets: data, information, knowledge, and intelligence. Any and all can have value. But some may not be worth the investment if they add little to competitive capabilities because the industry is mature or other, more critical, requirements for success exist. But the data are available to evaluate industry conditions and firm standing within an industry for all of these intangibles, allowing careful, strategic review of where, how, and when a firm should invest resources in a Big Data, KM, or CI capability.

Acknowledgment

The authors gratefully acknowledge the contributions of Fuld & Company for providing some of the data used in this study.

References

Andreou, A. N., Green, A. and Stankosky, M., 2007, A Framework of Intangible Valuation Areas and Antecedents. *Journal of Intellectual Capital*, 8(1), pp. 52–75.

Bernhardt, D., 1993, *Perfectly legal competitive intelligence—How to get it, use it and profit from it*, London: Pitman Publishing.

Beyer, M. A. and Laney, D., 2012, The Importance of 'Big Data': A Definition, retrieved from https://www.gartner.com/doc/2057415.

Boisot, M., 1995, Is Your Firm a Creative Destroyer? Competitive Learning and Knowledge Flows in the Technological Strategies of Firms. *Research Policy*, 24, pp. 489–506.

Bontis, N., 1999, Managing Organizational Knowledge by Diagnosing Intellectual Capital: Framing and Advancing the State of the Field. *International Journal of Technology Management,* 18(5–8), pp. 433–462.

Bose, R., 2009, Advanced Analytics: Opportunities and Challenges. *Industrial Management & Data Systems*, 109(2), pp. 155–172.

Brown, J. S. and Duguid, P., 1991, Organizational Learning and Communities-of-Practice: Toward a Unified View of Working, Learning, and Innovation. *Organizational Science*, 2(1), pp. 40–57.

Bussey, J., 2011, Seeking Safety in Clouds. *The Wall Street Journal*, September 16, p. B8.

Choi, B. and Lee, H., 2003, An Empirical Investigation of KM Styles and Their Effect on Corporate Performance. *Information & Management*, 40, pp. 403–417.

Cohen, W. M. and Levinthal, D. A., 1990, Absorptive Capacity: A New Perspective on Learning and Innovation. *Administrative Science Quarterly*, 35(1), pp. 128–152.

Edvinsson, L. and Malone, M., 1997, *Intellectual capital*. New York: Harper Business.

Erickson, G. S. and Rothberg, H. N., 2014, Big Data and Knowledge Management: Establishing a Conceptual Foundation. *Electronic Journal of Knowledge Management*, 12(2), pp. 115–123.

Erickson, G. S. and Rothberg, H. N., 2013, Competitors, intelligence, and big data. In: J. Liebowitz, ed., *Big data and business analytics*. Boca Raton, FL: CRC Press, pp. 103–116.

Erickson, G. S. and Rothberg, H. N., 2012, *Intelligence in action: Strategically managing knowledge assets*, London: Palgrave Macmillan.

Fleisher, C. S. and Bensoussan, B., 2002, *Strategic and competitive analysis: Methods and techniques for analyzing business competition*, Upper Saddle River, NJ: Prentice Hall.

Fuld, L. M., 1994, *The new competitor intelligence: The complete resource for finding, analyzing, and using information about your competitors*, New York: John Wiley.

Gilad, B., 2003, *Early warning: Using competitive intelligence to anticipate market shifts, control risk, and create powerful strategies*, New York: ANACOM.

Gilad, B. and Herring, J., eds., 1996, *The art and science of business intelligence*, Greenwich, CT: JAI Press.

Grant, R. M., 1996, Toward a Knowledge-Based Theory of the Firm. *Strategic Management Journal*, 17(Winter), pp. 109–122.

Jourdan, Z., Rainer, R. K. and Marshall, T. E., 2008, Business Intelligence: An Analysis of the Literature. *Information Systems Management*, 25(2), pp. 121–131.

Kogut, B. and Zander, U., 1992, Knowledge of the Firm, Combinative Capabilities, and the Replication of Technology. *Organization Science*, 3(3), pp. 383–397.

Laney, D., 2001, 3D Data Management: Controlling Data Volume, Velocity and Variety, retrieved November 1, 2013 from http://blogs.gartner.com/doug-laney/files/2012/01/ad949-3D-Data-Management-Controlling-Data-Volume-Velocity-and-Variety.pdf.

Liebowitz, J., ed., 2013, *Big data and business analytics*, Boca Raton, FL: CRC Press/Taylor & Francis.

Liebowitz, J., 2005, Linking Social Network Analysis with the Analytical Hierarchy Process for Knowledge Mapping in organizations. *Journal of Knowledge Management*, 9(1), pp. 76–86.

Manyika, J., Chui, M., Brown, B., Bughin, J., Dobbs, R., Roxburgh, C. and Hung Byers, A., 2011, *Big data: The next frontier for innovation, competition and productivity*, McKinsey Global Institute.

Matson, E., Patiath, P. and Shavers, T., 2003, Stimulating Knowledge Sharing: Strengthening Your Organizations' Internal Knowledge Market. *Organizational Dynamics*, 32(3), pp. 275–285.

McEvily, S. and Chakravarthy, B., 2002, The Persistence of Knowledge-Based Advantage: An Empirical Test for Product Performance and Technological Knowledge. *Strategic Management Journal*, 23(4), pp. 285–305.

McGonagle, J. and Vella, C., 2002, *Bottom line competitive intelligence*. Westport, CT: Quorum Books.

Nahapiet, J. and Ghoshal, S., 1998, Social Capital, Intellectual Capital, and the Organizational Advantage. *Academy of Management Review*, 23(2), pp. 242–266.

Nelson, R. R. and Winter, S. G., 1982, *An evolutionary theory of economic change*. Cambridge, MA: Harvard University Press.

Nonaka, I. and Takeuchi, H., 1995, *The knowledge-creating company: How Japanese companies create the dynamics of innovation*. New York: Oxford University Press.

Polanyi, M., 1967, *The tacit dimension*. New York: Doubleday.

Prescott, J. E. and Miller, S. H., 2001, *Proven strategies in competitive intelligence: Lessons from the trenches*. New York: John Wiley & Sons.

Raouch, D. and Santi, P., 2001, Competitive Intelligence Adds Value: Five Intelligence Attitudes. *European Management Journal*, 19(5), pp. 552–559.

Rothberg, H. N. and Erickson, G. S., 2005, *From knowledge to intelligence: Creating competitive advantage in the next economy*. Woburn, MA: Elsevier Butterworth-Heinemann.

Rothberg, H. N. and Erickson, G. S., 2002, Competitive capital: A fourth pillar of intellectual capital? In N. Bontis, ed., *World congress on intellectual capital readings*. Woburn, MA: Elsevier Butterworth-Heinemann.

Schulz, M. and Jobe, L. A., 2001, Codification and Tacitness as Knowledge Management Strategies: An Empirical Exploration. *Journal of High Technology Management Research*, 12, pp. 139–165.

Schumpeter, J. A., 1934, *The theory of economic development*. Cambridge, MA: Harvard University Press.

Stewart, T. A., 1997, *Intellectual capital: The new wealth of nations*. New York: Doubleday.

Teece, D. J., 1998, Capturing Value From Knowledge Assets: The New Economy, Markets for Know-How, and Intangible Assets. *California Management Review*, 40(3), pp. 55–79.

Thomas, J. C., Kellogg, W. A. and Erickson, T., 2001, The Knowledge Management Puzzle: Human and Social Factors in Knowledge Management. *IBM Systems Journal*, 40(4), pp. 863–884.

Vance, A., 2011a, The Data Knows. *Bloomberg Businessweek*, September 12, pp. 70–74.

Vance, A., 2011b, The Power of the Cloud. *Bloomberg Businessweek*, March 7, pp. 52–59.

Wernerfelt, B., 1984, The Resource-Based View of the Firm. *Strategic Management Journal*, 5(2), pp. 171–180.

Wright, S., Picton, D. and Callow, J., 2002, Competitive Intelligence in UK Firms, A Typology. *Marketing Intelligence and Planning*, 20(6), pp. 349–360.

Zack, M. H., 1999a, Developing a Knowledge Strategy. *California Management Review*, 41(3), pp. 125–145.

Zack, M. H., 1999b, Managing Codified Knowledge. *Sloan Management Review*, 40(4), pp. 45–58.

Zander, U. and Kogut, B., 1995, Knowledge and the Speed of Transfer and Imitation of Organizational Capabilities: An Empirical Test. *Organization Science*, 6(1), pp. 76–92.

Zhao, D., 2013, Frontiers of big data business analytics: Patterns and cases in online marketing. In: J. Liebowitz, ed., *Big data and business analytics*. Boca Raton, FL: CRC Press/ Taylor & Francis.

Chapter 5

The Rise of Big Data and Analytics in Higher Education

Ben K. Daniel and Russell J. Butson

Contents

5.1 Introduction

Institutions of higher education worldwide are operating in a rapidly changing and competitive environment, driven by political, cultural, economic, and technological factors. The complexity of these changes has far-reaching impacts that affect every aspect of provision, ranging from national systems of education to the curriculum and student learning. There are also growing regulatory demands for transparency and accountability as the sector experiences declining support from government, business, and the private sector (Daniel and Butson 2013; Daniel 2015). These radical transformations necessitate new ways of thinking, research theories, and approaches to manage unique challenges.

Further, as management strives to implement better evidence-based decision-making processes through the use of analytics, they are confronted with myriad data types and storage schemas that do not support data aggregation. Typically, data are stored in a variety of separate systems, for example, in student information systems, student social media, learning management systems, student library usage, individual computers, and administrative systems holding information on program completion rates and learning pathways.

The challenge is to develop metasystems that can aggregate the various data stores and formats in order to make them accessible for more intensive analysis. If achieved, we are likely to gain new insights from the "hidden" traces being generated through the growing digital infrastructures that currently underpin much of the action associated with teaching, learning, and research within higher education. It is only then that we would be in a position to address the complex challenges that institutions face.

The purpose of this chapter is to explore the current state of data aggregation within higher education—in particular, the theoretical understandings of the role Big Data plays or can play in addressing the challenges currently facing institutions of higher education. The chapter draws upon emergent literature in Big Data and discusses ways to better utilize the growing data available from various sources within an institution to help understand the complexity of influences on student-related outcomes, teaching, and the what-if questions for research experimentation. The chapter also presents opportunities and challenges associated with the implementation of Big Data analytics in higher education.

5.1.1 Development of Big Data

The use of data to inform decision making in organizations is not new; business organizations have been storing and analyzing large volumes of data since the advent of data warehouse systems in the early 1990s. However, the nature of data available to most organizations today is rapidly changing. According to IBM, 80% of the data organizations currently generating data are unstructured. Data also come in a variety of formats, such as text, video, audio, diagrams, images, and combinations of any two or more of these formats. With traditional solutions becoming too expensive to scale or adapt to rapidly evolving conditions, business organizations are looking for affordable technologies that will help them store, process, and query all of their data. Organizations store most of their data that are meant to support decision making in data warehouses. A data warehouse refers to a central repository of data or a centralized database system used for analyzing and reporting data. Data warehousing also represents an ideal vision of maintaining a central repository of data that provides an organization with a living memory of data that can be leveraged for better decision making.

Recent developments in database technologies made it possible to collect and maintain large and complex amounts of data in many forms and store them in multiple sources within multiple points in time and space. In addition, there are analytical tools available that can turn this complex data into meaningful patterns and value, a phenomenon referred to as Big Data. Theoretically, Big Data describes data that are fundamentally too big and move too fast, exceeding the processing capacity of conventional database systems (Manyika et al. 2010).

The notion of *big*, the term itself, is misleading as contested by critics as it does not reflect only data size, but complexity. Yang (2013) points out the definition of Big Data has little to do with the data itself because the analysis of large quantities of data is not new, but rather Big Data includes an emergent suite of technologies that can process massive volumes of data of various types at faster speeds than ever before.

5.2 Overview of Big Data Research

Big Data is an emergent knowledge system that is already changing the nature of knowledge and social theory in fields such as business, health, and government while also having the power to transform management decision-making theory. It is a set of techniques, procedures, and technologies dealing with voluminous amounts of data in physical or digital formats, data that is being stored in diverse repositories, ranging from tangible account bookkeeping records of an educational institution to class test or examination records to alumni records (Sagiroglu and Sinanc 2013).

The growing interest in Big Data is associated with the sophistication of technologies used to process large and complex quantities of data and the value accrued in utilizing such data. Big Data features many characteristics, but Douglas (2001) proposed what is commonly known as the "three Vs" (volume, velocity and variety). Generally, the literature presents a number of fundamental characteristics associated with the notion of Big Data, including the following (Figure 5.1):

- Volume, referring to a large amount of information that is often challenging to store, process, transfer, analyze, and present.
- Velocity, relating to the increasing rate at which information flows within an organization (e.g., institutions dealing with financial information and relating that to human resources and productivity).

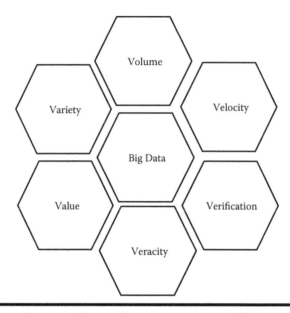

Figure 5.1 Key characteristics of Big Data. (From Daniel, B., *British Journal of Educational Technology,* **46, 5, 904–920, 2015.)**

- Veracity, referring to the biases, noise, and abnormality in data generated from various sources within an institution. It also looks at how data is stored and meaningfully mined to address problems being analyzed. Veracity also covers questions of trust and uncertainty associated with the collection, processing, and utilization of data.
- Variety, referring to data presented in diverse formats, both structured and unstructured.
- Verification, referring to data corroboration and security.
- Value, referring to the ability of data in generating useful insights, benefits, and business processes, etc., within an institution.

There are also other important properties of Big Data, such as data validity, which refers to the accuracy of data, and data volatility, a concept associated with the longevity of data and their relevance to the outcomes of analytics, especially the length of time required to store data in a useful form for further appropriate value-added analysis.

5.3 Analytics and Big Data in Higher Education

Data harvesting and storage has risen exponentially over recent years; as we once spoke of gigabytes (1000^3), we are now talking exabytes (1000^5), and zettabytes (1000^6). Contributing to this is the increasing focus on delivering learning online with the growing availability of online data repositories, educational digital libraries, and their associated tools (Borgman et al. 2008; Choudhury, Hobbs and Lorie 2002; Xu and Recker 2012). The increase in capturing, storing, distributing, managing, and analyzing these larger-sized data sets with diverse structures and the need for aggregation is fuelling innovative developments in Big Data techniques and technologies. For higher education, the concern is with the application of tools and techniques that c0an aggregate the various independent data sources and databases in order to engage in meta-analysis of these larger sets of complex data. The ultimate goal is to use this data to improve performance and governance of an institution's approaches to learning, teaching, research, and administration.

Big Data in higher education as an area of inquiry incorporates research areas, such as educational data mining, which is focused on developing new tools for discovering patterns in educational data, and learning analytics, a growing area of interest examining indicators of individual student and class performance (Luan 2002; Romero and Ventura 2010). In both of these cases, the utilization of Big Data in higher education involves the interpretation of a wide range of administrative and operational data aimed at assessing institutional performance and progress in order to predict future performance and identify potential issues related to academic programing, research, teaching, and learning (Hrabowski, Suess and Fritz 2011; Picciano 2012).

As a developing field within higher education, Big Data is well positioned to address some of the key challenges currently facing institutions of higher education (Siemens 2011; Siemens and Long 2011; Siemens, Dawson and Lynch 2013; Daniel 2015). Wagner and Ice (2012) note that technological developments have served as catalysts for the move toward the growth of analytics in higher education. Capturing and storing data in a data warehouse and applying data mining techniques are the foundations for future activities involved with higher education (Tulasi 2013). Analytics are also attractive approaches in education due to the ability of tools and techniques for data processing and analysis. Mayer (2009) notes that the increase in attention to analytics is also driven by advances in computation. For instance, smartphones today exceed the computational power of desktop computers, and because they are more powerful, they can accomplish tasks that were impossible only a few years ago (Baker and Inventado 2014).

Further, there is a growing number of systems intended to leverage Big Data. Systems such as Apache Hadoop, Hortonworks, MapReduce, and Tableau Software are designed to support the use of analytics tools. Further, SAS and IBM SPSS address the substantial challenges of managing data on the scale of the Internet (Dean and Ghemawat 2010). Nonetheless, currently, the best platforms for harnessing the power of Big Data are open and flexible. They also blend the right technologies, tools, and features to turn data compilation into data insight.

5.3.1 Conceptualizing Big Data in Higher Education

In order to understand the added value of Big Data in higher education, we proposed a conceptual framework that provides a foundation for understanding the fundamental components of Big Data in higher education (see Figure 5.2) (Daniel 2015), the data sources that contribute to Big Data in higher education institution environments (Figure 5.3), and the schema needed to harvest and process data into meaningful outputs (Figure 5.4).

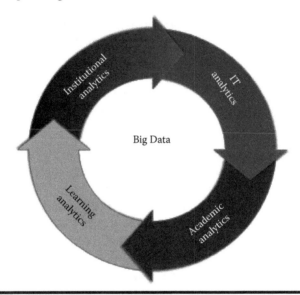

Figure 5.2 Components of Data in higher education. (From Daniel, B., *British Journal of Educational Technology,* **46, 5, 904–920, 2015.)**

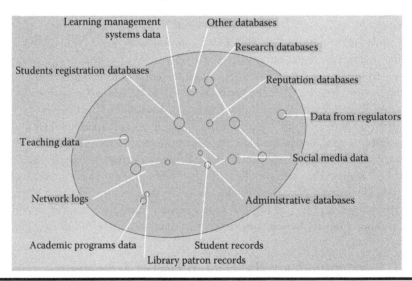

Figure 5.3 Sources of Data in higher education. (From Daniel, B., *British Journal of Educational Technology,* **46, 5, 904–920, 2015.)**

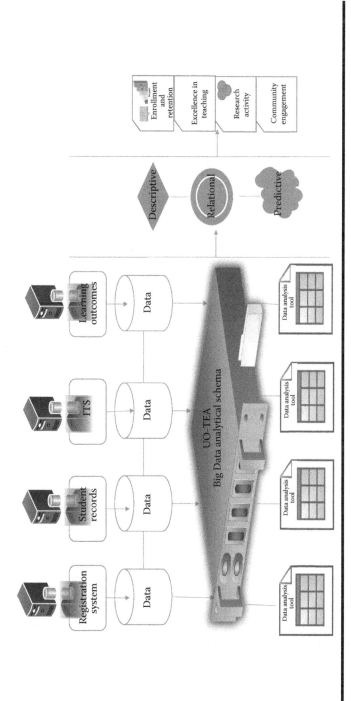

Figure 5.4   Schema for data processing.

5.3.2 Institutional Analytics

Institutional analytics refers to a variety of operational data that can be analyzed to help with effective decisions about making improvements at the institutional level. Institutional analytics include assessment policy analytics, instructional analytics, and structural analytics. They make use of reports, data warehouses, and data dashboards that provide an institution with the capability to make timely, data-driven decisions across all departments and divisions.

5.3.3 Information Technology Analytics

Information technology (IT) analytics covers usage and performance data, which helps with monitoring required for developing or deploying technology for institutional use, developing data standards, tools, processes, organizational synergies, and policies. IT analytics largely aims at integrating data from a variety of systems—student information, learning management, and alumni systems as well as systems managing learning experiences outside the classroom.

Furthermore, when students interact with learning technologies, they leave behind data trails, which can reveal their sentiments, social connections, intentions, and goals. Researchers can use such data to examine patterns of student performance over time—from one semester to another or from one year to another—and develop rigorous data modeling and analysis to reveal the obstacles to student access and usability and to evaluate any attempts at intervention.

5.3.4 Academic or Program Analytics

Academic analytics encapsulates all the activities in higher education affecting administration, research, resource allocation, and management (Tulasi 2013). It provides overall information about what is happening in a specific program and how to address performance challenges. Academic analytics combines large data sets with statistical techniques and predictive modeling to improve decision making and provide data that administrators can use to support the strategic decision-making process as well as to provide a method for benchmarking in comparison to other institutions.

5.3.5 Learning Analytics

Learning analytics is concerned with the measurement, collection, and analysis and reporting of data about learners and their contexts for purposes of understanding and optimizing learning and the environments in which it occurs (Siemens and Long 2011). More broadly, references are often made to learning analytics software and techniques, which are often used to improve processes and workflows, measuring academic and institutional data and generally improving organizational effectiveness. Although such usage is often referred to as learning analytics, it is more associated with academic analytics. Learning analytics is undertaken more at the teaching and learning level of an institution and is largely concerned with improving learner success (Jones 2012; Macfadyen and Dawson 2012).

5.4 Sources and Types of Big Data in Higher Education

Big Data within institutions of higher education is stored and accessed from various types of databases, such as administrative and operational databases. The widespread introduction of learning management systems (LMSs), such as Blackboard and Moodle, resulted in increasingly large sets of data. Each day, LMSs accumulate increasing amounts of students' interaction data, personal data, systems information, and academic information (Romero et al. 2008). LMSs keep a record of students' key actions. These include records of logging on to a system, posting and viewing messages, accessing materials, etc. Student data in an LMS could also include more detailed information on the content of students' postings or other writing, their choices and progress through a specific interactive unit or assignment, or their particular preferences and habits as manifested over a range of tasks and interactions or semester (Friesen 2013; Macfadyen and Dawson 2010).

Big Data also draws sources of data from social media posts, online news articles, digital scans of academic journals, student financial aid profiles, and student library usage. Data drawn from social media can also help us understand students' behaviors. Today, Facebook, Twitter, Instagram and LinkedIn are students' primary source of information, communication, and influence. Figure 5.3 summarizes possible types of data sources present in many institutions and constitute Big Data.

5.4.1 Opportunities

Big Data in higher education can be transformative, altering the existing processes of administration, teaching, learning, and academic work (Baer and Campbell 2011), contributing to policy and practice outcomes and helping address contemporary challenges facing higher education (Daniel and Butson 2013). For instance, at the departmental level, Big Data can provide dashboards that reveal patterns confirming program strengths or deficiencies. By designing programs that collect data at every step of the students' learning processes, institutions can address student needs with customized modules, assignments, feedback, and learning trees in the curriculum that will promote better and richer learning. Similarly, at the institutional level, predictive models can be developed that help institutions align resources, such as tutorials, online discussions, and library assistances, thus personalizing learning pathways.

Furthermore, the added value of Big Data in higher education is the ability to identify useful data and turn it into useable information by identifying patterns and deviations from patterns. Schleicher (2013) reports that "Big Data is the foundation on which education can reinvent its business model and build the coalition of governments, businesses, and social entrepreneurs that can bring together the evidence, innovation, and resources to make lifelong learning a reality for all. So the next educational superpower might be the one that can combine the hierarchy of institutions with the power of collaborative information flows and social networks." Siemens (2011) further indicates that "[learning] analytics are a foundational tool for informed change in education" and provide evidence on which to form understanding and make informed (rather than instinctive) decisions.

Additionally, when used effectively, Big Data can help institutions enhance the learning experience and improve student performance across the board, reducing dropout rates and increasing graduation numbers. Analytics also provides researchers with opportunities to carry out retrospective analysis of student data, producing predictive models capable of identifying students at risk and providing appropriate intervention (EDUCAUSE 2011; U.S. Department of Education 2012). Further, Big Data analytics could be applied to examining student entry on a course assessment and discussion board entries, blog entries, or wiki activity could be recorded, generating thousands of transactions per student, per course. This data would be collected in real or near real time as it is transacted and then analyzed to suggest courses of action.

For the individual student, dashboards can help them track their own progress and personalize their own learning pathways. Further, the availability of student interaction data can be used to understand students' learning patterns online. For instance, by measuring the time a student spends on a module or question, educators can assess how well an assignment performs for any one subgroup of students and identify areas of difficulty for a class or individual learner.

Furthermore, data left in LMSs and database technologies will prepare institutions to proactively plan and stay relevant to their students. For instance, an analysis of a student's attendance, test results, laboratory performance, and class participation (and more), can indicate whether or not he or she will graduate on time. Early intervention can improve retention, and her overall experience. Within an LMS, data obtained could be used to do the following:

- Help predict student success in an online course
- Monitor a student's behavior and engagement level
- Notify a lecturer when a student seems to be less engaged with learning
- Personalize the learning process
- Reduce classroom administrative work
- Help the lecturer refine content and keep relevant
- Monitor students' progress and provide real-time feedback

5.5 Challenges of Implementation

There are a number of anticipated challenges associated with collection and implementation of Big Data in higher education. For instance, the costs associated with collecting, storing, and developing algorithms to mine data can be time-consuming and complex. Furthermore, most institutional data systems are not interoperable, so aggregating administrative data and classroom and online data can pose additional challenges (Daniel and Butson 2013; Daniel 2015). Although combining data sets from across a variety of unconnected systems can be extremely difficult, it offers better comprehensive insights that inevitably lead to improved capabilities of predictive modeling. Dringus (2012) suggests that one way of overcoming these problems is to increase institutional transparency by clearly demonstrating the changes that analytics can help to achieve.

Although Big Data also has the potential to help learners and instructors recognize early warning signs (Wagner and Ice 2012), wide institutional acceptance of analytics requires a clear institutional strategy that helps different parties within an institution to work together (Ali et al. 2013). For instance, it requires the involvement of information technology services departments in planning for data collection when use is deemed critical. This observation is consistent with a recent U.S. Department of Education (2013) report suggesting that the successful implementation of Big Data in higher institutions would depend on collaborative initiatives between various departments in a given institution.

It should also be noted that the implementation of Big Data depends on the ability of an institution to co-create data-governing structures and delivery of more progressive and better policies and strategies for data utilization and governance (Daniel and Butson 2013). Wagner and Ice (2012) also point out that increasing collaborative ventures on Big Data initiatives helps all groups take ownership of any challenge that might involve student performance and persistence. Similarly, Dringus (2012) suggests that the practice of Big Data, particularly learning analytics, should be transparent and flexible to make it accessible to educators (Dringus 2012; Dyckhoff et al. 2012).

However, in many instances, there is still a divide between those who know how to extract data and what data is available and those who know what data is required and how it would best be used. Lack of an institutional vision for the added value of data and an inability to leverage collective institutional efforts make collaboration difficult. Romero and Ventura (2010) note that analytics has traditionally been difficult for nonspecialists to generate (in a meaningful context), to visualize in compelling ways, or to understand, limiting their observability and decreasing the institutional impact of analytics (Macfadyen and Dawson 2010).

Finally, Big Data raises issues on ethics associated with quality of data, privacy, security, and data ownership. It also raises the question of an institution's responsibility for taking action on issues based on the information available (Jones 2012).

5.6 Summary and Future Directions

Big Data is being used to convey all sorts of concepts, such as huge quantities of data, social media data, advanced databases, and algorithms. Regardless of the label, business organizations are starting to systematically understand and explore how to process and analyze a vast array of information in new ways that can help them use this data as evidence to improve decision making. Institutions of higher education are still lagging behind although they are faced with growing challenges that require the same evidence-based decision making.

Large stores of data already exist in most institutions of higher education. By analyzing this data, analytics applications have the potential to provide various types of dashboards (institution, program, teacher, and student), which provides a predictive view of upcoming challenges. For instance, the ability to mine unstructured and informal connections and information produced by students, including social media, machine sensors, and location-based data, will allow educators to uncover useful facts and patterns they have not been able to identify in the past. Further, the application of Big Data in higher education opens a window into students' interaction with content, peers, and educators as well as presenting an opportunity to measure those interactions and draw conclusions about what they mean for student retention and success as well as the ability to proactively address policy challenges.

Despite the potential of Big Data in higher education, there are potential challenges that need to be addressed. These include issues around data management and governance structures associated with Big Data in higher education as well as maintenance of privacy. As the amount of data available for use is ever-increasing, the benefits will come from good learning management, reliable data warehousing and management, flexible and transparent data mining and extraction, and accurate and responsible reporting.

An institutional research project at the University (Daniel and Butson 2013) is being undertaken to develop and test conceptual and theoretical underpinnings of Big Data and analytics in higher education as well as developing key performance indicators; metrics; and methods for capturing, processing, and visualizing data. In addition, a set of diagnostic tools, an integrated technology-enhanced data analytic framework, and ultimately, a data warehouse for Big Data and analytics are being pursued.

The research team is also currently engaged in identifying and establishing policies that specify who is accountable for various portions or aspects of the institutional data and information, including its accuracy, accessibility, consistency, completeness, and maintenance. This research will also be looking at defining processes concerning how data and information are stored, archived, backed up, and protected as well as developing standards and procedures that define how the data and information are used by authorized personnel and implement a set of audit and control procedures to ensure ongoing compliance with governmental regulations and industrial standards.

Author's Notes

Work presented in the chapter draws from a large ongoing research programme at the University of Otago. Some of the ideas also appear in previously published work.

References

Ali, L., Adasi, M., Gasevic, D., Jovanovic, J., and Hatala, M., 2013, Factors influencing beliefs for adoption of a learning analytics tool: An empirical study, *Computers & Education*, 62, pp. 130–148.

Baer, L., and Campbell, J., 2011, Game Changers, EDUCAUSE.

Baker, R. S. J. D., and Inventado, P. S., 2014, Educational Data Mining and Learning Analytics. In J. A. Larusson, and B. White (Eds.) *Learning Analytics: From Research to Practice*. Berlin, Springer.

Borgman, C. L., Abelson, H., Dirks, L., Johnson, R., Koedinger, K. R., Linn, M. C., Lynch, C. A., Oblinger, D. G., Pea, R. D., Salen, K., Smith, M. S., and Szalay, A., 2008, Fostering Learning in the Networked World: The Cyberlearning Opportunity and Challenge. A 21st Century Agenda for the National Science Foundation. Report of the NSF Task Force on Cyberlearning. Office of Cyberinfrastructure and Directorate for Education and Human Resources. National Science Foundation. Retrieved July 12, 2014, from http://www.nsf.gov/publications/pub_summ.jsp?ods_key=nsf08204.

Choudhury, S., Hobbs, B., and Lorie, M., 2002, A framework for evaluating digital library services. *D-Lib Magazine*, 8. Retrieved July 12, 2014, from http://www.dlib.org/dlib/july02/choudhury/07choudhury.html.

Daniel, B., 2015, Big Data and analytics in higher education: Opportunities and challenges, *British Journal of Educational Technology*, 46 (5), pp. 904–920.

Daniel, B. K., and Butson, R., 2013, Technology Enhanced Analytics (TEA) in Higher Education, *Proceedings of the International Conference on Educational Technologies*, November 29–December 1, 2013, Kuala Lumpur, Malaysia, pp. 89–96.

Dean, J., and Ghemawat, S., 2010, MapReduce: A flexible data processing tool. *Communications of the ACM*, 53 (1), pp. 72–77.

Douglas, L., 2001, 3D data management: Controlling data volume, velocity and variety, *Gartner Report*. Retrieved 30 December 2013 from http://blogs.gartner.com/doug-laney/files/2012/01/ad949-3D-Data-Management-Controlling-Data-Volume-Velocity-and-Variety.pdf.

Dringus, L., 2012, Learning analytics considered harmful, *Journal of Asynchronous Learning Networks*, 16 (3), pp. 87–100.

Dyckhoff, A. L., Zielke, D., Bültmann, M., Chatti, M. A., and Schroeder, U., 2012, Design and implementation of a learning analytics toolkit for teachers. *Educational Technology & Society*, 15 (3), pp. 58–76.

EDUCAUSE, 2011, Learning Initiative, 7 Things You Should Know about First-Generation Learning Analytics, December 2011. Retrieved on July 14 from http://www.deloitte.com/assets/DcomIreland/Local%20Assets/Documents/Public%20sector/IE_PS_making%20the%20grade_IRL_0411_WEB.pdf.

Friesen, N., 2013, Learning analytics: Readiness and rewards, *Canadian Journal of Learning Technology*, 39 (4). Retrieved from http://www.cjlt.ca/index.php/cjlt/article/view/774.

Hrabowski, F. A., III, Suess, J., and Fritz, J., 2011, Assessment and analytics in institutional transformation. *EDUCAUSE Review*, 46 (5) (September/October).

Jones, S., 2012, Technology review: The possibilities of learning analytics to improve learner-centered decision-making, *Community College Enterprise*, 18 (1), pp 89–92.

Luan, J., 2002, Data mining and its applications in higher education. In A. Serban and J. Luan (Eds.), *Knowledge management: Building a competitive advantage in higher education* (pp. 17–36). San Francisco, PA: Jossey-Bass.

Macfadyen, L. P., and Dawson, S., 2010, Mining LMS data to develop an "early warning system" for educators: A proof of concept, *Computers & Education*, 54, pp. 588–599.

Macfadyen, L. P., and Dawson, S., 2012, Numbers are not enough. Why e-learning analytics failed to inform an institutional strategic plan, *Educational Technology & Society*, 15 (3), pp. 149–163.

Manyika, J., Chui, M., Brown, B., Bughin, J., Dobbs, R., Roxburgh, C., and Byers, A. H., 2011, Big Data: The Next Frontier for Innovation, Competition, and Productivity. McKinsey Global Institute. Retrieved on July 14, 2014, from http://www.mckinsey.com/Insights/MGI /Research/Technology_and_Innovation/Big_data_The_next_frontier_for_innovation.

Mayer, M., 2009, The physics of Big Data. Retrieved on July 14, 2014, from http://www .parc.com/event/936/innovation-atgoogle.html.

Picciano, A. G., 2012, The evolution of Big Data and learning analytics in American higher education, *Journal of Asynchronous Learning Networks*, 16 (3), pp. 9–20.

Romero, C., and Ventura, S., 2010, Educational data mining: A review of the state of the art, *IEEE Transactions on Systems, Man and Cybernetics, Part C: Applications and Reviews*, 40 (6), pp. 601–618.

Romero, C., Ventura, S., and García, E., 2008, Data mining in course management systems: Moodle case study and tutorial. Computers & Education, 51(1), 368–384.

Sagiroglu, S., and Sinanc, D., 2013, Big Data: A review. *Proceedings of the international conference on collaboration technologies and systems (CTS)*, pp. 42–47.

Schleicher, A., 2013, Big Data and PISA. Retrieved on August 4, 2013, from http://oecd educationtoday.blogspot.co.nz/2013/07/big-data-and-pisa.html?m=1.

Siemens, G., Dawson, G., and Lynch, G., 2013, Improving the Quality and Productivity of the Higher Education Sector Policy and Strategy for Systems-Level Deployment of Learning Analytics Society for Learning Analytics Research [online]. Available at: http://www.voced.edu.au/content/ngv64739.

Siemens, G., 2011, How data and analytics can improve education, July 2011, Retrieved August 8 from http://radar.oreilly.com/2011/07/education-data-analytics-learning.html.

Siemens, G., and Long, P., 2011, Penetrating the fog: Analytics in learning and education. EDUCAUSE Review, 46 (5), p. 30.

Tulasi, B., 2013, Significance of Big Data and analytics in higher education. *International Journal of Computer Applications* 68 (14), pp. 23–25.

U.S. Department of Education, 2012, Office of Educational Technology, Enhancing Teaching and Learning through Educational Data Mining and Learning Analytics: An Issue Brief, Washington, D.C.

Wagner, E., and Ice, P., 2012, Data changes everything: Delivering on the promise of learning analytics in higher education. *EDUCAUSE Review*, July/August, pp. 33–42.

Xu, B., and Recker, M., 2012, Teaching analytics: A clustering and triangulation study of digital library user data, *Educational Technology & Society*, 15 (3), pp. 103–115.

Yang, L., 2013, Big Data Analytics: What is the Big Deal? Retrieved July 12, 2014, from http:// knowledge.ckgsb.edu.cn/2013/12/30/technology/big-data-analytics-whats-big-deal/.

Chapter 6

Google Analytics as a Prosumption Tool for Web Analytics

Joanna Palonka, Marcin Lora, and Tomasz Oziębło

Contents

Context

The problem is located in social sciences and humanities, that is, organization management, e-marketing, and business informatics.

Purpose

The aim of this chapter is to verify a hypothesis that Google Analytics (GA) is a prosumption tool for Internet data analysis that can be used by a company to effectively (in a simple way and on its own) manage its website, that is, manage the website content and traffic.

Design

To test the hypothesis, an experiment was designed and conducted on the website of Soluzioni IT, on which GA was installed and activated. The main goal was set, and then it was translated into particular goals. Next, measurable KPIs were assigned to the goals. During the experiment, the GA indicators were monitored, the impact of the changes on the GA values was assessed, and subsequent changes were designed and implemented. It involved active modification of website content and graphic design. The process was cyclically repeated in the four stages of the study.

Findings

Web analytics and GA allow owners to comprehensively monitor the parameters of any website. The software can track a user's path on Internet platforms and visualize the results. Thanks to GA results, it is possible to precisely target advertisements and use various means to strengthen marketing initiatives and design websites, which can generate more conversions. GA provides information on how users find a site and what their interactions are. It enables comparison of changes in users' behavior due to, for example, improvements in site content and design. It is a good analytics tool that ensures comprehensive analysis of the whole site from multiple perspectives, depending on users' needs.

Research Limitations/Implications

GA is an analytics tool used to analyze Internet data from various perspectives. This chapter focuses on the analysis of data to optimize website content and traffic. In addition, GA analyses are able to answer other questions that are of critical importance to running a business, for example, at what stage and why do users abandon purchases in a store? Moreover, GA itself is not able to arrive at any conclusions. Using this tool requires the ability to interpret data from individual reports and identify relationships between particular data as well as knowledge about products, services, and customers' needs. A lack of such skills and knowledge can lead to wrong decisions, which will negatively affect website goals. It implies the necessity for continuous further research.

Practical Implications

GA is a supporting tool that supplies detailed information about, for example, the behavior of visitors to a particular website, the usability of the content provided, etc. The users themselves can set website goals, assign KPI to the goals, monitor and compare the data they need, analyze goal conversion, etc. This knowledge helps to improve the decision-making process and optimize the management of marketing activities.

Originality/Value

The results of web analyses help improve the quality of services, save resources, or make some business processes more efficient. Based on the data, business can be improved. But it is also necessary to assess the path between the data and improvement activities, that is, those increasing company efficiency. There is one principle: Analytics should lead to continuous optimization. When a report is ready, the data should be analyzed, and recommendations for changes made and then implemented (this is a key moment of the entire process and the most important stage as it brings a company real profits).

6.1 Introduction

6.1.1 Purpose of the Study

Nowadays, every organization that wants to reach new customers, retain its existing ones, and gain a competitive edge over competitors must have some tools at hand in order to study the particular behavior of its website visitors. An analysis of

Internet data allows for comprehensive monitoring of website operations, in particular the goals defined for the website as well as the needs of the organization, its customers, and business partners. Depending on their needs, users can gather any data and next analyze and evaluate them. But they need IT tools for web analytics, which can provide the required data. The reason to perform this work was to verify whether or not GA is a prosumption tool for Internet data analysis. It is a free IT tool, and a company can use it to effectively (in a simple way and on its own) manage its website, that is, manage the website content and traffic. The results can improve the decision-making process and help streamline marketing operations in terms of promotion and advertising and sales operations as well as planning of new website goals.

6.1.2 About the Background of This Work

The study was carried out in stages comprising the following:

- Preliminary analysis and website assessment: Stage I May 1, 2012–September 30, 2012
- Modification of the website content and a change of its graphic design: Stage II October 1, 2012–November 30, 2012
- Website popularization on other sites: Stage III December 1, 2012–February 28, 2013
- Work on website positioning in the Google search engine: Stage IV March 1, 2013–May 31, 2013

6.1.3 What Is the Scope of This Work?

The assumption was that thanks to GA an organization can effectively (in a simple way and on its own) manage its website, that is, manage the website content and traffic. Operations that were undertaken based on the GA analyses were to result in website traffic optimization, that is, a rise in traffic due to improved positioning in search engines and a greater number of users interested in its content. The traffic optimization effect was to be reflected in an increasing number of visitors, a larger number of new users, or a larger number of returning visitors. At the same time, site visitor retention was evaluated, and content that would meet visitors' requirements was provided. This, in turn, was to increase the number of page views per visit, reduce the bounce rate, and increase time spent on the site. As a result, the goals set by the owner were to be achieved.

6.1.4 Definition of the Key Concepts

Web analytics involves traffic monitoring and visitor behavior tracking on a particular website with the aim of optimizing an organization's marketing strategies.

The stages of Internet data analysis are conducted cyclically: measurement, analysis, reporting, hypotheses/action, and testing.

Prosumption is understood as production for one's own use, in accordance with the motto "Do it yourself."

Key performance indicators (KPIs) that were assigned to the website goals include the total number of visits, the number of new visitors, the percentage of new visitors, visits from the Google search engine, direct traffic, the average time spent on the website, the average number of pages viewed during a visit, and the bounce rate.

A unique user (UU) is an individual that has visited a website or received specific content. For a UU on a website, UU information consists of, at least, the IP address associated with his or her computer and a further ID, such as a browser ID.

The traffic optimization effect was to be reflected in an increasing number of visitors, a larger number of new users, or a larger number of returning visitors.

The content optimization effect was to be reflected in an increasing number of page views per visit, reduction in the bounce rate, and increasing time spent on the site.

6.2 What Is the Work Performed in This Field?

6.2.1 General Assumptions about Web Analytics

Web analytics involves traffic monitoring and visitor behavior tracking on a particular website with the aim of optimizing an organization's marketing strategies (Kaushik 2009). Web analytics activities are conducted cyclically (Figure 6.1) and

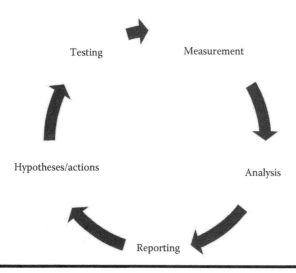

Figure 6.1   Web analytics as a continuous process.

must not be implemented piecemeal. They can be divided into five stages, which have to be carried out in accordance with the following principles (Kowalczyk 2012):

1. Combine analytics with business
2. Share knowledge about analytics
3. Customize reports for different recipients in an organization (an analyst, a supervisor, HIPPO)
4. Set business objectives and indicators
5. Measure and analyze conversion
6. Segment data
7. Integrate off-line and online data

6.2.2 Measurement

Measurement is the first stage of Internet data analysis. It involves defining the website objectives (strategic and marketing) that an organization is going to achieve (Lewiński 2013). Strategic objectives should be doable, understandable, manageable, and beneficial. Next, KPIs for the entire project should be defined (Lovett 2011; Peterson 2004) and translated into the language of statistics tools. Thus, a decision about what is going to be measured during the analysis of a particular site is made. At this stage, an organization has to determine what values of particular indicators will be considered satisfactory in a specific period of time (Clifton 2008) (Table 6.1).

Table 6.1 Examples of KPI Plans

Strategic Objectives	Marketing Objectives	KPI	KPI Targets
Product sales	Profit increase	Total revenue	PLN 20,000/month
	Sales volume increase	Visit value	PLN 100 per visit value
Effective Internet marketing	Creation of a prospect database	Number of new visitor registrations	1,000 registrations/month
Brand building	Rise in the willingness to buy	Conversion rate	2%
	Increased involvement	Time on site	>1 minute

6.2.3 Analysis

During the second stage—analysis—an analytics tool is chosen and configured. According to the principle of "rubbish in, rubbish out," if a mistake is made at that point, even the best analysis will lead to erroneous conclusions (Trzósło 2014). When an account is set up, it must be configured, that is, it is necessary to determine an account structure and create profiles assigned to users of a selected part of the website, configure goals, create alerts, describe filters, etc. Tools can be combined to obtain more complex data on pay-per-click (PPC) campaigns and free search results, for example, GA with Google Adwords (Bailyn and Bailyn 2012; Clifton 2008).

6.2.4 Reporting

During the third stage—reporting—website statistical reports are generated. Modern analytics tools offer a wide range of standard reports and enable creation of custom reports as well. There are various possibilities of data visualization (Few 2009). Reports can give answers to different questions, including the following (Cutroni 2010):

- Where are our users from?
- How much time do they spend on particular pages?
- What percentage of them abandon their shopping cart at the last stage?
- How many UUs convert to the site goals?
- Which channel (for example, organic positioning, Adwords, or a banner campaign) is best, and which has to be immediately given up?
- What do people search for using our internal search engine?

6.2.5 Conclusion Development

However, reports themselves do not suffice. An overall look at the data must be taken to draw conclusions that will be profitable for a company (Burby 2007). The results of analyses can help improve the quality of services, save resources, or make some business processes more efficient. Based on the data, business can be improved (Krug 2013). But it is also necessary to assess the path between the data and improvement activities, for example, those increasing company efficiency. There is one principle: Analytics should lead to continuous optimization. When a report is ready, the data should be analyzed and recommendations for changes made and then implemented (this is a key moment of the entire process and the most important stage as it brings a company real profits) (Ash, Ginty, and Page 2012).

6.2.6 The Accomplishment of Case Study Goals

In stage 5, the progress in goal accomplishment is checked. Usability tests are done, site content and design are tested (online tests—A/B or multivariate), and surveys are conducted (Beasley 2013).

Web analytics is carried out by means of IT tools. So far, the analysis and evaluation of Internet data have been conducted by specialized consulting firms. Nowadays, organizations themselves are getting more involved in such operations as a result of employees' increasing knowledge and competence and wider availability of tools that are used for this kind of analysis (Dykes 2011; Rosenfeld 2011). There are free tools, such as GA, Piwik, and Open Web Analytics, and paid ones, such as Gemius, Coremetrics, Adobe Online Marketing Suite, Webtrends, etc. (Oberoi 2014). IT tools provide valuable data, but making and implementing recommendations are critical to web analytics. The synergy of these elements allows for continuous creation of innovative ideas and higher profits.

GA is gaining recognition among Polish entrepreneurs as a tool for the analysis of global Internet traffic. It is an online analytics service, which enables users to manage their website, that is, its content and traffic, on their own. It can be used to measure and assess various aspects of Internet projects and perform comprehensive website analysis. It provides detailed information on web traffic by means of segmentation, custom reports, charts, and comparison tools. Its data analysis features offer instant access to a great number of data, metrics, KPIs, etc. (Kaushik 2010).

GA can be used to do the following (Clifton 2008; Gąsiewski 2013; Ledford and Tyler 2009):

1. Calculate return on investment: Sophisticated data analysis and reporting features enable companies to find out which keywords, used, for example, in sponsored links, are the most profitable. The information allows for more effective marketing investment. It is also possible to calculate customer acquisition cost.
2. Check traffic sources: That is, determine where exactly users are coming from, not only their geographic location, but the referring sites as well. As a result, a company gets information about where it should advertise and where its advertisements really pay off.
3. Check content effectiveness: That is, identify pages that have a high bounce rate and those that have content that is particularly interesting to users. Having such knowledge, an organization can change the content of pages with a high bounce rate or expose those that appeal to Internet users.
4. Set goals and create goal paths: This should be done for each site that has an implemented GA code for specific goals, for example, product sales, form completion, and reaching a certain page, and a path to completing the goals can be set (Tonkin, Whitemore, and Jutroni 2010). Thus, an organization can find out at which stage it loses users and take steps to keep them on the site.

Figure 6.2   GA: basic questions.

In addition, GA can send customized emails and export data in various formats. Data can be visualized by means of interactive maps and site overlays or presented graphically as charts (bar charts and pie charts) and tables. The service allows for continuous monitoring and analysis of the website traffic, identification of most frequently viewed pages, etc.

Depending on the site goals, GA answers numerous questions (Figure 6.2).

GA answers two questions that are of critical importance to running a business (Davenport, Morison, and Harris 2010; Kowalczyk 2012):

1. What happens on the website in terms of users' activities?
   a. Why did you enter my site?
   b. Did you get what you were looking for?
   c. If not, tell me why?
2. How to edit a website and what marketing operations to undertake in order to reach goals.

6.3 Description of the Problem and Method to Solve It

6.3.1 Definition of the Problem That Is Analyzed

Over the last few years, one can observe increased involvement of direct IT system users in activities that used to be outsourced. This happens in business with regard to IT technologies and tools, which are designed in such a way that users are able to collate data and conduct analyses for their own needs. The IT tools of this kind are called prosumption tools (Gajewski 2009; Szymusiak and Toffler 2013; Toffler 1997). They offer a chance to continuously create innovative ideas and realize higher profits. The service makes innovation more likely to succeed because users, not employees of R&D departments and consultation firms, define specific needs. Depending on their needs, users can gather any data and next analyze and evaluate them. The results can help streamline the marketing operations in terms of promotion, advertising, and sales operations and planning new website goals. The assumption was that thanks to GA an organization can effectively manage its website, that is, manage the website content and traffic, in a simple way and on its own.

6.3.2 Research Questions or Hypotheses

This chapter attempts to test a hypothesis that GA is a prosumption tool for Internet data analysis that a company can use to effectively manage its website.

6.3.3 What Was the Methodology of the Problem Resolution?

An experiment was performed to test the hypothesis. It was carried out on the website of Soluzioni IT, which provided custom-built IT products and services. The optimization work on the Soluzioni.pl website, by means of GA service, was conducted from May 1, 2012, to May 31, 2013. First, major indicators related to the main goal were monitored and, later on, those connected with the website content and the website visitors' behavior. The website was cyclically assessed and redesigned. Mistakes and shortcomings on the website were cyclically eliminated. As a result, researchers were able to understand visitors' behavior and identify areas of great potential for improved traffic.

6.3.4 How Was the Research Designed?

The experiment was carried out in four stages.

During the first stage, after installing and activating GA, a preliminary analysis of the website was made, and the initial values of metrics were determined. In order to accurately identify the project objectives, a general category of the owner's desired objective was determined (Lovett 2011). The main goal was set—to increase website traffic—and then it was translated into particular goals, that is, optimization of the website content and structure according to users' requirements, web positioning, and online promotion through social media. Next, measurable KPIs were assigned to the goals, including the total number of visits, the number of new visitors, the percentage of new visitors, visits from the Google search engine, direct traffic, the average time spent on the website, the average number of pages viewed during a visit, and bounce rate. Constant monitoring and control of the KPIs' values ensured proper assessment of the website optimization effects with respect to the changes taking place over time.

First, the indicators related to the main goal were monitored and, later on, those connected with the website content and the website visitors' behavior.

Consequently, within the Soluzioni.pl profile, the following website goals were set, and progress toward them was being monitored over time:

Goal 1: Visitors moving from the Offer page to the Contact page (the goal for which the custom alert was defined).

Goal 2: Visitors spending more than five minutes on the site.

Goal 3: Visitors not entering the site via the Google search engine.

Goal 4: Visitors from the Google search engine—the goal that permits examination of web positioning effectiveness.

During stage II, changes recommended as a result of the preliminary analysis were implemented. In that period, the website content and the overall graphic design were modified.

Stage III focused on visit sources and on the popularization of the site on social networking sites. The study was based on Facebook.com and Internet forums. The aim of this stage was to establish communication with potential customers: community members.

Moreover, activities were undertaken on various Internet forums, which were to attract more visitors from other websites (i.e., referral sources). The promotion of the site in social media was to increase its traffic.

During stage IV, attention was focused on positioning the website in the Google search engine. At the same time, the Facebook campaign was continued. The main aim was to introduce changes that would ensure better search engine visibility of the site and reduce the bounce rate.

6.3.5 What Data Was Used?

The data was obtained from different reports that were generated by GS.

What were the models and concepts used in this study?

KPI, web analytics

What was the way to test or answer the hypotheses or research questions?

The level of goal achievement was measured at the end of each stage when the work was completed. Values of the KPIs for the periods under study and their changes during the study were monitored and analyzed, which gave a reliable assessment of the impact that the researchers' activities had on goal achievement and thus verified the hypothesis.

About Validity and Reliability in This Work

The website management procedure was implemented by Soluzioni IT and fully met its IT expectations/needs.

6.4 What Were the Results and Their Meaning/Context?

6.4.1 Why Is This Approach to the Solution Valuable?

This approach is valuable for the solution because GA is a free IT tool for web analytics; it is easy to use, user friendly, and available in different language versions. The users themselves can compare the data they need, analyze goal conversion, and make decisions concerning online activities. The experiment presented in this chapter shows activities undertaken in order to optimize content and improve traffic to the website.

6.4.2 What Are the Results and Their Interpretation?

Summing up the findings of the first stage, a conclusion was reached that the biggest problem was site visibility in the search engine (goals 3 and 4 had not been achieved). It was necessary to start working on search engine optimization (SEO), which would lead to a reduced bounce rate and a drop in the number of visitors leaving the site. Referral sources were pointed out as the right direction for site traffic optimization and increase. It was decided that the site should be promoted on selected platforms (e.g., facebook.com, peb.pl). Therefore, work had to be undertaken to enhance the chance of the site being found on Google and, at the same time, to increase the number of visitors referred by other sources.

Text modification was another important step toward improving site traffic and search capability. Changes in the content of the site and the pages as well as in the general layout were proposed with the aim of contributing to goal 1 achievement.

In the time period under study, goal 1 was not achieved, which mainly resulted from low website traffic and difficult contact through the Contact page. It was decided that the Contact page had to be altered and displayed in a place visible to users.

The preliminary analysis led to the identification of the areas and pages that needed change. Particular operations were recommended for the subsequent stages of the study to reach the set goals.

In the second period, the website content and the overall graphic design were modified. After completing the work, the level of goal achievement was measured. The results were as follows:

Goal 1: 21 visitors
Goal 2: 31 visitors
Goal 3: 247 visitors
Goal 4: 56 visitors

The comparison of the data from the first period and the second one shows that progress was made. A thorough analysis indicated that site traffic increased, and so did the number of page views per visit; the bounce rate fell; users spent more time on the site; and the number of potential clients rose due to the fact that goal 1 was attained. In addition, changes in visit sources were observed. It was stated that further work on the site should produce even better results.

The aim of the third stage was to establish communication with potential customers—community members. Moreover, activities were undertaken on various Internet forums, which were to attract more visitors from other websites (i.e., referral sources). The promotion of the site in social media was to increase its traffic.

In that period, there were 17 visitors moving from the Offer page to the Contact page (goal 1), 24 visitors spending more than five minutes on site (goal 2), 263 visitors not entering the site via the Google search engine (goal 3), and 103 visitors from the Google search engine (goal 4).

Comparing the data from periods I and III, a positive impact of the changes was observed. They brought about more traffic, a larger number of page views per visit, and longer visit duration.

The number of goals achieved was similar to the previous period, which indicates the right trend in site development.

The main goal was to increase the number of visitors from referral sources, yet it grew by less than 4%. Therefore, a decision was made to continue the promotion of the services on Facebook.

The main aim of fourth stage was to introduce changes that would ensure better search engine visibility of the site and reduce the bounce rate. The measurement of the goal achievement level showed the following:

Goal 1: 17 visitors moved from the Offer page to the Contact page.
Goal 2: 31 visitors stayed on the site for more than five minutes.
Goal 3: 285 visitors did not access the site via the Google search engine.
Goal 4: 156 visitors came to the site from the Google search engine.

The comparison of data from period I and period IV showed a dramatic increase in site traffic. The number of visits was the highest ever. In addition, compared to the previous period, more than 50 users entered the site through the Google search engine, which shows how important site positioning is for traffic optimization.

Table 6.2 presents values of the KPIs for the periods under study and their changes during the study, which gives a reliable assessment of their impact on traffic optimization and goal achievement.

The values for the total number of visits show that the changes inspired by the GA findings led to a significant increase in site traffic. The number of visits kept rising steadily to become almost four times bigger than in the first period of time. The most dramatic growth (of 132%) could be observed after the first site optimization

Table 6.2 The Values of KPIs for the Time Periods under Study

	Period I	Period II	% Change	Period III	% Change	Period IV	% Change
Total number of visits	133	309	132%	374	21%	455	22%
Number of new visitors	122	235	93%	322	37%	372	16%
Percentage of new visitors	92%	76%	−16%	86%	13%	82%	−5%
Visits from the Google search engine	33	56	70%	103	84%	156	51%
Direct traffic	43	76	77%	138	82%	194	41%
Average time on site	00:31	02:26	363%	01:32	−37%	01:18	−15%
Average page views per visit	2.11	3.61	71%	3.02	−16%	2.61	−14%
Exit rate	68.42%	44.66%	−35%	51.87%	16%	51.69%	−0.35%

(period II). This was accompanied by a considerable increase in the number of new visitors (from 122 in the first period to 372 in the last one).

The percentage of new visitors was falling (except for period III). However, the drop was of a few percentage points only and thus of minor significance; the biggest change could be observed between the first two time periods (–16%) due to building a relatively strong base of returning users.

The average time on site in the first time period rose by 363%, which might result from the new layout of the site. However, after that, the visits were getting shorter to finally level off at 1:15. The figures could mean that the site content was well structured, and the users visiting it were able to quickly find the information they needed.

Visits from the Google search engine and direct traffic rose in each period. This proves that the adopted optimization strategy, also based on the GA data, was effective. An increase in the number of visits from the Google search engine shows the effectiveness of positioning and makes it an essential method for boosting online visibility.

Throughout the whole period of time, the average number of page views per visit ranged from two to three pages and cannot be regarded as a satisfying score. Due to the modification of the site content, the exit rate was almost halved compared to the first period, which is quite a good result.

In summary, the analysis of the GA data helped to achieve all the goals set at the beginning of the study. Gradually, the problems on the website were eliminated, new marketing operations were implemented, and the site content was optimized. As a result, site traffic increased, and the scope of site access was extended. As the data in Table 6.2 show, owing to the site modifications, the values of all KPIs improved.

In most cases, the values did not rise sharply between the time periods. However, in a few cases, an increase of more than 100% compared to the previous period could be observed, for example, growth in the total number of visits between the first two periods, which shows how effective the undertaken site optimization was.

6.4.3 How Are These Results Meaningful for Organizations and for Future Research?

Web analytics can be used to manage the implementation of an organization's strategy. By undertaking specific activities, it focuses on the achievement of particular goals. The decisions regarding those activities are based on the knowledge acquired from various analyses. Moreover, it provides the ability to monitor the extent to which the goals are being achieved. Such a view indicates that web analytics should be well organized and structured, and its processes should be of a continuous character. This can be attained with the help of IT.

6.4.4 Where, How, and When to Use It?

Every organization that wants to reach new customers, retain its existing ones, and gain a competitive edge over competitors must use IT tools in order to study the particular behavior of its website visitors. An analysis of Internet data allows for comprehensive monitoring of website operations, in particular the goals defined for the website as well as the needs of the organization, its customers, and business partners. GA is an effective tool for optimizing the management of corporate website content and traffic.

6.5 Conclusions and Recommendations

6.5.1 Are the Objectives of the Research Achieved?

The analysis of the GA data helped to achieve all the goals set at the beginning of the study.

6.5.2 Operational and Tactical

Site traffic increased, the site content was optimized, and the scope of site access was extended.

6.5.3 Strategic

Web analytics can be regarded as a modern instrument in the management of online operations.

References

Ash, T., Ginty, M. and Page, R., 2012, *Landing Page Optimization: The Definitive Guide to Testing and Tuning for Conversions*, Sybex.

Bailyn, E. and Bailyn, B., 2012, Przechytrzyć Google. Odkryj skuteczną strategię SEO i zdobądź szczyty wyszukiwarek, Helion, Gliwice.

Beasley, M., 2013, *Practical Web Analytics for User Experience*, [ebook], Morgan Kaufmann Publishers.

Burby, J., 2007, *Actionable Web Analytics: Using Data to Make Smart Business Decisions*, Sybex.

Clifton, B., 2008, *Advanced Web Metrics with Google Analytics*, John Wiley & Sons.

Cutroni, J., 2010, *Google Analytics*, O'Reilly Media.

Davenport, T. H., Morison, R. and Harris, J. G., 2010, *Analytics at Work: Smarter Decisions, Better Results*, Harvard Business Review Press.

Dykes, B., 2011, *Web Analytics Action Hero: Using Analytics to Gain Insight and Optimize Your Business*, AdobePress.

Few, S., 2009, *Now You See It: Simple Visualization for Techniques for Quantitative Analysis*, Analytics Press.

Gajewski, Ł., 2009, Prosumpcja—Praktyki konsumenckiej innowacyjności [online], http://www.e-mentor.edu.pl/artykul/index/numer/29/id/631.

Gąsiewski, M., 2013, Przewodnik po Google Analytics [online], www.ittechnology.us/ebook-google-analytics/.

Kaushik, A., 2009, *Godzina dziennie z Web Analytics. Stwórz dobrą strategię e-marketingową*, Helion, Gliwice.

Kaushik, A., 2010, *Web Analytics. Świadome rozwijanie witryn internetowych*, Helion, Gliwice.

Kowalczyk, D., 2012, Najważniejsze zasady analityki internetowej [online], www.damiankowalczyk.pl/2012/05/najwazniejsze-zasady-analityki.html#.UZ—TpyjvDg.

Krug, S., 2013, *Don't Make Me Think, Revisited; A Common Sense Approach to Web Usability*, New Riders Publishing.

Ledford, J. and Tyler, M., 2009, *Google Analytics 2.0*, Wiley Publishing.

Lewiński, M., 2013, *Google Analytics, Materiały szkoleniowe Akademia Analityki*, Warszawa.

Lovett, J., 2011, *Social Media Metrics Secrets*, John Wiley & Sons.

Oberoi, A., 2014, Top 30 Web Analytics Tools [online], www.adpushup.com/blog/web-analytics-tools-google-analytics-alternatives/.

Peterson, E. T., 2004, *Web Analytics Demystified: A Marketer's Guide to Understanding How Your Web Site Affects Your Business*, Ingram.

Rosenfeld, L., 2011, Search Analytics for Your Site [online], http://rosenfeldmedia.com/books/search-analytics/.

Szymusiak, T. and Toffler, A., 2013, *Prosument czy Lead User współczesnej ekonomii?*, *Creativetime*, Kraków.

Toffler, A., 1997, *Trzecia fala*, PIW, Warszawa.

Tonkin, S., Whitmore, C. and Jutroni, J., 2010, *Performance Marketing with Google Analytics: Strategies and Techniques for Maximizing Online ROI*, Wiley Publishing.

Trzósło, T., 2014, Analityka internetowa [online], http://semkonsultant.pl/uslugi/analityka-internetowa/.

Chapter 7

Knowledge-Based Cause–Effect Analysis Enriched by Generating Multilayered DSS Models

Axel Benjamins

Contents

Context

Computer-based analysis to support decision making in organizations is a crucial competitive factor. Cause–effect analysis is an important component of these analyses as it identifies cause–effect relationships among data, which can be applied in decision-making situations to improve the decision-making quality.

Purpose

This chapter envisions a concept for the support of cause–effect analyses, which is based on an integrated knowledge base with cause–effect relationships and a knowledge reasoning process, according to the human approach to solving problems.

Design

The knowledge base integrates both structured and unstructured knowledge from a variety of organizational sources. The knowledge reasoning is divided into three phases during which the decision situation is (1) isolated and matched into the knowledge base, (2) explored for potential causes (including their validation), and finally, (3) verified and, if necessary, adjusted by the user. As a proof of concept, this concept is applied manually to the slightly extended example data set from Microsoft for the SQL Server 2012. For the creation of the knowledge base, knowledge about the cause–effect relationships is extracted manually from the database schemas and integrated with additional expert knowledge about further cause–effect relationships.

Findings

The result is an ontology with cause–effect relationships for this specific data set. Based on a fictitious decision scenario, the phases of the knowledge reasoning are played through. The exploration of the ontology will typically identify cause–effect chains with various potential explanations alongside the levels of the chain. These potential cause–effect chains are implemented in a DSS model with multiple layers. The resulting DSS model enables the evaluation of the impact of the identified cause–effect chains for the specific decision scenario.

7.1 Introduction

7.1.1 Purpose of the Study

The impending shortage of employees with analytical competencies (Chen et al. 2012) and the importance of cause–effect analyses for the understanding of a decision-making situation leads to the conclusion that it might be necessary to offer computer-supported cause–effect analysis to all decision makers to sustain a competitive advantage.

7.1.2 About the Background of This Work

Companies that apply analytics to gain a competitive advantage (Davenport and Harris 2007) can make more effective and timely decisions (Vercellis 2009). Cause–effect analysis is an important component in these analyses as it clarifies and defines a decision-making situation (Mintzberg et al. 1976) through the identification of potential causes for a specific effect.

7.1.3 What Is the Scope of This Work?

This chapter demonstrates the feasibility of the concept for a knowledge-based cause–effect analysis from Benjamins (2014). The concept is manually applied to an example data set to support a fictitious decision scenario by generating a multilayered decision support system (DSS) model.

7.1.4 Definition of the Key Concepts

The following is an overview of the concept for a knowledge-based cause–effect analysis. A detailed description can be found in Benjamins (2014). The concept uses the separation of the knowledge representation and the knowledge reasoning, which is typical for a knowledge-based system (Brachman et al. 2004).

For the knowledge representation, knowledge about cause–effect relationships is extracted from a variety of sources within a company, transformed into a unified structure, and loaded into the knowledge base. The unified structure consists of knowledge elements, relationships between these elements, and different relationship types. The sources can contain structured and unstructured knowledge. Most importantly, formulas of DSS models provide structured knowledge about quantified relationships between data. OLAP cubes also implicate potential cause–effect relationships within their dimensional structure and even ETL processes from a data warehouse (DW) implicitly contain cause–effect knowledge within their transformations. Linked (open) data from the World Wide Web can add external influences. This is enriched with unstructured knowledge about cause–effect relationships from experts to add relationships between data from different sources. The result is a homogeneous knowledge base with knowledge about cause–effect relationships from a variety of sources (Figure 7.1).

The knowledge reasoning is applied to the knowledge base in order to identify relevant causes in a specific decision-making situation. The reasoning is based on the separation of a decision-making process into the three phases: intelligence design, choice (Simon 1977), and the human approach to solving problems by using

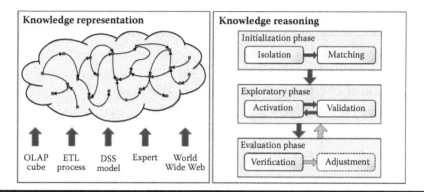

Figure 7.1 **Overview of a knowledge-based cause–effect analysis. (Adapted from Benjamins, A., Knowledge-based cause-effect analysis for context-driven decision support. In *DSS 2.0—Supporting Decision Making with New Technologies, Supplemental Proceedings*. Paris: IFIP Working Group 8.3 digital publications, http://dss20conference.files.wordpress.com/2014/05/benjamins.pdf, 2014.)**

a specific problem context (Newell and Simon 1972). The reasoning is divided into three phases with two steps in each (Figure 7.1). During the initialization phase, a decision-making situation is isolated and matched into the knowledge base. This identifies the relevant factors for the decision-making situation within the knowledge base. The exploratory phase uses these identified factors in the activation and validation steps. During activation, all relationships between elements directly connected to the identified factors are marked as unconfirmed cause–effect relationships. These unconfirmed relationships are statistically validated with the help of time series data, for example, from a DW or operational systems. If they are confirmed, the connected elements are promoted to relevant factors and used for another activation step. The result is a targeted activation along a chain of promising factors in a specific decision-making situation. The evaluation phase offers the user the possibility to verify the confirmed cause–effect relationships and, if necessary, to adjust the affected relationships in the knowledge base.

7.2 What Data Was Used?

The sample database for the fictitious company Adventure Works Cycles is available for all major versions of the Microsoft SQL Server (Microsoft 2014). Adventure Works Cycles is a global company that manufactures and sells bicycles. The bicycles are manufactured in Mexico and the base operation is in the United States with additional regional sales teams. There are sample databases for an online transaction processing (OLTP) database and a DW. The OLTP database contains data about human resources, purchasing, production, persons, and sales. The DW includes the subjects finance and sales with multiple fact tables for each. For this proof of concept, the sample databases for the OLTP as well as the DW are used in the versions for the Microsoft SQL Server 2012. The OLTP database was slightly extended with a table about working shifts for the manufacturing process.

Based on this example data set, a fictitious scenario of dropped sales in a specific product subcategory in a specific sales territory will be analyzed to discover possible causes.

7.3 What Were the Models and Concepts Used in This Study?

7.3.1 Knowledge Representation

Knowledge about cause–effect relationships is extracted from the OLTP and DW data model, transferred into a unified structure, and thus, a knowledge base is created. This is done by representing a database table as an ontology class and important table columns as annotation to a class (Gómez-Pérez et al. 2003). Additionally, a relationship between two tables in the data model is represented as a connection between the two correspondent classes (Gómez-Pérez et al. 2003); for example, a connection between the fact table FactResellerSales and the dimension table DimReseller depicts that reseller sales are potentially influenced by the reseller or vice versa. The direction of the influence must be defined by an expert. The data and relationships are then checked for duplicates and possibilities to unify nodes. The result is used for the creation of an OWL ontology (W3C OWL Working Group 2009) to represent the knowledge about types of cause–effect relationships and corresponding impact calculations based on these data models (Figure 7.2; different relationship types, e.g., solid versus dashed lines, represents different impact calculations). The impact calculations are used to compute the correlation between two related factors.

The ontology is extended with abstract nodes, which do not originally belong to the data models, but are added by a human expert; for example, _Quality is non-existing in the data models but does potentially have an influence on sales (especially _ProductQuality).

7.3.2 Knowledge Reasoning

The knowledge reasoning is manually applied to the created knowledge base for the fictitious scenario, thus showing the procedure of the reasoning phases: initialization, exploration, and evaluation.

The initialization phase maps the scenario into the knowledge base. First, the factors of the fictitious scenario of dropped sales are identified (isolated); they are sales, product subcategory, and sales territory. Then, the knowledge base is searched for

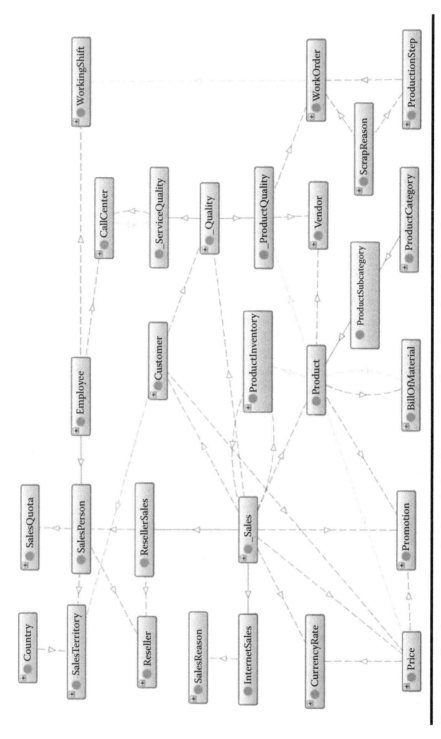

Figure 7.2 Ontology representing knowledge about cause–effect relationships for the AdventureWorks database.

these identified factors, which are matched with appropriate elements. The matched elements _Sales, SalesTerritory, and ProductSubcategory are used as starting points for the exploration iterations. All elements connected to these starting points are activated for further analysis; for example, the factor _Sales activates the elements InternetSales, ResellerSales, Customer, _Quality, ProductInventory, Product, Promotion, Price, and CurrencyRate (Figure 7.2). The relevance of the activated elements in the specific scenario is validated by calculating the impact of an activated element on the initial factor, for example, the impact of Customer on _Sales. The calculation for the impact depends on the relationship type between the two elements; for example, the impact of Customer on _Sales is calculated with the Pearson correlation because of the relationship of the type is_influenced_by. The data for the calculation is fetched from the OLTP or DW databases. An activated element is successfully validated if a user-defined threshold is reached; for example, the correlation r between Customer and _Sales is $r = |0.87|$ and therefore higher than the threshold $t = 0.6$. The validated elements are promoted to factors and used as a starting point for the next iteration; for example, the factor Customer is one starting point for the second iteration. In the next iteration, the elements connected to the factor Customer are activated and validated; for example, the element _Quality is newly activated (SalesTerritory and Price were already activated—see above), and the validation of _Quality is successful.

In this proof of concept, the evaluation phase is done without any changes. The possible adjustments from an expert would be comparable to the adjustments already done during the creation of the knowledge representation.

7.3.3 DSS Model Output

A DSS model is generated to improve the decision-making ability of the user (Holsapple and Whinston 1996). It supports the design phase of a decision to propose alternatives or show the effects of various alternatives (Holsapple and Whinston 1996). The model is based on the activated as well as validated factors and consists of multiple layers due to the multiple iterations during the exploration phase. Each layer adds more detailed explanations for the analyzed effect by including more and more causes (Figure 7.3).

The first layer represents the initial DSS model including only the scenario without any explanations. The second layer explains the effect of dropping sales with decreasing product quality by adding the activated and validated factors from the first iteration of the exploration phase to the model. The third layer extends the model with activated and validated factors from the second iteration. The decreasing product quality is caused by a change in the working shifts. This DSS model can be used to simulate potential solutions to the problem; for example, the cost of the number of employees who would have to be hired to compensate for the change in the working shifts could be compared to a possible increase of the service quality. What are the results and their interpretation?

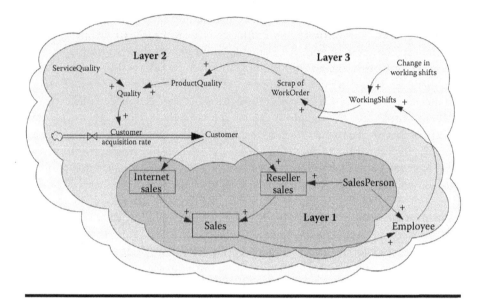

Figure 7.3 The resulting DSS model for a specific product subcategory and a specific sales territory with multiple layers.

The feasibility of this concept for a knowledge-based cause–effect analysis was proven by manually applying the concept to an example data set. An automatic extraction of knowledge about cause–effect relationships from database structures, ETL processes, and DSS models for the integration into a unified knowledge base is envisioned in the concept. The automatic creation of the knowledge base could be done for a specific environment (e.g., in the context of a company) and then extended with domain-specific knowledge from experts. These experts require a user-friendly interface to adjust the knowledge representation and add domain-specific knowledge.

This proof of concept also showed that there are many different parameters during the knowledge reasoning (e.g., the activation strategy, the validation calculation). Because of a very complex architecture and environment, a prototype of the knowledge-based cause–effect analysis will be developed to evaluate the effectiveness of these parameters. This will be done by using a component-based architecture to easily exchange components and compare the results of using different components for the same step (similar to Markus et al. 2002 for emergent knowledge processes).

The research is concluded by evaluating the prototype concerning the support during the design and choice phases of decisions (Holsapple and Whinston 1996). This is done by demonstrating the prototype as a realizable and valid solution to predefined situations (Vaishnavi and Kuechler 2007). Additionally, an experiment could be used to evaluate the prototype (Boudreau et al. 2001), for example, with real-life data in a selected company or in a laboratory setting.

References

Benjamins, A., 2014, Knowledge-based cause-effect analysis for context-driven decision support. In *DSS 2.0—Supporting Decision Making with New Technologies, Supplemental Proceedings*. Paris: IFIP Working Group 8.3 digital publications. Available at http://dss20conference.files.wordpress.com/2014/05/benjamins.pdf [accessed June 18, 2014].

Boudreau, M. C., Gefen, D. and Straub, D. W., 2001, Validation in Information Systems Research: A State-of-the-Art Assessment. *MIS Quarterly*, 25(1), pp. 1–16.

Brachman, R. J., Levesque, H. J. and Pagnucco, M., 2004, *Knowledge Representation and Reasoning*, Boston, MA: Morgan Kaufmann.

Chen, H., Chiang, R. H. L. and Storey, V. C., 2012, Business Intelligence and Analytics: From Big Data to Big Impact. *MIS Quarterly*, 36(4), pp. 1165–1188.

Davenport, T. H. and Harris, J. G., 2007, *Competing on Analytics: The New Science of Winning*, Boston, MA: Harvard Business School Press.

Gómez-Pérez, A., Fernández-López, M. and Corcho, O., 2003, *Ontological Engineering: With examples from the areas of Knowledge Management, e-Commerce and the Semantic Web*, London: Springer.

Holsapple, C. W. and Whinston, A. B., 1996, *Decision Support Systems: A Knowledge-based Approach*, St. Paul, MN: West Publishing Company.

Markus, M. L., Majchrzak, A. and Gasser, L., 2002, A Design Theory for Systems That Support Emergent Knowledge Processes. *MIS Quarterly*, 26(3), pp. 179–212.

Microsoft, 2014, *Microsoft SQL Server Product Samples Database*. Available at https://msftdbprodsamples.codeplex.com [accessed March 26, 2014].

Mintzberg, H., Raisinghani, D. and Theoret, A., 1976, The Structure of "Unstructured" Decision Processes. *Administrative Science Quarterly*, 21(2), pp. 246–275.

Newell, A. and Simon, H. A., 1972, *Human Problem Solving*, 6th printing, Englewood Cliffs, NJ: Prentice-Hall.

Simon, H. A., 1977, *The New Science of Management Decision*, Revised Edition, Englewood Cliffs, NJ: Prentice-Hall.

Vaishnavi, V. K. and Kuechler, W., Jr., 2007, *Design Science Research Methods and Patterns: Innovating Information and Communication Technology*, Boca Raton, FL: Auerbach Publications.

Vercellis, C., 2009, *Business Intelligence: Data Mining and Optimization for Decision Making*, Chichester: John Wiley & Sons.

W3C OWL Working Group, 2009, *OWL 2* Web Ontology Language Document Overview. Available at http://www.w3.org/TR/owl2-overview [accessed March 26, 2014].

Chapter 8

Online Community Projects in Lithuania: Cyber Security Perspective

Aelita Skaržauskienė, Gintarė Paražinskaitė,
Agnė Tvaronavičienė, and Monika Mačiulienė

Contents

Context

Within the context of a smart and inclusive society, cyber security is an important issue, which must be analyzed and discussed in the field of science and in practice. Collective intelligence, which emerges in the activities of online communities, is a new quality of civic engagement that grants more effective decisions and compliance with societal needs. Various social technologies have created possibilities for society members to communicate despite the limitations of the physical world, but they have brought high prospects for sophisticated crimes and other violations of rights and obligations of users, administrators, and states as regulatory bodies.

Purpose

The purpose of this chapter is to connect several independent fields of research: analytics, social technologies, civil engagement, collective intelligence, and cyber security in order to reveal the main threats of using social technologies during the process of engaging society in socially responsible activities. The sources of data are growing, and data mining could be used in variety of ways. Analytics allow the combination of different observations in order to see new patterns.

Design

Research solutions were approached by fulfilling the analyses of regulatory framework for online communities, presenting Internet user analytics in Lithuania as well as identifying the cyber security perspective in online communication. As a result, the main trends were identified in the context of online community projects in Lithuania based on a quantitative public opinion survey conducted in 2013.

Findings

The quantitative research results helped to create a profile of frequent Internet users in Lithuania, where 58 out of every 100 people are using the Internet daily or a few times per week. Frequent Internet users are younger than 39 years old, well educated, and living in the biggest cities in the country. Mostly they use the Internet for communication or looking for professional or general information. Frequent Internet users use social networks and online communities in order to realize some personal interests, connected mostly with hobbies or other areas of personal interest. They perform passive activities, such as getting actual information or broadening one's view, and mostly avoid active behaviors, such as commenting or sharing information or knowledge. Despite the high accessibility of the web in Lithuania, people are not inclined to join socially oriented activities. This fact creates an obvious finding that accessibility is the condition but not a catalyst for increasing the social involvement of society. Even those respondents who are used to visiting websites oriented toward social problem solving, most are not active and mainly susceptible to observing the ongoing processes rather than taking part in them. People using the Internet every day are more often involved in socially oriented activities, and it could be concluded that digital competencies, in general, have a positive influence on online civic engagement.

From the cyber security perspective, respondents do not rank the legal risks as critically important, but they are aware of cyber security issues and strongly support most offered ideas about safe and secure operations online. This shows that people in Lithuania still lack experience in online civic activities and cannot identify independently what problems they might face in virtual space. A united effort is necessary—from the government and law enforcement to the general public—to meet the evolving challenges in securing cyberspace.

Research Limitations/Implications

This research mostly focuses on the context of online community projects in Lithuania (based on a quantitative public opinion survey conducted in 2013). The results of research in the future may be validated by further qualitative research as well as extended worldwide.

Practical Implications

This chapter stresses the importance of personal data protection in online networks and identifies the main legal problems that arise in networked society. These implications may be used in future investigations as well as in designing necessary legal regulations in this field.

Originality/Value

The topic of civic engagement through social networks is considered to be a novelty as is taking an analytic approach toward it. This research adds value to the stimulation of socially oriented activities on the Internet as well as identifying the main threats that the people involved may face.

8.1 Introduction

8.1.1 Purpose of the Study

The purpose of the study is to analyze in an interdisciplinary manner several independent fields of research (analytics, social technologies, civil engagement, collective intelligence, and cyber security) in order to reveal the main threats of using social technologies during the process of engaging society in socially responsible activities.

8.1.2 About the Background of This Work

Following the Internet expansion, organizations and movements have evolved from bureaucratic or centralized to both decentralized and distributed networks. This evolving change toward decentralization and democratization has started to impact business, governments, and society at large (Malone et al. 2010). "Since the future is basically unpredictable and uncertain, society must rely on creative initiatives from the citizens to be able to create the desired future" (Johannessen et al. 2001). Cyber security issues, within the context of a smart and inclusive society, are important aspects of our current reality, which must be analyzed and discussed in the field of science and in practice. Collective intelligence, which emerges in the activities of online communities, provides a new quality of civil engagement that grants more effectiveness and compliance with societal needs. Various social technologies have created possibilities for society members to communicate despite the limitations of the physical world, but they have brought high prospects for more sophisticated crimes and other violations of rights and obligations of users, administrators and states as regulatory bodies.

8.1.3 What Is the Scope of This Work?

The sources of data are growing, and data mining could be used for different reasons. Analytics allow mixing different observations together in order to see new patterns. Main expectations regarding this work were to find new information by fulfilling research not using a traditional legal approach, but analytics. That is why this study was dedicated to analyzing risks related to the processing of personal data in Lithuanian online community networks based on empirical research.

8.1.4 Definition of the Key Concepts

Collective intelligence in this chapter is defined based on Malone et al.'s (2010) definition: the general ability of the group acting collectively to perform a wide variety of tasks. This kind of collective intelligence is a property of the group itself, not just individuals in it.

Social technology is an interdisciplinary research field, which focuses on applying information, communication, and emerging technologies to serve the goals of society.

8.2 What Is the Work Performed in This Field?

8.2.1 Theories and Models Used for Approaching the Problem

Online communities provide useful tools for communication and information exchange; however, online networks and the use of such networks raise many questions regarding user data protection. Typical personal data published by users include user name, sex, birthday, age, contact information (e.g., e-mail address, telephone number, address), and instant messenger screen name. Depending on the community site, users may also be able to post additional information, such as their sexual orientation, where they work or attend school, and their religious and political affiliations (Henson et al. 2011). The core of online community sites is composed of user profiles showing an expressed list of user connections and relationships. The basic idea is that members will use their online profiles in order to become part of an online community of people with common interests (Trichkovska 2012).

Personal information, which is very sensitive and is processed in the context of online networks, may be used or transferred for illegal purposes. Personal data published on social network sites can be used by third parties for a variety of purposes, including commercial, and may pose major risks, such as identity theft, financial loss, loss of business or employment opportunities, and physical harm (Opinion 5 2009). The Article 29 Working Party is a platform for cooperation, composed of representatives of the EU member states national data protection authorities and the European Commission. This organization identifies several legal problems related to data protection in social online networks: the problem of security and default privacy settings, information to be provided by the virtual social network provider, the problem of sensitive data, processing of data of nonmembers, third-party access, legal grounds for direct marketing, retention of data, rights of users, etc. Also, there is the problem of jurisdiction, that is, whether the EU has jurisdiction over activities of international players originating from non-EU countries.

In the EU context, there are two directives regarding data protection: general data protection directive No. 95/46/EC and the directive on privacy and electronic communications No. 2002/58/EC. The provisions of the general data protection directive apply for social network providers in most cases. However, the directive was created when there were no social networks in cyberspace at all. Therefore, the main principles and provisions of the directive cannot solve data-protection issues of an online nature, and most of the issues remain uncovered (Trichkovska 2012). For example, it is unclear who controls data: the owner or manager of the online network, the application provider, or the user of such network. Because of such unresolved issues, directive 2002/58 on privacy and electronic communications, otherwise known as the e-privacy directive, is an EU directive on data protection and privacy in the digital age. It deals with the regulation of a number of important issues, such as confidentiality of information, treatment of traffic data, spam, and cookies. The directive complements the general data protection directive and applies to all matters that are not specifically covered by that directive.

We may note that not every privacy issue in online networks is related to electronic communications. However, the role of communications in online networks should not be undermined, and this directive should govern issues related to it.

The European Commission decided to revise the data protection legislation and was approached to draft and prepare new regulations for data protection. EU justice commissioner Viviane Reding, in a speech at a conference in London in 2011, pointed out a need for a more comprehensive and coherent approach in the EU policy for the fundamental right to personal data protection (Reding 2011). However, the regulation is under discussion in EU institutions now.

Other notable international efforts toward data protection viable legislation include a pioneering standard-setting report published by UNESCO on Internet freedom titled "Freedom of Connection–Freedom of Expression: The Changing Legal and Regulatory Ecology Shaping the Internet" and summary of 10 core principles, ranging from universality and equality, accessibility, and rights and social justice to diversity and network equality published by Access (also known as AccessNow.org), an international Internet advocacy group dedicated to an open and free Internet.

Actions discussed in this section clearly emphasize that attention must be paid to cyber security issues in order to develop a safe and reliable environment for people who wish to engage and wish to generate ideas for the greater welfare of society. The main challenge now is to exploit the potential of new media while not compromising civil liberties, including the right to freedom of expression, to education, and to privacy.

8.3 Description of the Problem

8.3.1 Definition of the Problem That Is Analyzed

In Lithuania and other Eastern and Central European countries of the post-Soviet bloc, civic engagement of society is low when compared with Western European partners. This problem is not new and often appears on the horizon for scientists who research society using different perspectives. One of the goals of the scientific project currently being carried out by our scientist group at Mykolas Romeris University (Lithuania) is to reveal the legal problems that might limit civic engagement via networks as well as to create obstacles for the emergence of collective intelligence as a more effective intellectual instrument for overcoming social challenges. Quantitative research on the extent and current trends and of the society's engagement and participation in building collective intelligence was carried out as part of this project. Having in mind the fact that such difficult and multidimensional questions can be resolved only after evaluation of the existing situation and factors influencing it, we chose to employ analytics of quantitative data as our research method.

8.3.2 Research Questions or Hypotheses

The main research questions are based on the issue of the frequent Internet user profile in Lithuania and are listed below:

- Who are the frequent Internet users in Lithuania?
- What activities do people usually carry out on the Internet?
- What main problems are people using the Internet facing?

All three questions were analyzed on two levels. First, a profile of the frequent Internet user was designed together with the set of activities considered most popular on the web. Answers to the empowered research group's list of problems needed to be taken into account while designing perspectives of a more inclusive society. Finally, the profile of the Internet user involved in socially oriented activities on the web and problems and barriers he or she faces while using online tools were defined. This profile allows us to proceed further with the research project and prepare grounds for a qualitative research stage in terms of identification of respondents for in-depth interviews.

8.4 What Was the Methodology of the Problem Resolution?

The main method used in performing this study was a public opinion survey. The selection of survey respondents was undertaken by respecting the general rules of a random stratification sample and the specifics related to the participation in the process of collective intelligence emergence. The sample ($N = 1,022$) included 478 males and 544 females aged 15–74 in all districts (urban and rural areas) of Lithuania, which guarantees a statistically reliable representation (with the confidence level of 95%) of the Lithuanian population. The public opinion survey was carried out using the method of direct interview at respondents' houses using computerized and standardized questionnaires. Interviewed respondents represented the overall Lithuanian population by major sociodemographic characteristics (using stratified random sampling). After collecting the survey data, a statistical study was carried out using SPSS for Windows. Statistical relationships between attributes were calculated by using chi-square (χ^2) tests. A significance level of $p < 0.05$ was chosen to calculate statistical reliability.

8.4.1 How Was the Research Designed?

The research was fulfilled by these major steps:

- Preparation work and design of research instrument (standardized questionnaire)
- Carrying out of quantitative research by public opinion company
- Data analysis
- Presentation of regulatory framework for online communities
- Fulfilling Internet user analytics in Lithuania
- Investigating the cyber security perspective in online community activities

8.4.2 What Were the Data, Models, and Tests Used?

The data from the results of the public opinion survey were used.

8.4.2.1 What Were the Models and Concepts Used in This Study?

The study focused on emergence of collective intelligence and cyber security aspects of these processes.

8.4.2.2 What Was the Way to Test/Answer the Hypotheses/Research Questions?

The research questions were tested by investigating the statistical data provided by the company, who carried out public opinion surveys.

8.5 What Were the Results and Their Meaning or Context?

8.5.1 Why Is This Approach to the Solution Valuable?

This approach to the solution is valuable because it joins the concepts of civic engagement, analytics, social technologies, collective intelligence, and cyber security in order to reveal the main threats of using social technologies during the process of engaging society in socially responsible activities. Using analytics in this field presents a combination of different observations and encourages reaching new results.

8.5.2 What Are the Results and Their Interpretation?

According to the results of the public opinion survey, all respondents can be divided into six groups based on Internet usage, but only three groups gathered more than 10% of respondents. Forty-four percent of respondents use the Internet every day, and only 34% use the Internet infrequently (less than one time per three months) or do not use it at all. The remaining 22% use the Internet less than a few times per week. It can be noted that the most frequent Internet users are younger (39 years old or less), well-educated people living in the three biggest cities in the country ($p < 0.05$). Respondents who do not use the Internet or use it very rarely usually are 50–74 years old, living in rural areas of the country and have a lower income ($p < 0.05$).

The most popular activities online appear to be communication related to professional aspects of life (67% of respondents chose this option). Activities related to generation of general information and knowledge are a close second (65%). However, Internet users who use the Internet more than a few times a week are not always active in visiting socially oriented websites ($p < 0.05$). As we discuss later, socially oriented activities are not listed among the most popular activities online. Only 21% of respondents answered that they share their opinion or knowledge online (comments in various websites, community forums, blogs, etc.). This reveals that Lithuanians are not inclined to participate in socially oriented activities either off-line or online. These findings encourage furthering the research on low civic engagement. Personal communication using online channels was indicated as one of the most popular options by respondents. Sixty-one percent of respondents using the Internet are using various websites for online communities and social networks, and only 33% of respondents are not registered in any network. Six percent of respondents said that they have accounts but do not use them. Most active users of social networks and online communities are people aged 15–29 ($p < 0.05$). The most popular and best-known social network in Lithuania is Facebook (82% of respondents using the Internet mentioned it).

A different situation can be observed when respondents were asked to name socially oriented networks operating in Lithuania. Only one well-advertised network, www.darom.lt, gathered 41% of respondents. Other projects were mentioned by less than 20% of respondents. Deeper analysis shows that respondents mostly use social networks and online communities in order to pursue personal interests related to hobbies or other areas of personal life (74%). Thus, socially oriented platforms were not mentioned often.

The number of people involved in online communities and social networks not oriented toward the solving of social problems is 54% of all respondents using the Internet. These high numbers show that respondents are actively communicating using social technologies. However, the number of respondents involved in activities of socially oriented virtual communities and social networks is only 7%. Obviously, people do not involve themselves in socially oriented activities even if they are organized in familiar online environments. The survey also revealed that more educated people use social networks more frequently ($p < 0.05$). It should be noted that people who are not members of social networks and online communities at all (38%) are usually 40 or older, have only a professional education, and are married or living with a partner ($p < 0.05$).

In order to proceed with analysis of quantitative data and for the sake of explicitness, the users were divided into three groups based on their activity in socially oriented online projects. "Strong users" were identified as respondents who visit socially oriented platforms every day. "Medium users" are involved in such activities a few times a week. "Weak users" join such socially oriented networks once a week or less. It is obvious that "strong users" are active in most activities online. That leads to a presumption that the Internet itself is inclusive, which means that people who are acquainted with this technology start to use it more extensively. "Weak users" of the Internet are very passive considering their involvement in socially oriented activities online.

Comparative analysis of public evaluation of possible applications of online communication to be conducted reveals that respondents know and understand the perspectives and benefits of Internet-based social involvement. For example, high positions were granted for such active behavior as finding like-minded people, expressing opinions, or proposing new ideas. Unfortunately, people do not indicate that they involve themselves in such activities. They rank all possible outcomes more positively than negatively but show no interest in realization of such expectations. Respondents who are using websites with socially oriented goals also were asked to identify what particular activities they perform there. Data shows that most popular activities are quite passive and related only to observation of processes happening on websites oriented toward social problem solving, for example, getting relevant information (56%), broadening views (54%), getting acquainted with interesting information and comments (49%), searching for like-minded people (31%), and getting more professional experience (28%) compared with such active activities as expressing one's own opinion (49%), voting for projects or ideas (29%), improving projects by using one's own knowledge and skills (only 24%), suggesting new ideas or projects (only 18%), and giving one's own input for social problem solving (only 15%). Such distinction shows that even those respondents who are using websites oriented toward tackling social problems are mostly inactive and mainly susceptible to observing the ongoing processes rather than taking part in them. This paradox encourages investigating the difficult questions: What does the Internet need in order to attract more users in socially oriented activities through the web?

Respondents to the public opinion survey were asked why they do not use online communities and social networks in general. The most popular answer was the "unacceptable culture of such communication method." Other popular answers include "lack of time" and "having no interest in such activities." From a legal perspective, 9% of respondents chose "the lack of privacy" as a reason for limited use of social networks and virtual communities. It is interesting that the least popular answers are related to the low level of governance feedback to any expressed opinion, dangers of expressing opinion, and low security of using it. Also, respondents were asked to list features of socially oriented online platforms.

From the legal perspective, only a few aspects of the survey can be discussed. First of all, it is the feedback on activities. Only 11% of respondents noticed that one of the weaknesses of socially oriented websites is the absence of practical influence of virtual activities on decision making. Second, the issues of security were mentioned. Only 19% of respondents identified this choice as a weakness, having in mind that websites oriented toward social problem solving are not secure. From such information, one conclusion can be drawn: Respondents do not consider the legal issues of online communication to be critically important. Thus, in this area, one more paradox arises. When respondents were directly asked about the advantages, in general, of using the Internet, they positively evaluated all answers related to socially orientated activities. This statement can also be confirmed by a short review of the public opinion survey on various aspects of online activity related to security and regulation (in-depth analysis of these aspects is provided in Skaržauskienė et al. 2014). Respondents find almost all listed legal risks equally important and had strong opinions (more than 70%) that strict liability of virtual community members must be envisaged if they violate the rights of other people. Also, it was recommended to think about the liability of the administrator of networks for the content of networks as well as the need for detailed regulation of activities of online communities. Thus, the opinion of respondents should be evaluated only having in mind the previous answers related to identification of the main reasons why people do not get involved in socially oriented Internet projects. If legal aspects were not dominant previously, it is not believable that legal aspects are so important for respondents who are not involved in socially oriented activities on the web and do not find such activity attractive. More likely, people who are not involved in such activities cannot identify by themselves independently what problems they might face.

8.5.3 How Are These Results Meaningful for Organizations and for Future Research?

The fact that Lithuanian people still lack experience in safe online activities shows the necessity—from the government and law enforcement to the general public—to meet the evolving challenges in securing cyberspace. In addition, it is still an open field for further research on cyber security issues in widespread online communities.

8.5.4 Where, How, and When to Use It?

The results of this chapter may be used in further scientific research as well as designing necessary legal regulation in this field.

8.6 Conclusions and Recommendations

8.6.1 Are the Objectives of the Research Achieved?

The main objectives of the research were successfully achieved.

The quantitative research results helped us to create the profile of frequent Internet users in Lithuania, where 58 out of every 100 people are using the Internet daily or a few times per week. Frequent Internet users are younger than 39 years old, well educated, and living in the biggest cities in the country. Mostly they use the Internet for communication or looking for professional or general information. Frequent Internet users use social networks and online communities in order to realize some personal interests, connected mostly with hobbies or other areas of personal interest. They perform passive activities, such as getting actual information or broadening their views, and mostly escape from active behaviors, such as commenting or sharing information or knowledge.

Despite the high accessibility of the web in Lithuania, people are not inclined to join socially oriented activities. This fact creates an obvious finding that accessibility is the condition but not a catalyst for increasing the social involvement of society. Even of those respondent who are used to visiting websites oriented toward social problem solving, most are not active and mainly susceptible to observing the ongoing processes rather than taking a part in it. People using the Internet every day are more often involved in socially oriented activities, and it could be concluded that digital competencies in general have a positive influence on online civic engagement.

From the cyber security perspective, respondents do not rank the legal risks as critically important, but they are aware of cyber security issues and strongly support most offered ideas about safe and secure operations online. It shows that people in Lithuania still lack experience in online civic activities and cannot identify independently what problems they might face in virtual space.

From the strategic and tactic points of view the united efforts are necessary—from the government and law enforcement, to the general public—to meet the evolving challenges in securing cyberspace.

References

Henson, B., Reyns, B. and Fisher, B., 2011, Security in the 21st Century: Examining the link between online social network activity, privacy, and interpersonal victimization, *Criminal Justice Review*, 36(3), pp. 253–268.

Johannessen, J. A., Olsen, B. and Olaisen, J., 2001, Mismanagement of tacit knowledge: The importance of tacit knowledge, the danger of information technology, and what to do about it, *International Journal of Information Management,* 21(1), pp. 3–20.

Malone, T. W., Laubacher, R. and Dellarocas, C., 2010, The Collective Intelligence Genome, *MIT Sloan Management Review,* 51(3), pp. 21–31.

Reding, V., 2011, Assuring data protection in the age of the Internet. London, June 20, 2011, [online] http://europa.eu/rapid/press-release_SPEECH-11-452_en.htm?locale=en.

Skaržauskienė, A., Tvaronavičienė, A. and Paražinskaitė, G., 2013, *Cyber Security and Civil Engagement: Case of Lithuanian Virtual Community Projects,* International Conference ECCWS, Greece.

Trichkovska, C., 2012, *Legal and privacy challenges of social networking sites,* Doctoral thesis, University of Oslo.

Chapter 9

Exploring Analytics in Health Information Delivery to Acute Health Care in Australia

Chandana Unnithan and Katerina Andronis

Contents

Context

The acute health care sector is a data-rich and information-poor environment in Australia. Conversely, information is a crucial yet under-utilized asset for managing patients in health care organizations. To ensure that information being mined and analyzed is of quality and to leverage the power of data analytics tools, a data governance framework needs to be in place. The "data concierge" function will provide such a framework for an organization in analyzing its data. Analytics and predictive analytics are used to manage current and future requirements both from a management and "changing models of care" perspective. Analytics can work hand-in-hand with an organization's strategic plan that can provide evidence-based data and information to support its plan.

Purpose

We aim to enhance the understanding of how data governance and analytics can help address current issues in the Australian context of health care in order to achieve better information outcomes in the acute health sector.

Design

In this exploratory research investigation, we present scenarios, that is, clinical and nonclinical case studies that demonstrate the use of multiple tools and methodologies for delivery of quality information to the acute health sector in Australia. These scenarios build the case for health data governance. Subsequently, we aim to enhance the understanding of how data governance and analytics can help address current issues in the Australian context of health care to achieve better information outcomes.

Findings

Data quality has become a common goal across all performance areas. For this purpose, it is best to adopt a framework, illustrated in this chapter, that provides the context of care for each activity undertaken. This can result in the convergence of good quality data that can result in better patient outcomes. For example, good quality data can be used for continuum of cancer care and in support of research for curing cancer.

Building governance arrangements into the regular business of health practices is advisable rather than managing information governance as a project. For this purpose, team participation is required with all stakeholders involved understanding their roles.

Prioritize and execute modestly scoped activities where there is relevance and support.

Data quality needs to be measured so that it gets managed efficiently. Even very basic data quality reporting helps instill it as a relevant business activity.

Keep it simple; for example, just go for a basic data dictionary in the first instance. Implement the governance organization as data subjects are addressed, and implement data quality reporting as subject areas are addressed.

Research Limitations/Implications

In addition to contributing to the body of knowledge, the findings will enable a better appreciation of the analytics and data governance framework and how they apply to health care practices.

Practical Implications

Practical recommendations are offered for establishing and operating analytics and data governance frameworks as well as approaches for justifying the investment for health practices.

Originality/Value

The Australian health care and acute care framework has a long way to go before the desired data quality is achieved. We have visualized some scenarios and a framework that can be applied to health care practices in this chapter. After the e-health records implementation occurs nationwide, the Australian health care sector needs to strive to achieve data quality, using the data governance and concierge techniques reviewed in this chapter. These techniques are valuable for the Australian health sector as, only then, the distant dream of acute health care management and continuum of care for Australians within their homes can become a reality.

9.1 Introduction

9.1.1 Purpose of the Study

In the acute health sector within Australia, quality data that is reliable for informing solutions is becoming imperative. Although there is data available, it is not integrated, and the reliability is questionable for the purposes for which it is used. This study was commissioned to explore the reasons for poor data quality and to better understand the solutions to addressing this problem.

9.1.2 About the Background of This Work

The acute care sector in Australia has experienced continuous change in the past few years with the implementation of quality systems to achieve accreditation while maintaining high standards of patient care. The current environment is also characterized by cost restraint balanced with increased accountability. To assist hospitals in providing acute care while also fulfilling regulatory requirements, there is a need for integrated systems and informed solutions (HCI 2014). Conversely, the acute health sector is considered data rich yet information poor (Duckett and Willcox 2011). Australian hospitals use ICD10-based codification of data so as to comply with reporting requirements. This data is of such high quality that it can be used not only for understanding the current status of patients and for predicting health within communities, but also to help establish appropriate models of care based on predictive analytics techniques.

Specifically, this captured data has the potential to become rich information that can subsequently inform policy frameworks. For example, in a particular area in a region where there are more reported cases of breast cancer, there may be a requirement for acute care facilities in this area of specialization. Similarly, if population health data typically on registered births and deaths from cancer registries are synthesized to build a rich picture, this information can predict the incidence of cancer and the continuum of care requirements into the future. Data is a crucial yet underutilized asset in the Australian health care sector because the rich data obtained from health organizations for managing patients does not effectively convert into quality information. We hold the view that only when the efficient conversion takes place and the data becomes high-quality information that can feed into the policy framework can it then be leveraged for research and care in the acute sector (HCI 2014).

We began this research based on the premise that the data that is available currently is not converting into good quality and reliable data for predictive analytics to work with. For enabling data conversion into good quality information that is reliable for predictive analytics to work with, the function of the data concierge comes into the picture. This function enables building good data structures and governance around data, and then, while predictive analytics can facilitate the evidence-based models of care, visual analytics applications, such as IBM Cognos, can enable better visualization of the models to inform policy frameworks.

The current aspiration in Australia is to keep people out of hospitals, fit and well within communities. Health facilities on the other hand aim to provide better patient experiences or patient-centric care. Leveraging the power of mobile applications, government, along with the health sector, is trying to facilitate this aim (ACHR 2011). For this purpose, there is a requirement for evidence-based models of care and policy frameworks for a continuum of care, that is, tracing a patient's journey from a general practitioner to a specialist to a hospital, aftercare facilities, and home-based care. This is where analytics comes into the equation.

9.1.3 What Is the Scope of This Work?

Our exploratory research presents evidence-based scenarios that initially mapped the justification for data governance. Thereafter, we looked at visualizing some of the hospital- and health organization-based data governance models that can enable the conversion of data into quality information, which can then inform the acute health care sector in particular.

9.1.4 Contextual Taxonomies

In this section, we have detailed the classifications that are relevant in this study within their contexts.

Health information management is a widely discussed topic although vigorous management of a health organization's data assets is perhaps less pervasive than expected (Andronis and Moysey 2013). There is increased recognition that data is significant to business process outcomes. However, many organizations in the Australian health sector are unsure when it comes to managing health information (or health data governance). Many of the initiatives that do occur are event-driven or short-lived. For example, a sudden change in weather could cause asthma, and this may trigger initiatives on chronic disease management. However, post that event, when it is contained, the quality of information collected ceases to be of any interest. Subsequently, unless another such event occurs, the data collected eventually gets archived and abandoned. There is no mechanism through which the data collected becomes quality information that can perhaps prevent the next instance of this event.

The health sector in Australia is complex with large primary health care providers. The entire clinical overlay with its obvious importance and potential for impact tends to overshadow other information governance perspectives (Andronis and Moysey 2013). This aspect may support the creation and use of clinical data for clinical purposes but generally does not address nonclinical information domains or properly manage clinical information to support broader use. Health care funding, delivery, and management are changing in ways that rely ever more critically on management information (Novak and Judah 2011). Detailed asset utilization management and strong financial analysis are necessary to properly understand service costs and optimize revenue, which is critical for financial viability under an activity-based funding regime (Novak and Judah 2011). A complete and unified set of good quality episodic data is an essential ingredient. However, data is primarily created in the context of individual service delivery processes and is therefore often fragmented and not sufficiently well formed to support the required analysis. Data is a lateral asset, spanning multiple functional areas, and it is used in multiple purposes in a health organization and in methods that may not be significant in the context of where it is created. Its effective management is challenging as the lateral characteristic does not align well with management requirements.

An insight into models of health care is presented as a prelude to understanding the context better. Models of care within Australia define the way health services are delivered. These outline best practice care and services for individuals or population groups as they progress through the stages of a condition, injury, or event. It aims to ensure people get the right care at the right time by the right team and in the right place (Duckett and Willcox 2011). Essentially, the models describe typical activities to be delivered to patients by a provider, health professional, or care team; the type of services to be provided by an organization; the appropriate stage for an activity or service to be delivered; the location or context in which the activity or service will be provided; the health care team and community partners that will provide the service; and the policy framework for the model of care (ACHR 2011). These models are based on clinical specialties and are developed by clinical teams collaborating in providing care pathways for the management of chronic diseases, trauma cases, etc. Every health department in Australia provides a state-wide framework of models of care for different conditions. Health facilities adopt these and modify them as required to fit for purpose for the care of their patients (Duckett and Willcox 2011).

The Data Management Association of Australia (DAMA 2014) defines data governance as the exercise of authority and control (planning, monitoring, and enforcement) over the management of data assets. The International Association of Information and Data Quality (IAIDQ 2014) proposes that data governance is the management and control of data as an enterprise asset. Drawing from these major definitions, we have applied the framework provided by IAIDQ (2014) to analyze and visualize the health care scenarios in next sections.

Within the data governance framework is a data concierge function that manages the information highway for data stakeholders, owners, and users (IAIDQ 2014). This is a very important function as it manages the information that comes from different environments that need to be analyzed and standardized before it enters the enterprise hub. Requirement teams (data concierges) work together to standardize data to ensure information is moving forward, which is based on standard quality. This is imperative when using data for clinical research and clinical decision making so that everyone understands the data elements and they are all on the same page. To achieve this, a data concierge team provides the following functions:

- Data custodians work with the data stewards and data owners to incorporate data.
- Data stewards work with the business users and data owners to standardize the data.
- Business users work with data stewards and data owners to define business requirements.
- Data custodians and application services work with architects and business users to develop solutions.
- Data owners and data stewards work with the business users to maintain the data.

9.2 What Is the Work Performed in This Field?

The work performed in this field is rather limited as the analytics approach to data quality itself is an emerging concept within Australia. This chapter is therefore an exploratory and pioneering effort in this field.

9.2.1 Theories and Models Used for Approaching the Problem

We have used the concept of scenario building and analysis toward building a strategy (Creswell 2013). We provide scenarios and plans, adjusting the vision as required gradually. Andronis and Moysey's (2013) model has also been adapted as required to inform our analysis.

In a similar context, Bierbooms et al. (2011) performed a scenario analysis of the future residential requirements for people with mental health problems in Eindhoven. There were four steps involved (Figure 9.1): (1) an exploration of the

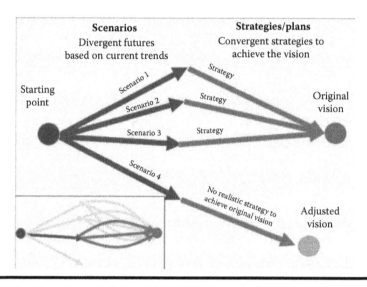

Figure 9.1 The process of scenario building, analysis, and planning. (Adapted from P. Moriarty, C. Batchelor, F. Abd-Alhadi, P. Laban and H. Fahmy, *The EMPOWERS Approach to Water Governance: Guidelines, Methods and Tools,* Presented at Inter-Islamic Network on Water Resources Development and Management [INWRDAM], Amman, Jordan, 2007.)

external environment, (2) the identification of key uncertainties, (3) the development of scenarios, and (4) the translation of scenarios into guidelines for planning organizational strategy. To explore the external environment, a document study was performed, and 15 semistructured interviews were conducted. During a workshop, a panel of experts identified two key uncertainties in the external environment and formulated four scenarios.

9.3 Description of the Problem

9.3.1 Definition of the Problem That Is Analyzed

The problem in this investigation is of data quality and how analytics can help with achieving the best solution for the poor data quality present in the health information management field.

9.3.2 Research Questions or Hypotheses

We hypothesized that visualizing a data governance model as applied to a health care context by eliciting varied scenarios may bring the solution to the problem.

9.3.3 What Was the Methodology of the Problem Resolution?

Taking the study of Bierbooms et al. (2011) as a guideline, this research was performed with the following steps: (1) We explored the environment, (2) we identified the key issues in data governance, (3) we developed scenarios based on them, and (4) we translated the scenarios into the contextualized guidelines and framework for data governance.

9.3.4 How Was the Research Designed?

In exploring the environment, 20 semistructured interviews were conducted over a time period of three years. A panel of experts then identified the key issues in a workshop and formulated the six scenarios, which were further validated individually with a set of one-on-one interviews with experts by the researchers.

9.3.5 What Data Was Used?

The data was obtained from interview transcripts of semistructured interviews as well as one-on-one interviews with experts. Furthermore, issues that were identified from the workshops were also synthesized and used.

9.3.6 What Were the Models and Concepts Used in This Study?

9.3.6.1 Visualizing Data Governance in Health Care Practices

In the context of Australian primary health care providers, Andronis and Moysey (2013) conducted an investigation based on a structured framework (IAIDQ 2014) to assess the indicative level of maturity of data governance. The framework posed questions derived from the content of performance domains and focusing on data governance as illustrated in Figure 9.2.

The key pattern indicates that overall maturity for data governance was quite low across all performance areas. Where it was relatively mature, it focused on aspects of privacy or clinical records, and there was action required. None of these warranted treating data as a crucial asset. This does not mean that data governance itself is uncontrolled or patient outcomes are at risk. Rather, the effect is a less obvious combination of multiple versions of data, poor quality data, loss of efficiency, and relinquished opportunities.

In Australia, there are significant changes in health and hospital administration and funding that have major implications for the use of data in reporting and management. Today, individually managed and operated sites that were funded based on size have been grouped into local health networks that operate as single, multicampus entities funded based on health care outputs; their reliance on data to function thus

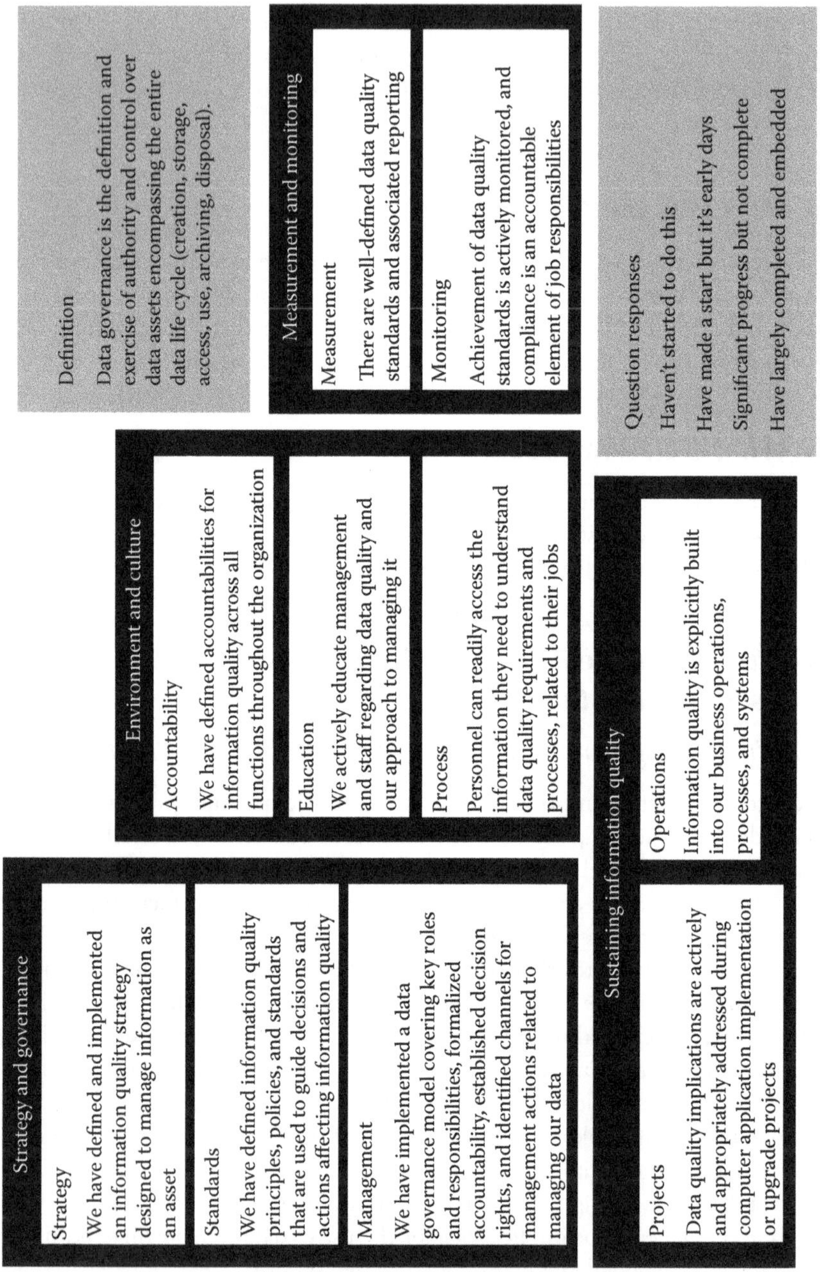

Strategy, and governance

Strategy

We have defined and implemented an information quality strategy designed to manage information as an asset

Standards

We have defined information quality principles, policies, and standards that are used to guide decisions and actions affecting information quality

Management

We have implemented a data governance model covering key roles and responsibilities, formalized accountability, established decision rights, and identified channels for management actions related to managing our data

Environment and culture

Accountability

We have defined accountabilities for information quality across all functions throughout the organization

Education

We actively educate management and staff regarding data quality and our approach to managing it

Process

Personnel can readily access the information they need to understand data quality requirements and processes, related to their jobs

Definition

Data governance is the definition and exercise of authority and control over data assets encompassing the entire data life cycle (creation, storage, access, use, archiving, disposal).

Measurement and monitoring

Measurement

There are well-defined data quality standards and associated reporting

Monitoring

Achievement of data quality standards is actively monitored, and compliance is an accountable element of job responsibilities

Question responses

Haven't started to do this

Have made a start but it's early days

Significant progress but not complete

Have largely completed and embedded

Sustaining information quality

Operations

Information quality is explicitly built into our business operations, processes, and systems

Projects

Data quality implications are actively and appropriately addressed during computer application implementation or upgrade projects

Figure 9.2   Structured framework for assessing data governance maturity.

has magnified. There is also additional government overlay in the form of 60+ local administration areas, known as Medicare locals, in order to better integrate primary health services on a localized basis. This generates a requirement for detailed data covering many services that were previously relatively scantily documented. The government administrators, on the other hand, want to make evidence-based decisions, which increases the need for complete granular data. Many data-intensive situations require the ability to combine data from multiple sources and, therefore, align definitions and compliant data recording and encoding (Andronis and Moysey 2013).

In the health environment, the key interest is to reuse once-entered data many times over. However, this is rather challenging in an environment in which non-integrated systems coexist. Andronis and Moysey (2013) presented a high level model for data governance as presented in Figure 9.3.

Subsequently, the authors applied this model to the context of a large health provider as in Figure 9.4.

In Figure 9.4, the application of the proposed data governance model to a health care provider is depicted and explained as follows.

CXX–executive sponsor: The executive sponsor has overall responsibility and authority for (in this case) data governance and exercises this through control of a group of line managers responsible for different business and clinical areas.

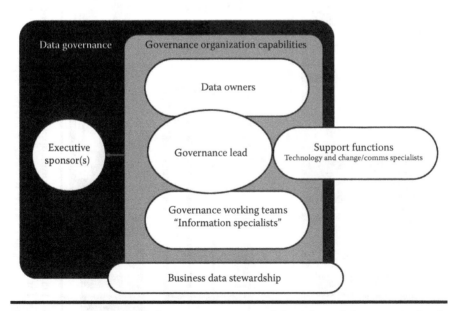

Figure 9.3   A high level data governance model. (Adapted from K. Andronis and K. Moysey, Data Governance for Health Care Providers, *Health Information Governance in a Digital Environment,* Studies in Health Technology and Informatics, Volume 193, IOS Press, Australia, 2013.)

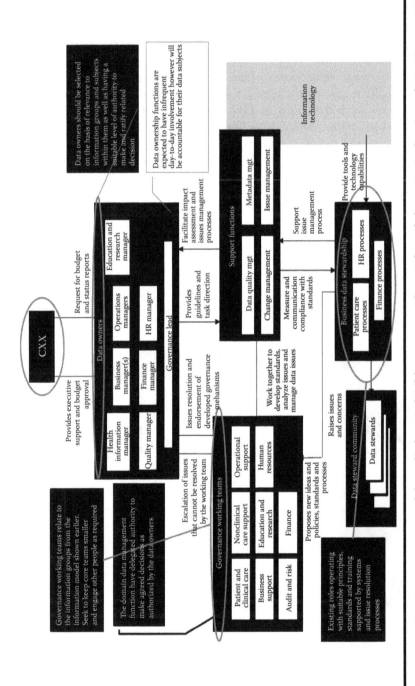

Figure 9.4 Data governance model applied to a health care provider. (Adapted from K. Andronis and K. Moysey, Data Governance for Health Care Providers, *Health Information Governance in a Digital Environment, Studies in Health Technology and Informatics*, Volume 193, IOS Press, Australia, 2013.)

Data owners: A data owner typically should be someone who is responsible for an area of the business that is a key user of the data domain. However, an important consideration for this role is the management of a data domain on behalf of the organization, not just for the area of direct responsibility.

Governance working teams: Governance working teams align with data domains, recognizing that knowledge of a data domain is usually spread across multiple individuals.

Business data stewards: Explicit inclusion of business data stewardship recognizes that day-to-day responsibility for creation of data rests with the people at the "coal face" of business and clinical processes.

9.4 How Were the Hypotheses/Research Questions Tested/Answered?

9.4.1 Scenario Analysis: The Need for Data Governance

The series of information-related scenarios are drawn from the primary health care provider contexts, and these cover clinical and nonclinical areas in order to demonstrate that there are significant dependencies and impacts for data across the board. Each scenario is considered from the perspective of how effective data governance contributes to a better outcome. The purpose is to show how data governance generates improvement. Although the discussion here focuses on data governance-related aspects, in all cases, there are other factors at play as well, such as related process improvement for acute care management.

9.4.1.1 Scenario 1: Scrutinizing the Business Case of an Operating Theater in the State of Victoria

An analysis was conducted of theater demand and usage, including forecasting. The conclusion was that investment in another theater was warranted with an expected payback period of five years. After construction of the theater was well under way, the analysis was revisited and found to be incorrect due to misinterpretation of the data. Corrected analysis showed that the return on investment for the additional theater would take five years longer to achieve than expected.

This scenario is one of conducting analysis that underlies an investment business case. This requires data representing past and likely future operational volumes and demand, case-mix and cost, and revenue elements. Such data is likely to come from a range of sources and needs to be correctly understood and applied in order to get a valid analysis outcome. A sound data governance regime would facilitate the identification of the people who really understand the required data, where to get the data from, and the associated definitions. It is also likely to improve the chances of consultation with the appropriate people to understand the business aspects relevant to such an analysis and ensure that the analysis is properly validated before being acted upon.

9.4.1.2 Scenario 2: Information Focus in a Public Primary Care Provider

In public primary care in Australia, the information focus is on inpatients, and there is generally comprehensive record-keeping. For outpatients (ambulatory), however, other than basic episodic data, record-keeping is relatively poor as it lacks a longitudinal view and health service outcome details. Although coding outpatient data would involve significant costs, without such detailed data a provider cannot get a precise picture of their service and cost base nor understand their case-mix for management or clinical research purposes.

Large public hospitals (and care providers generally) are subject to significant data collection obligations that include critical submissions that directly affect funding. Complying with these collections generates a substantial workload. Most (perhaps 80%) of the data required for these collections is drawn from data needed to deliver clinical care and support administration. Effective data governance contributes directly to ensuring data is correctly captured, sourced, and reported and that creators of data (including clinicians) understand what data is required and why. Executive sponsorship would ensure that this activity has an appropriate focus given its importance to the organization. One could also expect better overall efficiency through taking a more holistic view of data and collection and reporting processes. The quality and completeness of the reporting would be improved, reducing the rework associated with submitted data that fails validation checks.

9.4.1.3 Scenario 3: Influence of Genomic Data

There is increasing use of genetic data for characterization of pathogens and tumors and their application for biomarkers in patients, which directly influences clinical decisions on treatment. The genetic data itself and the translational correlation between genetic markers and treatment outcomes have intrinsic value. Relevant data sources are often spread across multiple systems that are generally not linked, but linking the data is the key to unlocking its clinical value. Health outcomes for the community will be improved by sharing these data. This creates an information management context that is very different from the past.

The use of genetic information is significantly increasing the quantity of data to be managed by care providers. It also requires sophisticated indexing and linking with other clinical and demographic data in order to be used effectively. There is a great opportunity to improve clinical outcomes but only with corresponding data governance. There is little point (and perhaps risk) in influencing clinical decisions with incorrect or incomplete data or data that has been incorrectly linked. Exact compliance is needed because the outcomes can be specific to the patient and the patient's circumstances. Precision is essential and is only achievable with appropriate data governance to help manage the quality of the underlying data, its interpretation, and apt use.

9.4.1.4 Scenario 4: Optimizing Income

With the shift to activity-based funding, care providers now find themselves being paid on the basis of delivered units of care. This necessitates a detailed understanding of care delivery costs down to episode level, careful selection of treatment and payment options for patients, and diligent clinical coding to maximize funding outcomes. Much of this lies outside the purely clinical information domain yet is critical to delivering the most effective health outcomes and simply staying in business. The collection of accurate data involves the whole patient episode journey and relies upon clinicians entering complete clinical data (including complications) into the patient's notes. This facilitates the accurate coding required to achieve optimized revenue outcomes for the hospital. There is often a material level of data governance around this coding process that is largely focused on the clinical rather than administrative significance.

The dramatic shifts in funding approaches to output- and volume-based models requires care providers to have an accurate and detailed handle on costs and be able to view costs from perspectives that include clinical characterization, outcome, patient, service, and time. Data governance needs to extend beyond the clinical domain and support more than clinical costing. Ensuring that revenue is diligently managed has become a critical capability. Given the reliance this has on data codification, integration, and interpretation, data governance is an essential enabler. It also enables essential knowledge to be captured and harnessed for reuse rather than locked away in the heads of individuals.

9.4.1.5 Scenario 5: Campus, Network, and Regional

In Australia, health care services have undergone dramatic change from individually funded and managed sites to networked groups of sites funded collectively. In addition, there is now a regional public health primary care overlay that is responsible for optimizing the health care services in each of 60+ areas across the country. Although these management structures are intended to improve efficiencies and better align services with demand, there is an underlying requirement to be able to report information consistently across these organizational structures as well as drill down to a detailed level by provider, site, service, patient type, etc. The information structures and facilities required to support this are not sufficiently mature.

Management reporting requirements for a large health care provider can be complex in keeping with the nature of the organization and the complex environment in which it operates. Structural changes that suddenly deal with groups of previously separate organizations as unified networks of campus-based organizations have generated significant challenges in management reporting. Data governance is necessary to define terminology and agree on business rules that enable common reporting frameworks and consolidation of reporting elements across multiple organizations. This is essential to meet external commitments. But it is also essential internally (within a network) simply to make sure that data available to management is actually correct and provides management insight into performance at a granular level. This is especially important because a major premise for the structural changes is that they yield efficiencies, not simply through scale or aggregation but by forcing optimization. Making really important management decisions about optimization (such as service portfolio changes) requires reliable information based on reliable data across sources of data that have previously not been integrated.

9.4.1.6 Scenario 6: Cancer Research Information Exchange Framework

A cancer center in Australia is currently embarking on a journey to implement a clinical and research information exchange framework. This framework would enable clinical information sharing across multiple hospitals for clinicians to make informed decisions for their patients as they move from one health facility to another. This project aims at implementing a research information exchange so as to share their research data with local and international research partners. To enable this, currently, a data governance framework has been established with a data concierge function that allows information to be shared in a secure manner for the development of clinical and research outcomes to assist in the cure of cancer.

The reason for effective data governance in this instance is to create a rapid learning environment for cancer that is founded on trusted data sets for those that support integrated cancer care across their cancer center partners or those that enable the creation of associations, rapid learning, and ultimately, high-impact cancer research. Delivering trusted data sets requires an effective data governance framework, encompassing the roles, policies, frameworks, and tools that collectively deliver high-quality and trusted data needed to deliver a successful rapid learning environment for cancer.

The experience of cancer organizations around the world recognized as having achieved a significant measure of success in the management of the data is actually the single most important success factor. Suitable technology and software applications are necessary to provide capability but can only do what the data allows. The true business of the cancer center itself is the management of data, and therefore, data governance constitutes a core management discipline and key operational processes. Given the nature of the data involved, the cancer center also has significant professional and regulatory responsibilities to comply with in relation to acquisition, storage, access, and use of this data. The key point, however, is that data governance is central to materializing the cancer center's vision, not just something that is necessary for compliance.

9.4.2 About the Validity and Reliability in This Work

This research was built upon conceptual frameworks built originally by experts in the field, which were then validated over numerous interviews with practitioners and field experts over three years.

The final validations conducted for the soundness of the model makes it reliable and valid in the context of Australia.

9.5 What Were the Results and Their Meaning/Context?

9.5.1 Why Is This Approach for the Solution Valuable?

The approach to visualizing the possible solutions was required with validation from practice so that the framework could be applied correctly. The practice validity of the solution makes it valuable in this field.

9.5.2 What Are the Results and Their Interpretation?

In the health context, and specifically acute health care, adhering to some recommendations can improve the data quality and improve health outcomes.

- Data quality has to become a common goal across all performance areas. For this purpose, it is best to adopt a framework, illustrated in this chapter, to provide the context of care for each activity undertaken. This can result in convergence of good quality data that can result in better patient outcomes. For example, good quality data can be used for continuum of cancer care and support of research for curing cancer.
- Do not resource managing information governance as a project. Rather build the governance arrangements into the regular business of the health practice as such. Ensure team participation as data governance is a team-based game. It can only be effective when stakeholders understand the purpose, know their roles, and feel that they are on board.
- Execute modestly scoped activities that have a clear priority. Although planning for data governance is reasonable, it should be recognized that you will only move forward when there is relevance and support.
- Take steps with permanence in mind as a one-off improvement in data quality achieves almost nothing. The adage that what gets measured gets managed is true when it comes to data quality. Even very basic data quality reporting helps instill it as a relevant business activity.
- Keep it simple; for example, just go for a basic data dictionary in the first instance. Implement the governance organization as data subjects are addressed and implement data quality reporting as subject areas are addressed.

In summary, the Australian health care and acute care framework has a long way to go before the desired data quality is achieved. We have visualized some scenarios and a framework that can be applied to health care practices in this chapter. After the e-health records implementation occurs nationwide, the Australian health care sector needs to strive to achieve data quality, using data governance and concierge techniques reviewed in this chapter. Only then can the distant dream of acute health care management and continuum of care for Australians within their homes become a reality.

9.6 How Are These Results Meaningful for Organizations and for Future Research?

Data management is crucial in the analytics process. The development of any analytics structure requires data governance to maintain the analytics process working and adding value. The recommendations provided based on results and their validation is useful for Australian health care organizations that are envisaging using analytics approaches to managing health information. Conversely, research in the area is nascent and emerging, which opens the door for future researchers in the area and collaborations. The research is also of significance to other countries, such as Canada, that are beginning to build the field of health analytics.

9.6.1 Where, How, and When to Use It?

The recommendations are timely and useful for acute health care environments in which data is crucial and quality of data is imperative to arrive at correct interventions.

9.7 Conclusions and Recommendations

9.7.1 Were the Objectives of the Research Achieved?

The objectives of this research were primarily to explore this emerging field, seeking health analytics solutions to an existing issue of data governance. The framework and visualization presented is the result of achieving these objectives.

9.7.2 Operational and Tactical

The recommendations and the frameworks given in this chapter can be used by health practices in a tactical manner and operationalized with immediacy.

9.7.3 Strategic

As the framework involves a rich visualization of all stakeholders and how they connect in this context to enhance the data quality, strategically, health practices can benefit from these solutions offered.

References

ACHR, 2011, *Healthcare in Australia—Prescriptions for Improvement*, Australian Centre for Health Research, South Melbourne, Victoria.

Andronis, K. and Moysey, K., 2013, Data Governance for Health Care Providers, in *Health Information Governance in a Digital Environment*, Studies in Health Technology and Informatics, Volume 193, IOS Press, Australia.

Bierbooms, J. P. A. J., Bongers, M. B. I. and van Oers, H. A. M., 2011, A scenario analysis of the future residential requirements for people with mental health problems in Eindhoven, *BMC Medical Informatics and Decision Making Journal*, 11(1).

Creswell, J. W., 2013, *Research design: Qualitative, quantitative and mixed method approaches*, 2nd Edition, Sage Publications, Thousand Oaks, CA.

DAMA, 2014, www.dama.org.au [online].

Duckett, S. J. and Willcox, S., 2011, *The Australian health care system*, 4th Edition, Oxford University Press, Melbourne.

HCI, 2014, Acute Care, Healthcareinformed.com, http://healthcareinformed.com.au/acute_care.html [online].

IAIDQ, 2014, http://iaidq.org [online].

Moriarty, P., Batchelor, C., Abd-Alhadi, F., Laban, P. and Fahmy, H., 2007, *The EMPOWERS Approach to Water Governance: Guidelines, Methods and Tools*, Presented at Inter-Islamic Network on Water Resources Development and Management (INWRDAM), Amman, Jordan.

Novak, J. and Judah, A., 2011, *Towards health productivity reform agenda for Australia*, Australian Centre for Health Research, South Melbourne.

Chapter 10

Information Visualization and Knowledge Reconstruction of RFID Technology Translation in Australian Hospitals

Chandana Unnithan, Arthur Tatnall,
and Stephen Burgess

Contents

Context

This research is located in Australian hospitals within the knowledge domain of health informatics and analytics. Radio frequency identification (RFID) is an evolving technology innovation that uses radio waves for data collection and transfer without human involvement. With its success worldwide in hospitals for improving efficiencies and thereby quality of care, the technology was piloted in Australian hospitals in the late 2000s. However, existing literature (in 2013) reflected limited success with full-scale implementation and the emerging view that the sociotechnical factors in implementation are not being considered.

Purpose

Information systems researchers in Australia had begun emphasizing sociotechnical approaches in innovation adoption and translation of technology in the context as well as visualizing the information using analytical techniques.

Design

A qualitative research study with a multiple case study method was set in this premise in 2007 and aimed at addressing the knowledge gap. Information for the case studies was obtained through a rigorous data collection process, through semistructured interviews, focus groups, concept mapping, and documentation analysis. The findings were then validated for currency with practitioners in the field in 2013. Innovation translation is an approach that posits that any innovation needs to be customized and translated into context before it can be adopted. To understand the "social" aspects that may be involved in adoption, a lens informed by the actor–network theory (ANT) helps reconstruct the implementation process, investigating social networks and relationships that influenced innovation translation. The innovation translation approach to theorization and knowledge abstraction, informed by the ANT removed the need for considering the "social" and the "technical" in separate modes. More importantly, an ANT-informed lens acted as an augmented filter, enabling an in-depth view of the data and information visualization of knowledge abstracted in this research investigation.

Findings

The network of actors and their relationships is extremely complex and is key to operations in Australian hospitals. As found in the initial period of investigations, both orderlies and nurses felt disempowered by technology introduction. The nurses did not endorse imposing a technology that disrupted the workflow. It had taken three years and a nurse-in-charge to redeploy the technology that was then accepted with ease by all stakeholders, including clinicians. As was also found to be true in the final phase of investigations, the introduction of the technology by a nurse enabled successful translation of RFID. The findings revealed a silent web of relationships between the key actors in hospitals in relation to promoting RFID technology. The constant communication flow between orderlies to orderlies, nurses to orderlies, and nurses to nurses across the private and public areas of Case 1 and nurse–nurse, nurse–clinician, and nurse–ICT relationships, which are not clearly visible at the onset, is indeed the most powerful social factor for RFID implementation.

Additionally, expert opinion/validation from the industry sector indicates that, in Australian hospitals, the nurse is the powerful and influential factor in technology translation. For example, the ICT department feels imposed upon by medical directors, but if the nurse is the person raising the issue, they will accept it, take it on board, and enable it. Doctors do not question nurses. Neither do the patient care orderlies. The nurse happens to be the lynchpin in Australian hospitals. This knowledge abstraction is significant from the Australian perspective, which would not have been possible without the interpretive stance of this investigation, visualizing the knowledge through an ANT-informed lens and eliciting the key social factors in translation further validated by industry experts. The finding is of significant value to large hospitals on the verge of RFID deployment. Conversely, the research extended the innovation translation theory framework and augmented the field of ANT through visualization techniques. This value addition has significant implications for academia as it added to the body of knowledge that is currently rather limited in the field of health informatics within Australia.

Research Limitations/Implications

This research investigation was done over a period of seven years when RFID as a technology was still being considered and not actively being deployed by Australian hospitals. However, after the publication of this study, hospitals in Australia have actively begun considering the technology in various parts of their operations. Further case investigations on this progress and the use of analytical techniques in visualization would be highly valuable for the health informatics sector.

From a global perspective, this study could become a framework for commissioning similar investigations based in other countries, such as Canada, within the health sector.

Practical Implications

It is evident that RFID innovation translation requires commitment of a key stakeholder in Australian hospital operations who is able to influence others, a view that is validated by industry practitioners. This key stakeholder is a nurse. Similarly, other countries and hospitals within Australia that are considering RFID deployment may find this as a strong practical consideration for their success.

Originality/Value

The contributions of this research are in that it addresses the sociotechnical gap evident in academic literature pertaining to RFID technology adoption in Australian hospitals; it augments the body of knowledge concerning innovation translation in health informatics informed by ANT analysis. The ANT lens visualizes that RFID was facilitating the renegotiation and improvement of network relationships between the people involved as well as the technology. The knowledge abstraction and visualization enabled by ANT is a major contribution to the field.

10.1 Introduction

10.1.1 Purpose of the Study

Technology adoption in hospitals is always challenging as reflected in the reviews from the last few decades (see, for example, Coustasse, Tomblin and Slack 2013; Yao, Chu and Li 2012). Academics have used adoption models, such as the technology acceptance model (TAM), which evaluates user acceptance of computer-based information systems (Davis 1986), or diffusion of innovation (Rogers 2003) to study and evaluate technology adoption within hospitals.

Hospitals are, no doubt, chaotic environments in which regularly scheduled processes undergo rapid changes in case of emergencies. For example, in the case of an emergency, it is not uncommon to page all available nursing staff. All procedures that were scheduled, with the exception of critical surgeries, could be postponed at this time. Clinicians posted in the outpatient area may be summoned to assist with emergencies. In this chaotic environment, technology cannot be implemented using the standard procedures or techniques used in other environments, such as retail or manufacturing. Although literature is prolific on the technical, legal, and economic impediments of technology implementation, the rather hectic social environment of hospitals (in which technology is implemented, making it unique) is often ignored. In this research, we take the view that technology implementation in hospitals involves a unique challenge. In industry sectors, such as retail or manufacturing, a routine adaptation is undertaken to redesign processes, and users are then trained to fit in with the new technologies. However, health services cannot be interfered with, stalled, or put on hold temporarily; this may cost a life! Given the perilous nature of hospitals, we were of the view that any new technology has to be customized and implemented with the involvement of all ground-level users or stakeholders.

Radio frequency identification (RFID) is regarded as an accepted mobile technology solution to improve process efficiency in supply chain management. It uses radio waves for data collection and transfer, efficiently and automatically without human intervention (Yao, Chu and Li 2011). From 2005, health care providers globally began to realize the benefits of adopting RFID in their operations, to enhance efficiency and provide better services (Degaspari 2011). By 2010, RFID systems had been trialed to track medical equipment and supplies more efficiently in hospitals (Yao, Chu and Li 2012) as RFID was expected to lead reduction in clinical errors, reduced costs, and increased efficiencies.

A literature review from 2000 to 2013 (Coustasse, Tomblin and Slack 2013) ratified the acceptance of RFID as an innovation accentuated by global recession that called for cost efficiencies without compromising on quality of care. Nonetheless, in the Australian context, privacy and health industry regulations have mainly constrained the innovation diffusion. Australian hospitals are still transitioning into e-health records and unified health systems (Dunlevy 2013).

RFID integration issues with legacy clinical systems and the costs involved in large-scale implementation resulted in hospitals putting RFID on hold as they prioritized funding toward the transition to e-health records (Duckett and Willcox 2011; Novak and Judah 2011).

The motivation for this investigation arose in 2007 from RFID's status as a still nascent innovation in Australian hospitals. There were only a small number of largely unsuccessful and abandoned cases or pilot studies reported in Australia involving large hospitals, through biased vendor or technical reports. Even in 2013, focused research reporting on RFID adaptation in Australian hospitals is yet to emerge and is limited to typical diffusion studies or uses essentialist approaches, which are indifferent to or dismissive of sociotechnical factors (Dunlevy 2013). Therefore, this study was and remains significant to date because the findings throw light upon the underexplored, yet critical, interplay of sociotechnical factors that have a prominent role in the adaptation of RFID technology in Australian hospitals.

Conversely, academic literature in Australia was demanding more qualitative approaches and interpretive studies. In the early 1990s, influential researchers in Australia (for example, Parker, Wafula, Swatman and Swatman 1994) alluded to the fact that information systems research has to move away from technical issues and focus more on behavioral issues. Moreover IS methodologists called for a move away from scientific/positivist research methods toward interpretivism. As Davis, Gorgone, Cougar, Feinstein and Longnecker (1997) pointed out, the problem of handling complexities due to interconnected technologies, how they relate to humans and organizations, and how humans relate to them, has come into focus. However, as Tatnall (2011a) pointed out, even interpretive studies have focused on innovation diffusion and technology-related factors, taking on an "essentialist" approach that suggests innovation diffusion occurs because of the technology's salient features, making it acceptable. These approaches, such as diffusion studies or TAM, did not reveal possible and deeply covert human and social factors and perceptions. In other words, the quintessence of "innovation translation" (i.e., how RFID as an innovation can translate into Australian hospitals in which "implicit sociotechnical factors" play a significant role) was rather absent from published academic literature.

Taking the gaps in literature into account, this investigation took a holistic approach, wherein we observed and analyzed the adaptation process of RFID in two different large hospitals with several departments; this proved revelatory. The study, which has evolved over five to six years, made significant discoveries through participant and nonparticipant observations. Further, strong validation from practitioners in the health sector (hospitals, health consulting, and professionals) on the findings and recommendations in 2013 has made it relevant to the current situation. Moreover, the study not only applied the innovation translation concept to the field, but also visualized the interplay of human beings and the technology, using the actor–network theory (ANT) lens. ANT has been criticized as insufficient for explaining the relationship formation between actors and changes that occur in relationship networks (Tatnall 2011b). The investigation addressed this deficiency in relation to information systems research, in that it incorporated an ANT lens for visualization of the innovation translation theory as an augmented filter, enabling an in-depth view of the data, thus making an important academic contribution to the field of ANT—a sociotechnical approach.

10.1.2 About the Background of This Work

Toward the end of the 1990s, the application of sociotechnical perspectives was arguably promoted as a means to appreciate and extenuate the poor uptake and performance of information systems within health sectors (Berg 1999). Emerging sociotechnical foci also seem to have influenced research as more qualitative studies began to emerge alongside conventionally quantitative-focused global health sector research (Whetton and Georgeou 2010).

10.1.3 The Australian Health Milieu

Over the past decade (2001–2010), it is evident through the progress of varied organizations, such as the Health Informatics Society of Australia, the National E-Health Transition Authority (NeHTA), etc., that Australia is progressing toward a fully electronic health record system nationally (Prgoment, Georgiou and Westbrook 2009), albeit slowly. Mobile technologies are the fastest growing category of the ICT revolution. Both public and private health care providers are increasing their investment in technology, particularly in mobile communication, to enable process efficiency in their workforces (Ho 2012). Debatably, two of the largest issues facing hospitals are enhancing worker productivity and reducing human error (Ho 2012).

It was only toward the end of 2006 that mobile technologies were initially explored in Australian hospitals (Cangialosi, Monaly and Yang 2007). In 2009, with the Wi-Fi evolution, wireless devices and mobile technologies, such as RFID, gained momentum in Australia (Yao, Chu and Li 2012). Unlike other technologies, which may address a particular area (such as physicians or nurses with a PDA), or a technological system that is meant for physiotherapy or surgery, RFID is a tracking technology that has the potential to track objects and people in a hospital. By the sheer nature of its tracking ability, it has the potential to pervade hospitals, touching every department dealing with patient care. It was in the decade of 2001–2010 that technology refreshments had begun to occur in earnest with the imminent national health records system. Additionally, in Australia, health care is heavily affected by privacy regulations (Privacy Act of Australia 1988; Privacy.Gov 2013) and the Privacy Act is more formidable. Often it is so doctrinaire that any data regarding an adult patient is not even provided to parents unless they are named as carers and if the patients are unable to handle themselves. This poses significant difficulties in emergencies (Duckett and Willcox 2011). In such restrictive conditions affecting the health sector, a piece of technology, such as RFID with its surveillance potential, was unacceptable in its original form to Australian hospitals. They had to be compliant with the existing privacy laws and standards.

RFID, as an innovation, was still being trialed toward the end of the 2000s and was not yet fully accepted as a standard way of asset tracking in hospitals (at the time when this research study was conducted, i.e., 2007–2012) (Duckett and Willcox 2011). An early report of RFID-enabled functions in Australia by Bacheldor (2006) reported that the Rockhampton Base Hospital in Queensland, Australia, used RFID to improve nurse safety in mental health ward buildings. Many pilot implementations, such as those at RMH and Barwon Health in Victoria (and others in Western Australia and Queensland) were introduced for not only asset tracking but also patient tracking (infants, geriatrics, and the mentally disabled). However, most of these pilots did not result in full-scale implementation. Bendigo Hospital in regional Victoria has successfully deployed RFID progressively in all departments across the hospital (Friedlos 2010). Despite Australian hospitals piloting the technology toward the end of the decade, unsuccessful and abandoned examples persisted.

10.1.4 What Is the Scope of This Work?

The scope of this work is limited to finding the sociotechnical factors that impacted successful translation of technology, namely RFID, in the context of Australian hospitals. Additionally, it was required to visualize the knowledge abstracted such that it becomes clear to academia, practitioners, and strategists who were considering the technology deployment during the past few years within Australia so as to improve the quality of service offered in hospitals through the improvement of worker productivity.

10.1.5 Definition of the Key Concepts

RFID technology refers to an acronym and a broad term for classifying technologies that use radio waves to automatically recognize objects and people.

Information visualization in this chapter refers to the knowledge abstracted from this investigation being visualized through a set of graphical images showing relationships.

ANT refers to a theory developed by Bruno Latour (1986) and developed by Law and Callon (1988) in an attempt to give voice to artifacts. ANT holds that humans and technology should be considered equally as "actors" that influence successful deployment of technologies in any context.

Innovation translation refers to the seminal work of Callon (1986) named as the "sociology of translations" in which effective deployment of technology is considered through four moments of translation, namely, problematization, interessement, enrollment, and mobilization.

10.2 What Is the Work Performed in This Field?

When the sociotechnical factors are considered in the field of health informatics in Australia, research is still emerging. RFID is almost a noninterventional technology in the health sector for tracking equipment, so it may be accepted for that purpose (Coustasse, Tomblin and Slack 2013). However, the sociotechnical factors or actors in the milieu (stakeholders) hold the key to effective RFID deployment in the Australian context.

Within hospitals, a business case might encourage management to consider the technology; however, it is rendered useless if abandoned by users. Therefore, in this research, we investigated the sociotechnical factors and how the interplay between RFID technology and actors (people) affects successful deployment.

10.3 Description of the Problem

10.3.1 Definition of the Problem That Is Analyzed

The problem that is being analyzed is as to why RFID technology deployments are being unsuccessful within Australian hospitals, particularly when it is regarded as a technology that is relatively unobtrusive to hospital operations.

10.3.2 Research Questions or Hypotheses

The research questions were as follows:

> RFID technology in Australian hospitals is still nascent and seemingly viewed with scepticism: What sociotechnical factors interact to affect the adoption of RFID in Australian hospitals, and how is this achieved?
> What are the key factors that affect adoption?
> How do these factors interact and negotiate to eventuate in adoption?

10.4 What Was the Methodology of the Problem Resolution?

We have chosen a multiple case study methodology for this inquiry, using two landmark case sites (hospitals) in Australia. The choice was based on an Australian milieu being different for implementing RFID technology as it touches every department in terms of tracking ability as well as people. The issue under investigation was innovation translation of RFID in a complex sociotechnical context. This is not well understood, and the aim is to gain an in-depth understanding regarding actors, their opinions and relationships, and changes to their relationships and interactions. The research questions involved understanding how the actors in the network of translation negotiate with each other in order to achieve successful RFID translation. The process of negotiation and translation involves complex issues in the hospital context: a chaotic environment in which people continuously negotiate with each other. Information relating to these issues of translation is best obtained through qualitative fieldwork (Creswell 2013). The lead researcher not only interviewed people in their settings, but also observed and recoded behaviors.

The choice of the case study method is justified by Yin (2009) as an appropriate method when we tried to answer how and why questions, and we had less control over events being observed and when the project was a contemporary phenomenon with a real-life context. All of the above elements are present in this research that investigates RFID translation into Australian hospital contexts. Moreover, we have resorted to *purposeful sampling*, which is a concept in which researchers select sites for the study because they can purposefully inform an understanding of the research problem and the central phenomenon in the study (Creswell 2013). In this investigation, the determining criteria were that RFID implementation was partially or fully completed or at least initiated in the hospitals. We were able to find a pioneering, partially complete and a successful, fully completed situation to draw cross-case comparisons later. As described in Creswell's (2013) compendium of data collection approaches of qualitative research, from six sources of evidence for cases as prescribed by Yin (2009), and drawing from many authors in the field, we have chosen observation, interviews, and documents for data collection. For observation purposes, the principal researcher was a semiparticipative observer (Case 1) and a nonparticipative observer (Case 2) and gathered field notes. A semistructured approach was resorted to for interviews. Focus groups were also used for validation.

For analyzing the interview data, the concept mapping technique was used to reveal hidden patterns. These were then presented using ANT-based information visuals, thus abstracting the data to the next level of information. This technique helped in the abstraction of real information without breaching confidentiality and did not affect the sensitivity of the health environment.

10.5 How Was the Research Designed?

10.5.1 Developing the Conceptual Framework

Callon (1986) outlined a novel approach to the study of power: the "sociology of translation." This pivotal work describes a scientific and economic controversy about the causes for the declining population of scallops in St. Brieuc Bay and the efforts by three marine biologists to develop a conservation strategy for that population. We have drawn from this seminal work to build the conceptual framework described below. The research quest was to *determine* the sociotechnical factors that affect adoption of RFID in Australian hospitals and *how* they interact to eventuate successful translation.

- *Problematization* is when a group of key actors define the nature of the problem (in this situation, the issue that RFID proposed to address) and the role of all actors in the context. All factors in this situation are regarded more as actors.
- *Interessement* is whereby the factors or actors defined in the problematization process impose the identities and roles defined on other actors, thus building a network of relationships in which all actors become involved. In this context, the champions of RFID in the context try to negotiate with others in the network.
- *Enrollment* occurs after the success of interessement, when a process of coercion, seduction, and consent leads to the establishment of a stable alliance. In this situation, this is the moment of translation whereby the key network of actors enrolls all others into accepting an RFID solution, either by imposing it or through influencing them.
- *Mobilization* occurs when the solution gains wider acceptance. In this situation, RFID gains wider acceptance as a solution for the proposed reason within the hospital context.

Thus, we took an approach to theorizing innovation that had the advantage over essentialist approaches, such as innovation diffusion.

10.5.2 What Data Was Used?

In this research investigation, the lead researcher went through a series of interviews and observations to collect relevant data. This data was transcribed and reconstituted in a "movie script" format with acts or scenes, actors, and dialogue (see Figure 10.1 as an example). This unique method of presentation was then funneled into information visualization through an ANT-informed lens.

Cameo:	*What is your opinion on RFID being deployed here in ED?*
Head-ED:	*This is an area where there is frequent movement of equipment, people and other resources on a regular basis. In this chaotic environment, it is an expectation that equipment can be tracked immediately, and these are sterilized and the correct equipment. For example, often this department loses its wheelchairs while transporting patients, and over the last year, there has been a loss of 11 wheelchairs. Similarly, there is equipment that gets lost in the laundry area of wastebaskets due to the nature of emergency. There are no tracking or information systems in place at present, and collaborative care is therefore dependent on the goodwill of existing orderlies only (not RFID).*

Figure 10.1   Case 1 (Scene 3): Meeting the head of the emergency department and a business analyst.

10.6 What Were the Models and Concepts Used in This Study?

10.6.1 Intersection of Innovation Translation and ANT

In the much-acclaimed diffusion of innovations theory (Rogers 1995, 2003), an innovation is defined as "an idea, practice or object that is perceived as new" (Rogers 1995). Tatnall (2011) posits that the process of innovation involves getting new ideas accepted and new technologies adapted and used. A challenge to adapting a new technology or applying it to an existing context is that it is often not accepted in the form first proposed (Latour 1986, 1996) and has to be *translated* into a suitable form for the environment. Unlike diffusion, translation can only occur if it interests all involved stakeholders.

In this research, it was studied how RFID technology translated into large Australian hospitals, retaining the essential element of innovation, namely location tracking, while adapting itself to the environment. Elements of ANT were incorporated into the conceptual framework, thereby visualizing the interplay that occurred between actors. ANT was developed by Latour (1986) in an attempt to give a voice to technical artifacts, considering humans and nonhumans as equally important in the translation of innovative technologies. As Tatnall (2011) points out, ANT offered an advantage over other theories as there is no dividing line between human and nonhuman entities, nor is there an essence attributed to either that determines the adoption rate of an innovation. However, one criticism of ANT is its inability to explain relationship formation between actors and over changes of events in relationship networks (Greenhalgh and Stones 2010). In this research, this criticism has been addressed in relation to information systems research, in that the conceptual framework incorporates an ANT lens for visualization to the innovation translation theory as an augmented filter enabling an in-depth view of data.

10.6.2 In What Way Were the Hypotheses/Research Questions Tested/Answered?

In Table 10.1, the conceptual framework incorporating the innovation translation moments and ANT visualization lens is presented along with the relevant excerpts from the literature.

The moments of translation in Table 10.1 reveal that despite the promotion by technology vendors and, to an extent, ICT departments or people in hospitals, RFID technology is yet to gain momentum due to user reluctance and nonacceptance (nurses or orderlies) within the Australian system. To a large extent, this solution is yet to gain wide acceptance in hospitals. It was evident in the moments of translation that the key moments of *interessement* and *enrollment* are often a product of coercion or a top-down approach rather than *mobilization* of allies in the

Table 10.1 Conceptual Framework: Innovation Translation Moments and ANT

	Moment 1 Problematization	*Moment 2 Interessement*	*Moment 3 Enrollment*	*Moment 4 Mobilization*
Literature review (2005–13); see, for example, Nagy et al. 2006; Fisher and Monahan 2008; Cox 2008; Cheng and Chai 2012; Yao et al. 2012; Martinez-Perez et al. 2012; Ustundag 2013)	The key actors in hospitals seem to be technology vendors, systems integrators, and administrators in hospitals. Users of the RFID system, such as nurses and orderlies, are ignored or forced to use the system. The moment is characterized by the acceptance of technology for tracking equipment in order to reduce costs and improve efficiencies by hospital administrators and strategists.	As the literature revealed, there is little evidence of getting users (nurses and orderlies) interested in RFID solution. Rather, driven by vendors and administrators of hospitals, other key actors are largely forced into the moment.	Enrollment into the RFID enablement network is forced or pushed through by vendors and administrators.	The RFID solution has relatively low acceptance or rather skepticism from users. Because the users were skeptical, the solution did not get promoted. Literature reveals that, despite the skepticism, RFID as a technology was being promoted in the health sector via IT strategists and vendors.

environment. This factor made it imperative to study RFID implementation and its translation into the Australian health context.

10.6.3 About Validity and Reliability in This Work

Expert opinion/validation from the industry sector indicates that in Australian hospitals, the nurse is the most powerful and influential factor in technology translation. For example, the ICT department feels imposed upon by medical directors, but if the nurse is the person raising the issue, they will accept it, take it on board, and enable it. Doctors do not question nurses; neither do the patient care orderlies. The nurse happens to be the lynchpin in Australian hospitals. This validation was undertaken in real time in 2013 with 15 different hospitals in Australia and consultancy groups, which makes it valid. In addition, a few hospitals have taken the findings and operationalized the recommendations in their context, which adds to its reliability.

10.7 What Were the Results and Their Meaning/Context?

10.7.1 Why Is This Approach for the Solution Valuable?

This knowledge abstraction is significant from the Australian perspective, which would not have been possible without the interpretive stance of this investigation, visualizing the knowledge through an ANT-informed lens and eliciting the key social factors in translation further validated by industry experts. The finding is of significant value to large hospitals on the verge of RFID deployment. Conversely, the research extended innovation translation theory framework and augmented the field of ANT by visualization techniques. This value addition is of significant importance for academia as it adds to the body of knowledge that is currently rather limited in the field of health informatics within Australia.

10.7.2 What Are the Results and Their Interpretation?

The lead researcher appears in the script as *Cameo*, and RFID is the *debut* actor. The varied stakeholders, such as technology implementers, CIOs, nurses, and orderlies, are the human actors, and there are also nonhuman actors, such as artifacts, interfaces, etc. Table 10.2 presents the entry and exit of actors for Case 1 in the black box of the hospital. Figure 10.2 visualizes the interplay between actors, the formation of networks, and the complexity of negotiation from Case 1.

In this hospital, RFID deployment was initiated by the ICT department for the private wing and was abandoned by users over time although the equipment remained in the hospital. The CIO and business analyst tried for two years by

Table 10.2   Case 1: Actor–Network Relationships

Human Actors	Existed	Entered	Exited	Sustained
CIO (The Champion)	X			X
PM (Technology Company)				
External company teams				
Head (SSD)	X			X
Nursing Unit Manager–Private	X			X
Orderlies (Private)	X			X
Nurses (Private)	X			X
SysAnalyst (Implementation Projects)	X			X
Business Analyst	X			X
Cameo		X	X	
Wards-in-Charge (Public)		X		X
Head (ED)		X		X
Nonhuman Actors				
RFID Tags and Equipment The Debut Actor		X		X
RTLS Report		X		X
Web-Based Clinical System	X			X
Bo-Beep Interface	X			X
Touch Screens	X			X
New Funding Group (Sirens)		X		X

pumping in discretionary funding into the cause of championing RFID without any results. After two years, a nurse in charge of wound care wards communicated with the head of emergency (also a nurse) in the public wing to reinitiate RFID in the hospital. Subsequently, RFID became the buzzword again as they communicated in a different language with the operations people—namely orderlies—in the hospital. This triggered the redeployment of external funding within the public hospital. It is interesting to note that the hospital management, the CIO and ICT department, other department heads, clinicians, and orderlies heeded the nurses'

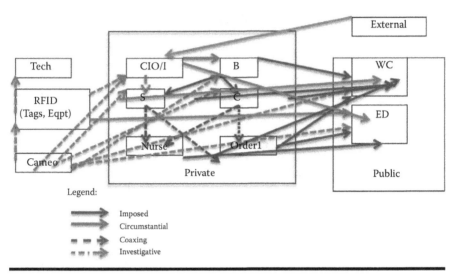

Figure 10.2   Interplay of actors, network formation, and relationships negotiated (Case 1; dotted line means indirect relationship).

communication. It only took the wound care ward nurse in charge a few months before the stage was reset to deploy RFID again.

Subsequently, in Table 10.3, we present the actor–network relationships in Case 2, followed by Figure 10.3, visualizing the actor–network relationships formed and their complexity.

In this hospital, RFID had been introduced by an orthopedic nurse, and the technology itself had evolved, taking on many facets. It was found useful by varied departments as it translated into many formats, such as temperature tags, asset tags, and alarms. It also enabled a web of relationships subtly and indirectly via its champion: the nurse.

10.8 How Are These Results Meaningful for Organizations and for Future Research?

The network of actors and their relationships is extremely complex and is key to operations in a hospital. In this investigation, in Case 1, both orderlies and nurses felt disempowered by technology introduction. The nurses did not endorse imposing a technology that disrupted the workflow. It took three years and a nurse in charge to redeploy the technology that was then accepted with ease by all stakeholders, including clinicians. In Case 2, the introduction by a nurse enabled successful translation of RFID. The findings revealed a silent web of relationships between the key actors in hospitals in relation to promoting RFID technology. The

Table 10.3   Case 2 Actor–Network Relationships

Actors	Existed (in the black box)	Entered	Exited	Sustained/ Transformed
DHS/PPPs		X		X
Symposium Article		X		X
RFID (tags, eqpt.) (External Company)		X		X
RFID Results		X		X
RFID Maps		X		X
Infection Control	X			X
Cameo		X	X	
Nursing Staff	X			
Orderlies	X			
Pharmacy	X	X		X
Pathology	X	X		X
Food Services	X	X		X
Engineering	X	X		X
CIO (new)	X	X		X
OHS	X			X
ICU	X			X
High Care	X			X

constant communication flow between orderlies to orderlies, nurses to orderlies, and nurses to nurses across the private and public areas of Case 1 and nurse–nurse, nurse–clinician, and nurse–ICT relationships, which are not clearly visible at the onset, is indeed the most powerful social factor for RFID implementation.

10.8.1 Where, How, and When to Use It?

Expert opinion/validation from the industry sector indicates that in Australian hospitals, the nurse is a powerful and influential factor in technology translation. For example, the ICT department feels imposed upon by medical directors, but if the nurse is the person raising the issue, they will take it on board and enable it. Doctors do not question nurses, and neither do the patient care orderlies. Nurse

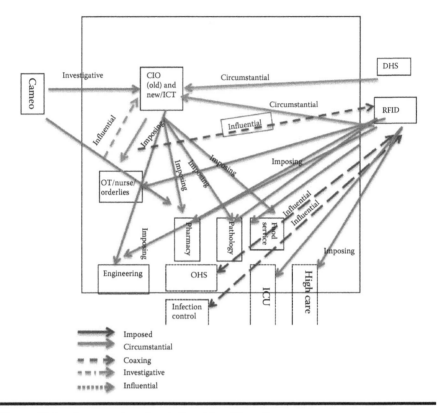

Figure 10.3   Actor–network relationships (Case 2).

happens to be the lynchpin in Australian hospitals. This knowledge abstraction is significant from the Australian perspective, which would not have been possible without the interpretive stance of this investigation, visualizing the knowledge through an ANT-informed lens and eliciting the key social factors in translation further validated by industry experts.

The finding is of significant value to large hospitals on the verge of RFID deployment. Conversely, the research extended the innovation translation theory framework and augmented the field of ANT by visualization techniques. This value addition has a significant implication for academia as it added to the body of knowledge that is currently rather limited in the field of health informatics within Australia.

10.9 Conclusions and Recommendations

10.9.1 Are the Objectives of the Research Achieved?

This research investigation was seeking an answer to the unsuccessful attempts in Australian hospitals to deploy RFID as a technology to boost worker productivity and enhance the quality of service. The technology was not translating well, and a rather sociotechnical approach was warranted. The investigation achieved its objective in finding the key to a successful translation, namely the nurse, the lynchpin in technology translation within the Australian context. If the technology was initiated and propagated through a nurse, it was successful. The knowledge abstraction and visualization through a sociotechnical approach of ANT and innovation translation rendered this objective possible.

10.9.2 Operational and Tactical

As suggested earlier in the chapter, hospitals in Australia, particularly in the State of Victoria, have operationalized the findings thus far. One of the regional hospitals has been extremely successful in tactically presenting the technology through a nurse and has successfully deployed it into the entire hospital.

10.9.3 Strategic

In the strategic planning of hospitals, it is often overlooked that hospitals are run by orderlies and nurses on a daily basis. Without these people, none of the technology or other deployments can translate well into quality of care. Strategically, hospitals are better positioned if they take the social consideration that is crucial to hospital operations as the study revealed. The learning is also useful to other hospitals in Australia as well as other countries, such as Canada, which may be in similar situations contemplating how to best deploy technologies.

References

Bacheldor, B., 2006, RFID fills security gap at psychiatric ward, *RFID Journal*, Retrieved October 24, 2007 from http://www.rfidjournal.com/article/articleview/2750/1/1.

Berg, M., 1999, Patient care information systems and health care work: A sociotechnical approach, *International Journal of Medical Informatics*, 55(2), pp. 87–101.

Callon, M., 1986, Some elements of a sociology of translation: Domestication of the scallops and the fishermen of St Brieuc Bay, in J. Law, *Power, action and belief: A new sociology of knowledge?* Routledge, London, pp. 196–223.

Cangialosi, A., Monaly, J. E. and Yang, S. C., 2007, Leveraging RFID in hospitals: Patient lifecycle and mobility perspectives, *IEEE Communications Magazine*, 45(9), pp. 18–23.

Cheng, C. Y. C. and Chai, J. W. J., 2012, Deployment of RFID in healthcare facilities—Experimental design in MRI department, *Journal of Medical Systems*, 36(6), pp. 3423–3433.

Coustasse, A., Tomblin, S. and Slack, C., 2013, A review of Radio Frequency Identification Technologies and Impacts on the Hospital Supply Chain: 2002–2012, *Proceedings of Academic and Business Research Institute (AABRI) International Conference*, MMM Track, January 3–5, Orlando, Florida.

Cox, J., 2008, RFID proving to be Rx for hospitals, *Network World*, August 25, 25(33), p. 24.

Creswell, J. W., 2013, *Research Design: Qualitative, quantitative and mixed method approaches*, 2nd Edition, Sage Publications, Thousand Oaks, CA.

Davis, F., 1986, *A technology acceptance model for empirically testing new end user information systems: Theory and Results*, MIT Press, Boston.

Davis, G. B., Gorgone, J., Couger, D., Feinstein, D. and Longenecker, H. Jr., 1997, IS 1997 model curriculum and guidelines for undergraduate degree in information systems. ACM, AIS and AITP, Association for Computing Machinery.

Degaspari, J. J., 2011, Keeping track. Barcodes and RFID tags make inroads in hospitals. *Healthcare informatics: The business magazine for information and communication systems*, 28(3), pp. 44–47.

Duckett, S. J. and Willcox, S., 2011, *The Australian health care system*, 4th Edition, Oxford University Press, Melbourne.

Dunlevy, S., 2013, Outrage as eHealth record sign-up squads hit Australian hospital patients in bid to boost numbers, News.com.au, Retrieved April 30 2013 from http://www .news.com.au/national-news/outrage-as-ehealth-record-sign-up-squads-hit-australian -hospital-patients-in-bid-to-boost-numbers/story-fncynjr2-1226619874616.

Fisher J. A. and Monahan, T., 2008, Tracking the social dimensions of RFID systems in hospitals, *International Journal of Medical Informatics*, 77(3), pp. 176–183.

Friedlos, D., 2010, Australia's Bendigo health improves efficiency through RFID, *RFID Journal*, December.

Greenhalgh, T. and Stones, R., 2010, Theorising big IT programmes in healthcare: Strong structuration theory meets actor–network theory, *Social Science & Medicine*, 70(9), pp. 1285–1294.

Ho, G., 2012, Can technology help overcome Australia's health care challenges? Australian Broadcasting Corporation (ABC)—Technology and Games, 27 April 2012, Retrieved in January 2014 from http://www.abc.net.au/technology/articles/2012/04/27/3490209 .htm.

Latour, B., 1986, The power of association, in Law, J. ed., *Power, Action and Belief—A New Sociology of Knowledge* (Sociological Review Monograph 32), Routledge and Kegan Paul, London, pp. 264–280.

Latour, B., 1996, Aramis or the love of technology, Harvard University Press Cambridge, MA.

Law, J. and Callon, M., 1988, Engineering and sociology in a military aircraft project: A network analysis of technological change, *Social Problems*, 35(3), pp. 284–297.

Martinez-Perez, M., Cabrero-Canosa, M., Vizoso, H. J., Carrajo, G. L., Liamas, G. D., Vazquez, G. G. and Martin Herranz, I., 2012, Application of RFID technology in patient tracking and medication traceability in emergency care, *Journal of Medical Systems*, December, pp. 3983–3993.

Nagy, P., George, I., Bernstein, W., Caban, J., Klein, R., Mezrich, R. and Park, A., 2006, Radio frequency identification systems technology in the surgical setting, *Surgical Innovation*, 13(1), pp. 61–67.

Novak, J. and Judah, A., 2011, *Towards a health productivity reform agenda for Australia*, South Melbourne: Australian Centre for Health Research.

Parker, C. M., Wafula, E. N., Swatman, P. and Swatman, P. M. C., 1994, Information Systems Research Methods: The Technology Transfer Problem, *Proceedings of the Australasian Conference on Information Systems (ACIS)*, Australia.

Prgoment, M., Georgiou, A. and Westbrook, J. I. 2009, The impact of mobile handheld technology on hospital physicians work practices and patient care: A systematic review, *American Medical Information Association*, 16(6), pp. 792–801.

Privacy Act of Australia, 1988, http://www.privacy.gov.au/law/act.

Privacy.Gov, 2013, State and Territory Laws, Office of the Australian Privacy Commissioner, Australia, http://www.privacy.gov.au/law/states.

Rogers, E. M., 1995, Diffusion of innovations, Free Press, New York.

Rogers, E. M., 2003, Diffusion of innovations, Free Press, New York.

Tatnall, A., 2011a, Innovation translation, innovation diffusion, and the technology acceptance model: Comparing three different approaches to theorising technological innovation, a chapter in *Actor–Network Theory and Technology Innovation: Advancements and New Concepts*, Tatnall A (Ed) Information Science Reference, IGI Global Hershey, USA.

Tatnall, A., 2011b, *Information Systems Research, Technological Innovation and Actor–Network Theory*, Heidelberg Press, Victoria, Australia.

Ustundag, A., 2013, *The Value of RFID*, Springer-Verlag, London.

Whetton S. and Georgiou, A., 2010, Conceptual challenges for advancing the socio-technical underpinnings of health informatics, *The Open Medical Informatics Journal*, 4, pp. 221–224.

Yao, W., Chu, C.-H. and Li, Z., 2011, Leveraging complex event processing for smart hospitals using RFID, *Journal of Network and Computer Applications*, 34(3), May, pp. 799–810.

Yao, W., Chu, C.-H. and Li, Z., 2012, The adoption and implementation of RFID technologies in Healthcare: A literature review, *Journal of Medical Systems*, 36, pp. 3507–3525, Springer Publications, USA.

Yin, R. K., 2009, *Case study research design and methods*, 4th Edition, Sage Publications Inc, USA.

Chapter 11

Health Care Analytics and Big Data Management in Influenza Vaccination Programs: Use of Information– Entropy Approach

Sharon Hovav, Hanan Tell, Eugene Levner,
Alexander Ptuskin, and Avi Herbon

Contents

Context

Annual influenza epidemics impose great losses in both human and financial terms. A key question arising in large-scale vaccination programs is the need to balance program costs and public benefits. Risks occur in the vaccination supply chain due to the stochastic nature of the vaccination process, which fluctuates from year to year, depending on many factors that are difficult to predict and control. Large data sets representing the information involved are Big Data sets of sizes far beyond the ability of commonly used software packages to capture, process, and manage data within a reasonable computing time. We suggest an entropic approach to handle this challenging problem.

Purpose

For a vaccination supply chain consisting of manufacturers, distribution centers, warehouses, pharmacies, clinics, and customers, we seek to reduce the problem size and then decrease the total expenses of all stakeholders while taking into account public benefits on a nationwide level. We propose an analytics-driven research approach for enhancing the efficiency of influenza vaccination programs, using supply chain concepts. We seek to minimize the total cost of the vaccination supply chain while upholding the individual interests of its stakeholders.

Design

Information entropy is widely used in information control and management as a measure of uncertainty in a random environment. Extending Shannon's classical information entropy concept used in information theory, we use the term to quantify and evaluate the expected value of the information contained in a supply chain with uncertain but predictable data about the costs and benefits. An integer-programing model is developed in which the problem of minimizing the total loss is effectively solved in a reduced vaccination supply chain.

Findings

Knowing the history of adverse events, we estimate the entropy and knowledge about the risks occurring in the vaccination supply chain, reduce the problem size, define the most vulnerable components in the supply chain, and evaluate the economic loss. This new analytics approach permits us to estimate and balance the manufacturing, inventory, and distribution costs with possible public benefits and reduce the incurred losses.

Research Limitations/Implications

In this chapter, we assume that the data on the vaccination demands are deterministic and known in advance to a decision maker. In our future research, we intend to lift this limitation and accomplish a more scrupulous analysis of links between the entropy as a data uncertainty measure and the costs in medical supply chains. Moreover, we intend to perform a more sophisticated cost–benefit–risk analysis of the vaccination supply chains, taking into account the stochastic behavior of demands for different population groups.

Practical Implications

A case study has been implemented to test the suggested methodology; we successfully used our approach to analyze and improve the nationwide vaccination program carried out by the CLALIT Health Services (Israel). We believe that the suggested analytics methodology can be used for wider applications in other types of health care supply chains.

Originality/Value

This chapter develops a novel integrated approach for optimizing costs and public benefits within the influenza vaccine supply chain. The methodology is applicable for wider health care management applications.

11.1 Introduction

11.1.1 Purpose of the Study

Influenza is a highly contagious airborne viral infection. Seasonal influenza epidemics cause up to 500,000 deaths per year worldwide and impose great economic losses as a result of health care costs and lost productivity (Chick et al. 2008). Billions of dollars are spent annually for influenza vaccination in an attempt to avoid even greater losses. The current work proposes an analytics-driven research approach for enhancing the efficiency of influenza vaccination programs, using supply chain (SC) concepts and techniques. We seek to minimize the total cost of the vaccination supply chain (VSC) while upholding the individual interests of its stakeholders with their risks being taking into account.

The influenza VSC includes vaccine manufacturers, health care organizations (HCOs) (consisting of distribution centers [DCs], pharmacies, clinics, and hospitals), and end users. The latter is the population of individuals to be vaccinated. It is segmented into subpopulations, each characterized by an age range. The cost of the vaccination program includes direct and indirect medical costs of the vaccination process and direct and indirect nonmedical costs of the VSC (these terms are discussed below). The costs of the vaccination program must be balanced against its public benefits. These benefits include, among other factors, reductions in the number of patient visits, in the number of hospitalization days among different groups of people, in the number of working days lost, and in mortality.

The seasonal flu viruses change from one season to another and can also change within the course of one season (CDC 2014). This means that no inventory surplus of the flu vaccine can be used during the following flu season. It is obvious that none of the stakeholders of the VSC is ready to bear the losses that stem from the costs of purchasing as well as disposing of unused vaccine inventories. Thus, the vaccine production will match the demand on the basis of advanced orders, and in cases of unexpected high demand, there can be large shortages. Similar shortages can result from contamination problems during the production process, such as those that happened in 2004 at a British manufacturing facility and resulted in shortages of millions of vaccines.

On the other hand, there can be large surplus inventories due to unexpected reluctances of the public to take the vaccines: A case at hand, when during the first week of vaccination in 2012 in Israel three people died within 24 hours of getting the vaccination, and, as a result, most of the population was reluctant to get the vaccine.

In this study, we consider a basic single manufacturer, multicustomer VSC. A manufacturer produces the vaccine, whose type and production rate are established according to the requirements of the World Health Organization (WHO). A simplified influenza vaccination timeline (a timed SC) is illustrated in Figure 11.1.

As an illustration, consider the SC vaccination timeline for the Northern Hemisphere:

Stage 1: February 2014. The WHO recommends viruses for inclusion in influenza vaccines for the forthcoming influenza season (2014–2015). The recommendation is based on all seasonal influenza viruses detected worldwide between September 2013 and February 2014 (WHO 2014). The process for the southern hemisphere is similar, but the recommendation is made in September 2014 for the 2015 flu season.

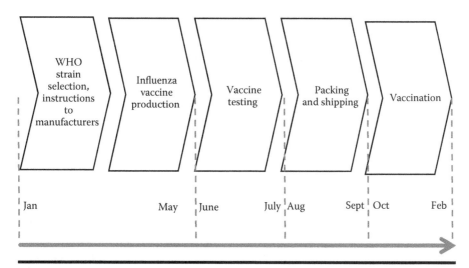

Figure 11.1 Influenza vaccine timeline. (Adapted from E. Levner, H. Tell, S. Hovav, D. Tsadikovich, Balancing the costs and public benefits of a vaccination program using a supply chain approach. Poster presented at the INFORMS-2012 conference, Huntington, USA, April 15–17, 2012. Accessed November 29, 2014 at http://meetings2.informs.org/Analytics2012/posters.html.)

Stage 2: February–May 2014. Viruses are manipulated for high-yield in eggs and distributed to manufacturers who cultivate each virus separately and then blend them together. The manufacturing is lengthy, and there are no short cuts. Research efforts are being directed toward finding alternative ways to shorten the process (Trenor 2004).

Stage 3: June–July 2014. Vaccine test and verification is conducted.

Stage 4: August 2014. Packing and shipping to DCs is done. Sometimes, the distribution process can be phased out over a number of months, especially if the volume of the vaccines is high (CDC 2014).

Stage 5: September 2014–March 2015. Deployment of vaccines to clinics, and finally, the vaccination of the designated population is conducted.

Our study is based on the following premises and assumptions.

■ We seek to balance the costs and benefits of the vaccination program from the perspective of the HCO, which is a key component between the manufacturer and end users.

■ The hierarchical health care SC can be presented as a tree-type graph.

■ The DC's role, as part of the HCO, is reflected in the general objective function by the DC's direct nonmedical costs, that is, inventory holding costs.

■ Clinics are responsible for the direct medical costs related to the service of administering vaccine injections to consumers and for the corresponding inventory costs.

Given weekly (or monthly) forecasts of customer demand and limited capacities of the manufacturer, DCs and clinics, the objective is to minimize the costs of the vaccination program while taking into account the program's main public benefits and population risks. We model the problem and present the case study based on data from the CLALIT Health Services, a leading HCO in Israel's national influenza VSC. This case study indicates that the integrated approach we propose can lead to substantial savings (up to millions of dollars annually). One of the key planning problems in managing a vaccination supply chain is to coordinate and integrate individual interests of all the players within an entire supply chain, that is, the geographically distributed SC components.

The budget for decision making aimed at reducing the risks is limited, and therefore, the processing of the complete volume of information for all the components of the SC can be prohibitively time- and resource-consuming. Large data sets representing the involved information are Big Data sets of sizes far beyond the ability of commonly used software packages to capture, process, and manage data within a reasonable computing time (Liebowitz, 2013). We suggest an entropic approach to handle this challenging problem.

In spite of the importance of the latter issue, the majority of published analytical works did not handle this, assuming that the size of the SC is known in advance. A motive for the present research, distinguishing it from other works is asking how to reduce the huge size of an original SC model so as not to discard meaningful predictive information and to identify those SC components that are the major causes of loss in the chain. This is the key question to answer for which we use Shannon's information entropy (Shannon 1951) as a measure of our knowledge about risks and their impact. The main idea is that there is no need to elaborate a more and more detailed SC model if a huge model does not lead to an essential change in entropy value, and, hence, in our knowledge.

11.2 About the Background of This Work

In recent decades, researchers have used a variety of analytical approaches to study service quality in health care SCs, the prevailing approach being optimization techniques, heuristics and metaheuristics, and simulation-based analytics. Our study belongs to the first group. Gerdil (2003) presents the main steps of the vaccine production process. This study focuses on product design and manufacturing as a complex cyclical process but does not explore crucial subsequent steps in the vaccination process over the entire SC. In contrast, in the present study we explicitly introduce additional stakeholders into the SC, namely, the DCs, hospitals, pharmacies, clinics, and population groups.

A paper by Chick et al. (2008) studies an influenza SC and focuses on a specific issue of designing a contract between a manufacturer and a government. This interaction is modeled as a game. They show that a global social optimum can be achieved by using the contract to share production risks between the manufacturer and the government and consider in depth various game theoretic aspects of the VSC management.

Recall some basic definitions. An *event* is the observable discrete change in the state of a VSC or its components. An *adverse event* is an undesirable unforeseen event, such as disruptions, breakdowns, defects, mistakes in the design and planning, shortages of material in the HSC, etc. A *risk driver* is a factor or a driving force that may be a cause of the adverse event. We study situations in which we can register the adverse events in the considered VSC, during a prespecified period of time. The registration list is called *a risk protocol*, which provides information about adverse events, their risk drivers, and possible losses. Statistics accumulated in the risk protocols permit us to quantitatively evaluate the contribution of each driver and the total entropy-based observable information in the SC. The idea is that the prognostic information about the risk probabilities can be inferred from the patterns (events) of past observations and can be used to forecast the future probabilities.

As have many other authors, we accept that the *risk* is the expected value of an undesirable outcome, that is, the product of two entities: the *probability* of an undesirable event and the *impact* or *severity*—that is, an expected loss in the case of the disruption affecting the performance of a supply network (Levner and Proth 2005; Kogan and Tapiero 2007). Due to increasing dynamics and growing uncertainty in the health care SC environment, risk management became a key concern. In order to reduce the risk level in the SC, we need to process data about failures and faults and their causes and economic consequences, locations, and occurrence frequencies.

There exists a wide diversity of risk types in the SC. Their taxonomy lies beyond the scope of this paper; we refer to Olson (2012). We will look at Shannon's information entropy as a tool for measuring the whole information about the risks and potential loss. Many works used the entropy for evaluating the *SC complexity* (Allesina et al. 2010; Isik, 2010).

Durowoju et al. (2012) and Herbon et al. (2012) explored the fact that a high level of entropy (or chaos) in the SC has the effect of impeding perfect SC performance by building obstacles to its supply and delivery; the bigger the obstacle, the more uncertain the state of the entire SC, and as a consequence, a larger amount of information is required to monitor and manage the system. From this perspective, the entropy is regarded as a measure of estimating the knowledge about risks. Durowoju et al. (2012) and Herbon et al. (2012) considered the simplest linear SCs containing only four components—the retailer, distributor, manufacturer, and supplier—and did not handle the specificity of risk management in multilayer SCs *with precedence constraints* between the SC nodes. This limitation is overcome in the present study.

11.3 What Is the Scope of This Work?

The present study continues and extends the latter works by taking a network structure and precedence relationships into account. We suggest an iterative method that computes the entropy for the nodes belonging to the same layer of the hierarchical SC successively, layer by layer. The main aim is to reduce the SC size and pick out the most risky components in the reduced SC model. The method respects the precedence relationships between the nodes and reduces the SC size without the loss of essential information about the risks. Then the min-cost problem is solved on the reduced SC.

Minimizing the expenses is a critical element in achieving health care supply chain effectiveness. The SC literature offers various models and solution methods for solving the min-cost problems. The efficiency and effectiveness of influenza vaccination have been well documented by Nichol (2008). Colombo et al. (2006) uses the cost–benefit analysis of the influenza vaccination comparing the universal mass vaccination policy and the targeted vaccine program, a policy that focuses on high-risk groups only. Our research also addresses this issue from the SC managerial point of view. The corresponding literature is vast, and we refer to the recent excellent reviews by Tang and Musa (2010), Olson (2012), and Matinrada et al. (2013) that provide a summary of the most commonly used optimization models and methods in SCs published in recent years.

11.4 Definition of the Key Concepts

In our analysis, in line with studies in the field of analytical medical management, we divide vaccination costs into four categories: direct and indirect medical costs and direct and indirect nonmedical costs. Direct medical costs include product costs and costs of service from nurses and physicians (calculated as average service time multiplied by the average salary of nurses and physicians). Indirect medical costs consist of administration and organizational costs. Direct nonmedical costs are logistical costs incurred by the DC, hospitals, and clinics. Indirect nonmedical costs are organizational or administrative costs by the DC, hospitals, and clinics.

Although the papers discussed above provide valuable insights into the costs and benefits of vaccination programs, they do not provide sufficient quantitative analysis that can be used for optimization purposes. Our study is an attempt to bridge this gap, focusing on direct medical and direct nonmedical costs in the framework of a cost–benefit analysis.

Our SC model includes multiple manufacturers and multiple customers. The influenza vaccination SC is illustrated in Figure 11.2.

The VSC has a hierarchical structure and, therefore, can be presented as a tree-like graph in which the upper node (a "root node") depicts the entire VSC without

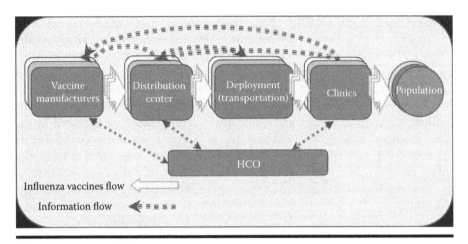

Figure 11.2   A typical vaccination supply network.

identifying its elements; the first tier of nodes contains its main components, that is, manufacturers, DCs, clinics, and the population. Each subsequent tier presents the same VSC in a more detailed form. As an illustration, Figure 11.3 shows a fragment of a SC in which all the clinics are depicted hierarchically.

For completeness in the entire exposition, we start with a definition of risk.

Risk is the expected value of an undesirable outcome, that is, the product of two entities: the *probability* of an undesirable event and the *impact* or *severity* (that is, an expected loss in the case of the disruption affecting the performance of a supply network).

In order to reduce the risk level in the SC, we need to process data about failures and faults and their causes and economic consequences, locations, and occurrence frequencies.

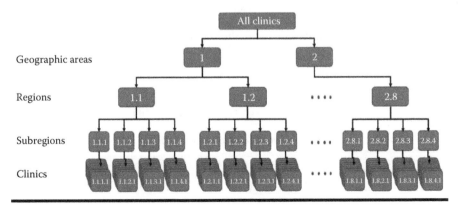

Figure 11.3   Hierarchical structure of a typical vaccination supply network.

Next, we give the definition of Shannon's entropy and its use for our aims. In information theory, *entropy* is a measure of the uncertainty, the chaos, and the absence of knowledge. It is commonly accepted that the entropy taken with the opposite sign is equivalent to the information content or the knowledge (Shannon 1951, Isik 2010, Stone 2014).

We have a volume of statistical data, namely, registered information about failures, disruptions, breaks, and other adverse events that have occurred in the VSC during some period. Consider a group of such random events and denote them by $E = \{e_1, \ldots, e_n\}$. Based on the entropy evaluation, we wish to estimate the information (knowledge) about the event occurrences, and as a result, we wish to forecast which risk types in the SCs that we can expect in the near future are most hazardous.

For a group of events $E = \{e_1, \ldots, e_n\}$, we assume a priori probabilities of event occurrence $P = \{p_1, \ldots, p_n\}$, $p_i \geq 0$, such that $p_1 + \ldots + p_n = 1$, being known. Then the entropy function H is defined as follows:

$$H = -\sum_{i=1,\ldots,n} p_i \log p_i. \tag{11.1}$$

Let R_v denote the total number of the adverse events occurring in node v of the multitiered hierarchical SC (see Figure 11.2) during the considered time period. If tier s contains $n(s)$ nodes, the total number E_s of adverse events in the tier s will be

$$E_s = \sum_{v=1,\ldots,n(s)} R_v.$$

Each adverse event is caused by some factor, which is called a *risk driver*. For the sake of simplicity, we assume that any adverse event is caused by a single driver. Let F be a total number of drivers; clearly, F is less than the total number of the registered adverse events in the SC. For each tier s and each risk driver f ($f = 1, \ldots, F$), using the list of the registered adverse events, we can determine the number $N_s(f)$ of adverse events caused by factor f in all the nodes of tier s; $E_s = \sum_{f=1,\ldots,F} N_s(f) = E_s$.

Because we are interested in estimating the risk impacts, we introduce another class of random events, denoted by $A(f,s)$, which are derived from the initial set of the registered adverse events:

$$A(f,s) = \{\text{the driver } f \text{ is the cause of different}$$

$$\text{adverse events in the nodes of tier } s\}.$$

Denote the probability of $A(f,s)$ by $p_s(f)$.

Using the list of registered adverse events, we can compute the relative frequency $N_s(f)/E_s$ of the event $A(f,s)$ and treat this value as an estimation of the probability $p_s(f)$ of the event $A(f,s)$, that is,

$$p_s(f) = N_s(f)/E_s. \tag{11.2}$$

Obviously, $\sum_f p_s(f) = 1$.

For simplicity, we assume that the considered events $A(f,s)$ are independent and that the loss due to the risks in the SC is summed up from the losses caused by different risk drivers in the system components.

Now we can turn to the computation of the SC entropy. The values $p_s(f)$, defined by Equation 11.2 are taken as a priori probabilities of the events participating in the calculation of the entropy function (Equation 11.1). We presume that the information content may be measured by the entropy at any tier, but the entropy value (and the information) varies from tier to tier because it reflects the contribution of different components (nodes) entering a tier. Recall that each tier describes the same SC but with a different degree of sharpness.

Consider the entropy $H(s)$ at tier s of the SC (the latter will be called below the entropy *for the s-truncated SC*), which is defined as follows:

$$H(s) = -\sum_{f=1,\ldots,F} p_s(f)\log p_s(f).$$

Notice that the summation is taken over all the risk types in the considered SC. In what follows, we shall observe a nontrivial dynamic pattern in the behavior of the entropy of the *s*-truncated SC.

11.5 Description of the Problem

The problem considered in this chapter is twofold: first, to reduce the model size without discarding essential prognostic information about possible losses and, second, to minimize the total costs for the vaccination on the reduced SC model before and within the epidemic season, subject to a population's demands in vaccines.

Given weekly forecasts of customer demand in vaccines and limited capacities of the DCs and clinics, the objective is to minimize the total costs of the vaccination program while maintaining a minimum required level of public benefits, expressed in the form of constraints of the model.

11.5.1 Research Questions or Hypotheses

In the next section, we consider the subproblem of identifying the most significant risk factors and most vulnerable components in a VSC and, therefore, in reducing the SC size, using the entropy approach. As a result, the set of selected VSC components becomes more compact and more controllable than the entire SC. We study the optimization problem aimed at reducing the total costs in the VSC. The problem becomes more compact, controllable, and easier to solve due to the decrease in the problem size.

11.6 What Was the Methodology of the Problem Resolution?

Based on the statistical information about adverse events in the SC, we wish to forecast which risk types in the SCs that we can expect in the near future are most hazardous. The volume of such information can be prohibitively large. The storage and analysis of all the information on the operation of the entire SC becomes a complex and often simply untreatable problem. A natural way to treat such a problem is to cut down the volume of the available information without losing any essential information. Our first goal is to identify those of the SC components that are major sources of information about the risks and losses in the chain. In recent years, the *information entropy* became a widespread measure of the knowledge about where the most important sources of risks in the SC are concentrated (Allesina et al. 2010; Isik 2010; Herbon et al. 2012). The Big Data sets representing the information involved, which are of sizes beyond the abilities of commonly used software packages and computers, can be dramatically reduced with the help of the entropic approach described below.

11.7 How Was the Research Designed?

A modeling process elaborated in this chapter consists of three basic stages presented in Figure 11.4.

11.7.1 What Data Was Used?

The data related to a real-life VSC in the HCO CLALIT (Israel) have been provided by the CLALIT's experts and used for the implementation and verification of the suggested analytics tool. In particular, the information regarding 1,262 CLALIT clinics (with five main population groups in each one) was aggregated sequentially according to six levels of aggregation (also called levels of resolution)

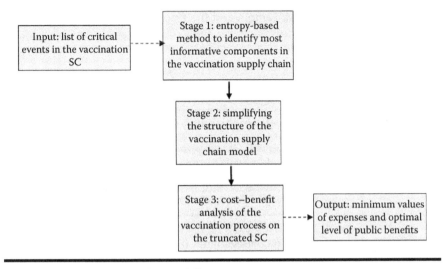

Figure 11.4   The logic of the modeling process.

corresponding to six tiers of the VSC: (1) all the clinics as a single entity, (2) the clinics divided into two geographic areas, (3) the clinics in the geographical areas divided into eight regions corresponding to eight realistic managerial units in the CLALIT organization, (4) the clinics divided into 26 subregions, (5) 1,262 real-life clinics, which are the smallest medical service units on hand. We also consider the sixth layer of the VSC, which comprises five groups of population assigned to each clinic.

Analysis of expert information permitted us to distinguish 20 main risk factors. Each factor is characterized by a probability (risk) of becoming ill for an unvaccinated customer during the epidemic season. Each risk factor can be defined at some layer of the VSC (i.e., level of aggregation), and its probability value remains unchanged at lower VSC layers. The factors and the corresponding layers at which they are defined are presented in Table 11.1.

The used method for the data collection was as follows: For each aggregation level, after risks (probabilities) are defined and evaluated for some risk factors, the probabilities for all other (undefined) factors are assumed to be equal and distributed uniformly at each layer. For example, at the layer "all clinics," we had two risk factors (#1 and #2) estimated; at the layer "geographic areas," #3 and #4 are estimated; and at the layer "regions," we had three more estimated risk factors, from #5 to #7. Hence, at the latter layer, the probabilities for the factors 1 to 7 are summed up to 0.51 (or 51%), and 13 factors from #8 to #20 are unknown, the remaining value of 0.49 (or 49%) is divided equally between the unknown factors, resulting in about 3.8% for each. Similarly, at the layer "subregions," which includes 26 entities, the factors from #8 to #10 are estimated by the experts so that the known risk

Table 11.1 The List of Risk Factors and the Corresponding Aggregation Level

Risk Factor	Aggregation Level	Description
1	All clinics	Shortages in manufacturers' supplies
2	All clinics	Delay of shipments
3	Geographic areas	Limited DC transportation capacity, leading to additional shortages over time
4	Geographic areas	Limited DC storage capacity, leading to additional shortages over time
5	Regions	Insufficient media campaign in a region (advertisements, blogs, local newspapers, etc.)
6	Regions	Human resources unavailability (i.e., unavailability of nurses)
7	Regions	Long waiting time in clinics that reduces customer motivation to be vaccinated
8	Subregions	Changing epidemic rates in an area, leading to changing (increasing or decreasing) customer response
9	Subregions	Local delays in deliveries in subregions
10	Subregions	Shortages of vaccines due to the misbalance in vaccination rates for risk groups and nonrisk groups of the population
11	Clinics	Mistakes in demand forecast and unbalanced inventory as a consequence of under- or overestimation of the vaccine demands per clinic
12	Clinics	Failures in local vaccine storage and delivery
13	Clinics	Poor local promotion activity in clinics (brochures in clinics, mail deliveries, etc.)
14	Clinics	Overload of clinic staff to meet demands over time
15	Clinics	Misbalance (overstock/stockout) of vaccines in clinics
16	Clinics	False information circulated in the community

(*Continued*)

Table 11.1 (Continued)   The List of Risk Factors and the Corresponding Aggregation Level

Risk Factor	Aggregation Level	Description
17	Clinics	Nonsynchronization of nurse availability with visits to doctors in clinics
18	Population subgroups	An excessive demand by nonrisk groups
19	Population subgroups	Willingness/unwillingness of subgroup to be vaccinated
20	Population subgroups	Inconvenient clinics/nurses working hours for some population groups

factor probabilities constitute a total of 79% whereas the remaining 21% is divided equally between other 10 factors.

Our next analytic step is to use the entropy as a measure of an uncertainty or no information at each aggregation level. It is well known that in the case in which all the probability is equal for each factor, the entropy reaches its maximal value. Our motivation to "drill down" to a lower (and more detailed) aggregation layer is to do this until the entropy value (or the entropy change when moving to the next layer) will be sufficiently low.

Table 11.2 shows the found probabilities and the corresponding entropy values defined for each aggregation level. For the reader's convenience, the table is broken into two parts (to fit on this page); the thick black line separates the experts' probability values from other, equally distributed probabilities.

Drilling down to a higher aggregation level, we observe that the entropy value drops. Figure 11.5 shows that when moving from "regions" to "subregions," the entropy decreases quickly, and when moving on to a higher aggregation level, the entropy drops more slowly.

In terms of the relational entropy decrease per entity (that is, the entropy value divided by the number of entities in the layer), the entropy change and, consequently, the information gain when moving from a layer to a lower layer can quickly become negligible (see Figure 11.6).

Entropy's dynamics. Consider an arbitrary VSC, and let the tier number s be monotonically increasing: $s = 1, 2, \ldots$. If the set of unknown risk factors shrinks when the s value grows, the entropy $H(s)$ of the s-truncated structure decreases.

This result follows from the following two observations:

First, consider the root node at tier $s = 1$ (see Figure 11.3). Although the general number of the risk drivers F is assumed to be known for the registered adverse

Table 11.2 The Probabilities and Entropy Values by Aggregation Level

Aggregation Level	1	2	3	4	5	6	7	8	9	10	11	12	13	14	15	16	17	18	19	20	Entropy
All clinics	8.0%	5.0%	4.8%	4.8%	4.8%	4.8%	4.8%	4.8%	4.8%	4.8%	4.8%	4.8%	4.8%	4.8%	4.8%	4.8%	4.8%	4.8%	4.8%	4.8%	4.31
Geographic areas	8.0%	5.0%	4.0%	1.0%	5.1%	5.1%	5.1%	5.1%	5.1%	5.1%	5.1%	5.1%	5.1%	5.1%	5.1%	5.1%	5.1%	5.1%	5.1%	5.1%	4.27
Regions	8.0%	5.0%	4.0%	1.0%	9.0%	12.0%	12.0%	3.8%	3.8%	3.8%	3.8%	3.8%	3.8%	3.8%	3.8%	3.8%	3.8%	3.8%	3.8%	3.8%	4.12
Subregions	8.0%	5.0%	4.0%	1.0%	9.0%	12.0%	12.0%	4.0%	10.0%	14.0%	2.1%	2.1%	2.1%	2.1%	2.1%	2.1%	2.1%	2.1%	2.1%	2.1%	3.89
Clinics	8.0%	5.0%	4.0%	1.0%	9.0%	12.0%	12.0%	4.0%	10.0%	14.0%	2.5%	0.3%	3.6%	2.0%	1.0%	2.0%	1.1%	2.8%	2.8%	2.8%	3.85
Population subgroups	8.0%	5.0%	4.0%	1.0%	9.0%	12.0%	12.0%	4.0%	10.0%	14.0%	2.5%	0.3%	3.6%	2.0%	1.0%	2.0%	1.1%	4.0%	4.00%	0.50%	3.83

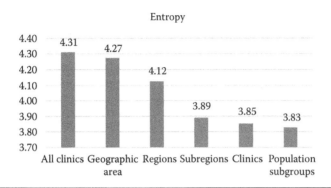

Figure 11.5   Entropy's dynamics.

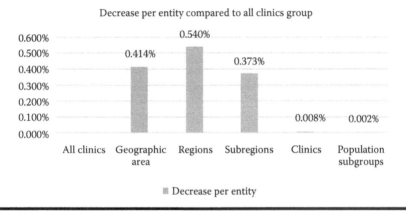

Figure 11.6   Relative entropy change.

events, at this level, the probabilities $p_s(f)$ for all f are yet unknown to the decision maker. Therefore, in the worst case, they are considered uniformly distributed for all the drivers, and the entropy at this tier is the following:

$$H(1) = -\sum_{f=1,\dots,F} p_s(f)\log p_1(f) = -\sum_{f=1,\dots,F} (1/F)\log(1/F) = \log F,$$

which is the maximum possible value and, hence, reflects the minimum of our knowledge about the risk type distribution in the SC.

Second, as long as we compute the entropy $H(s)$ for each tier s moving top down from one tier to the next one, our knowledge about the probabilities $p_s(f)$ for different f increases, the probabilities cease to be uniformly distributed as they become more diverse and, hence, father from $1/F$. As a result, the entropy decreases with the growth of s. This claim was confirmed through extensive experiments.

Taking the observed entropy's behavior into account, we can define which degree of resolution is sufficient when we sequentially compute the entropy for the SC, tier after tier, starting with the root node. Namely, this computation process can be terminated when the entropy decrease gradient becomes sufficiently small when moving to the next tier. Formally, we appoint an *allowed inaccuracy level*, denoted by ε, and may stop the computations at that tier s for which

$$(H(s) - H(s + 1))/H(1) < \varepsilon. \tag{11.3}$$

For example, in real-life computations in the HCO CLALIT, for the SC fragment presented in Figure 11.3, we obtained the following results:

We observe that $(H(4) - H(3))/H(1) = 0{,}023$. Therefore, if the allowed inaccuracy level $\varepsilon = 3\%$, then we may stop the entropy calculations at level $s = 3$. In practical terms, this means that it is sufficient to study the given SC model, limiting ourselves to three tiers only whereas the study of a larger model with four tiers, that is, 1,262 nodes, can add only 3% of additional knowledge about the risks.

We can offer another possible approach to the definition of the stopping rule in the procedure of reducing the SC model, which does not depend on the value of ε, given by an expert. For this aim, we introduce an assessment of the model accuracy $U(s)$, which is defined as a share of the total entropy value per one model unit (entity):

$$U(s) = H(s)/V(s),$$

where s is the number of the tier, $H(s)$ is the entropy value for tier s, and $V(s)$ is the number of entities of the model in tier s.

If during the transition from one tier to another, the outlet value $U(s)$ is reduced, this means that our knowledge about the risks and their sources in the SC counted per one entity of the model increases, and therefore one can observe the model refinement as a result of adding a next tier into the SC model. On the other hand, if the value $U(s)$ decreases nonessentially after adding a next tier, the amount of knowledge related to a single entity of the model is increased nonessentially; that is, the model becomes more complicated but not much more informative in respect to a single component of the SC used. Additional expenses for constructing a more complex and detailed SC in this case have not much sense.

Consider again a numerical example from Table 11.3. The corresponding values of $U(s)$ are presented in Table 11.3 and depicted in Figure 11.6. We see that the new stopping rule provides the same result as a previous stopping rule when $\varepsilon = 3\%$. However, it is worth noticing that the second stopping rule that uses the relative entropy values $U(s)$ does not depend upon a subjective ε value provided by experts.

In our extensive experiments with the real-life Big Data of the CLALIT, we steadily observed the same effect; namely, that almost all essential information (knowledge) about the risks in the SC can be found within three or four upper tiers of the model.

Table 11.3   Entropy's Dynamics

Number of the tier	$s = 1$	$s = 2$	$s = 3$	$s = 4$	$s = 5$	$s = 6$
Number of entities	1	2	8	26	1,262	6,310
Entropy value $H(s)$	4.31	4.27	4.12	3.89	3.85	3.83
Entropy decrease per unit, %		0.414	0.54	0.373	0.008	0.002

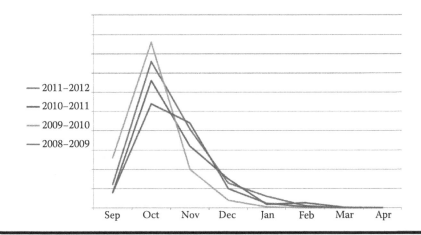

Figure 11.7   Monthly distribution of vaccinations 2008–2012.

Investigating the four-season demand data, we found a typical pattern of average seasonal demand. Monthly distributions of vaccinations over the years 2008–2012 are shown in Figure 11.7. A prototype demand profile for a typical year was calculated according to the average demand levels across 2008–2012. Table 11.4 presents the distribution of the average total vaccine demand in clinics over the course of a year, computed as a percentage for each month. Information has been partly censored for presentation purposes and to retain the confidentiality of certain commercial data.

Table 11.5 includes three clusters of clinics—small clinics, medium clinics, and large-sized clinics—and five age groups. Using Table 11.5, we can observe and analyze the demand in each clinic cluster, for each subgroup, each month.

11.8   What Were the Models and Concepts Used in This Study?

Following the logic of our modeling process described in Figure 11.4, in this section, we develop a mathematical programming model for the cost–benefit analysis

**Table 11.4 Average Distribution
of Vaccine Demand 2008–2012**

Month	Demand Rate
Sept.	6.7%
Oct.	45.4%
Nov.	37.0%
Dec.	8.4%
Jan.	2.0%
Feb.	0.4%
Mar.	0.1%
Apr.	0.0%

of the SC on the reduced network model, containing a reduced number of tiers. The objective is to minimize the total costs under vaccine balance and service level constraints. The objective function includes the following four components:

1. Delivery costs from the manufacturers and inventory holding costs in the DC.
2. Delivery and inventory holding costs within clinics.
3. Both (1) and (2) are direct nonmedical costs.
4. The shortage cost is dependent on customer waiting time. This cost includes additional medical costs associated with the service of infected people who were not vaccinated at earlier stages of the vaccination season.
5. The service cost is proportional to the amount of time required for nurses and physicians to administer the vaccine, multiplied by the average salary per time unit.

The constraints include the material balance in the DC and clinics, the predicted vaccine demand in each time period, the capacity limitations, and the requirements of the medical service level for different population groups.

From the analytical point of view, the model suggested below is an integer-programing problem. It differs from the standard inventory/delivery management problem in several ways. First, we consider three echelons of vaccine distribution and utilization: the DC, clinics, and population groups. Second, we introduce constraints that impose the required level of service and customer satisfaction. And, third, we explicitly introduce the time index in the supply network model reflecting time-varying costs, benefits, and demands.

Table 11.5 Monthly Demand Distribution per Population Subgroup

Clinic Size (i)	Age Group (j)	Sep	Oct	Nov	Dec	Jan	Feb	Mar	Apr
Small	<5	2,010	13,620	11,100	2,520	597	120	30	3
	5–17	2,546	17,252	14,060	3,192	756	152	38	4
	18–49	6,700	45,400	37,000	8,400	1,990	400	100	10
	50–64	5,360	36,320	29,600	6,720	1,592	320	80	8
	>65	11,390	77,180	62,900	14,280	3,383	680	170	17
Medium	<5	12,730	86,260	70,300	15,960	3,781	760	190	19
	5–17	15,276	103,512	84,360	19,152	4,537	912	228	23
	18–49	40,200	272,400	222,000	50,400	11,940	2,400	600	60
	50–64	32,160	217,920	177,600	40,320	9,552	1,920	480	48
	>65	72,360	490,320	399,600	90,720	21,492	4,320	1,080	108
Large	<5	6,030	40,860	33,300	7,560	1,791	360	90	9
	5–17	7,638	51,756	42,180	9,576	2,269	456	114	11
	18–49	20,100	136,200	111,000	25,200	5,970	1,200	300	30
	50–64	16,080	108,960	88,800	20,160	4,776	960	240	24
	>65	36,180	245,160	199,800	45,360	10,746	2,160	540	54

Indices:

j – Customer subgroup index, $j = 1,\ldots, G$
i – Clinic index, $i = 1,\ldots, I$
t – Time index, $t = 1,\ldots, T$

Parameters:

d_{ijt} – demand for vaccine units (doses) in period t by subgroup j in clinic i
h_i^{CL} – clinic inventory holding cost per vaccine unit per time period in clinic i
h^{DC} – DC inventory holding cost per vaccine unit per time period
Π_{jt} – HCO shortage cost per unvaccinated customer in subgroup j in period t
A_{ij} – service cost per customer in subgroup j by clinic i
k^{DC} – cost of purchasing and transporting a vaccine unit from the manufacturer
 to the DC
k_i^{CL} – cost of transporting a vaccine unit from the DC to clinic i
α_{jt} – minimum service level for subgroup j at time t
C_t^{DC}, C_{it}^{CL} – storage capacity at DC and in clinics, respectively, in period t
n_0 – average medical personnel treatment time per customer
N_{it} – medical personnel hours available in clinic i at period t (hours/day)
TQ – total quantity of vaccines purchased from the manufacturer

Decision variables:

I_t – Inventory in DC at the end of period t, $t = 1,\ldots, T$
I_{it} – Inventory in clinic i at the end of period t, $i = 1, \ldots, I, t = 1,\ldots, T$
q_t – Delivery (shipping) quantity of vaccine units from manufacturer to DC in
 period t
q_{it} – Delivery quantity of vaccine units from DC to clinic i in period t
s_{ijt} – Shortages in subgroup j in period t in clinic i
w_{ijt} – Consumption of vaccines linked to group j in clinic i in period t

The min-cost problem: Minimize the total costs:

$$J_{HCO} = \sum_{t=1}^{T} k^{DC} q_t + \sum_{t=1}^{T} h^{DC} I_t$$

$$+ \sum_{t=1}^{T} \sum_{i=1}^{I} k_i^{CL} q_{it} + \sum_{t=1}^{T} \sum_{i=1}^{I} h_i^{CL} I_{it} + \sum_{t=1}^{T} \sum_{i=1}^{I} \sum_{j=1}^{G} \Pi_{jt} s_{ijt} + \sum_{t=1}^{T} \sum_{i=1}^{I} \sum_{j=1}^{G} A_{ij} w_{ijt}$$

subject to
DC inventory balance:

$$I_{t-1} + q_t = I_t + \sum_{i=1}^{I} q_{it}$$

$$t = 1, \ldots, T \tag{11.4}$$

Clinic inventory balance:

$$I_{i,t-1} + q_{it} + \sum_{j=1}^{G} s_{ijt} = I_{it} + \sum_{j=1}^{G} d_{ijt} \; , \; i = 1, \ldots, I, t = 1, \ldots, T \tag{11.5}$$

Consumption balance:

$$w_{ijt} = d_{ijt} - s_{ijt}, i = 1, \ldots, I, t = 1, \ldots, T, j = 1, \ldots, G. \tag{11.6}$$

The minimal service level to subgroup j by time t in terms of vaccine availability (the minimal ratio of aggregated consumption divided by aggregated demand over all clinics and all periods):

$$\frac{\sum_{i-1}^{I} w_{ijt}}{\sum_{i=1}^{I} d_{ijt}} \geq \alpha_{jt} \; , \; j = 1, \ldots, G, t = 1, 2, \ldots, T \tag{11.7}$$

The quantity of vaccines delivered from the manufacturer to the DC is restricted to the total quantity purchased:

$$\sum_{t=1}^{T} q_t = TQ \tag{11.8}$$

Storage capacity constraints in the DC and in the clinics, respectively,

$$I_t \leq C_t^{DC}, \; t = 1, \ldots, T \tag{11.9}$$

$$I_{it} \leq C_{it}^{CL}, \; i = 1, \ldots, I, \; t = 1, \ldots, T \tag{11.10}$$

Medical personnel resource availability in clinic i:

$$\sum_{j=1}^{G} n_0 w_{ijt} \leq N_{it}, i = 1,\ldots,I, t = 1,\ldots,T \tag{11.11}$$

All the inventory, delivery, and consumption variables are non-negative and integer.

11.8.1 What Was the Way to Test/Answer the Hypotheses/Research Questions?

We solved the above mathematical programming problem for real-life data using the commercial software GAMS (www.gams.com).

11.9 What Are the Results and Their Interpretation?

We have applied the mathematical model from the previous section retroactively to the Big Data sets for the CLALIT Health Services, the largest HCO in Israel. We obtained an essential decrease in the VSC size. Whereas the initial four-tier supply chain constructed for real-life data for year 2013 contained 1,262 clinics located in different geographical places serving about one million people grouped into 6,000 population clusters, the reduced (three-tier) SC contained only 26 clinic clusters and 120 population subgroups.

The optimization model above has been formulated on the reduced SC and applied retroactively for the 2013 data. The mathematical programming problem has been solved by the GAMS software and permitted to decrease the annual total costs by 12%. It is worth noticing that the original SC model for the HCO CLALIT contained 6,310 nodes in each of which the information has been collected for 33 time periods (weeks) for the vaccination season of about eight months. The entropic approach permits us to reduce the original six-tier SC to a truncated SC with three tiers only. After reducing and reconfiguring the original network into the reduced three-tier network, the original optimization problem with 208,230 main variables was transformed to the corresponding problem defined for 26 subregions with a total of 4,290 variables. As a result, Big Data sets and problem complexity have been reduced without an essential loss of useful input information. Solving the optimization model on the retro-active CLALIT data of 2013 has led to savings of 12% or about $300,000 in the total costs of the vaccination program in comparison with the real-life annual expenses of 2013.

11.9.1 How Are These Results Meaningful for Organizations and for Future Research?

The analytic entropy-based approach for reducing the size of SC models described in this chapter is general and universal. The same is true for the mathematical programing-based optimization model. In this light, the suggested analytic approaches can be successfully used in wider medical and nonmedical applications.

11.10 Conclusions and Recommendations

11.10.1 Are the Objectives of the Research Achieved?

The objectives of the research have been achieved by using advanced analytics and operational research techniques. The chapter develops an integrated approach for optimizing costs and public benefits of an influenza VSC. The approach includes three stages, which distinguish it from earlier known works. At the first stage, we identify the most significant risk factors and most vulnerable components in a hierarchical VSC using the entropy approach. As a result, at the second stage, we select the most meaningful tiers, reduce the entire SC model, and decrease Big Data sets without an essential loss of meaningful information. At the third stage, we formulate and solve the optimization problem aimed at reducing the total costs in the reduced VSC. We believe that the suggested methodology is universal and applicable for processing and compressing other types of Big Data in different health care SCs.

A challenging problem to be further investigated is the inclusion of governmental structures into the SC model. It is a common practice that governments are reluctant to provide resources before the problem occurs. That is true for investments in infrastructure, education, and health. A solution can be achieved through more active government intervention with which a government can step in and guarantee payments for unused vaccines and buffer stocks. That may help to better balance vaccine supply and demand.

In our future research, we intend to study the latter problem using the analytics tools developed in this chapter. In addition, we plan to accomplish a more scrupulous analysis of links between entropy and costs in medical SCs. In addition, we intend to perform a more sophisticated cost–benefit–risk analysis of the VSCs, taking into account the inherent stochastic behavior of demands within different population groups.

Acknowledgment

The research of the fourth author is supported by the grant of Russian Humanitarian Scientific Fund (no. 14-12-40003a(p)).

References

Allesina, S., Azzi, A., Battini, D. and Regattieri, A., 2010, Performance measurement in supply chains: New network analysis and entropic indexes, *International Journal of Production Research*, 48(8), pp. 2297–2321.

CDC (Centers for Disease Control and Prevention), 2014, *Key factors about seasonal flu vaccine*, Accessed November 29, 2014 at www.cdc.gov/flu/protect/keyfacts.htm.

Chick, S. E., Mamani, H. and Simchi-Levi, D., 2008, Supply chain coordination and influenza vaccination, *Operations Research*, 56, pp. 1493–1506.

Colombo, G. L., Ferro, A., Vinci, M. and Serra, G., 2006, Cost-benefit analysis of influenza vaccination in a public healthcare unit, *Therapeutics and Clinical Risk Management*, 2, pp. 219–226.

Durowoju, O. A., Chan, H. K. and Wang, X., 2012, Entropy assessment of supply chain disruption, *Journal of Manufacturing Technology Management*, 23(8), pp. 998–1014.

Gerdil, C., 2003, The annual production cycle for influenza vaccine, *Vaccine*, 21, pp. 1776–1779.

Herbon, A., Levner, E., Hovav, S. and Lin, S., 2012, Selection of most informative components in risk mitigation analysis of supply networks: An information-gain approach, *International Journal of Innovation, Management and Technology*, 3(3), pp. 267–271.

Isik, F., 2010, An entropy-based approach for measuring complexity in supply chains, *International Journal of Production Research*, 48(12), pp. 3681–3696.

Kogan, K. and Tapiero, C. S., 2007, *Supply chain games. Operations management and risk valuation*, Springer, Berlin.

Levner, E. and Proth, J.-M., 2005, Strategic management of ecological systems: A supply chain perspective, In *Strategic management of marine ecosystems*, edited by E. Levner, I. Linkov, J.-M. Proth. Springer, Berlin, pp. 95–107.

Levner, E., Tell, H., Hovav, S. and Tsadikovich, D., 2012, *Balancing the costs and public benefits of a vaccination program using a supply chain approach*. Poster presented at the INFORMS-2012 conference, Huntington, USA, April 15–17, 2012. Accessed November 29, 2014 at http://meetings2.informs.org/Analytics2012/posters.html.

Liebowitz, J. (ed.), 2013, *Big Data and Business Analytics*, CRC Press, Boca Raton, FL.

Matinrada, N., Roghaniana, E. and Rasib, Z., 2013, Supply chain network optimization: A review of classification, models, solution techniques and future research, *Uncertain Supply Chain Management*, 1, pp. 1–24.

Nichol, K. L., 2008, Efficacy and effectiveness of influenza vaccination, *Vaccine*, 26, pp. 17–22.

Olson, D. L., 2012, *Supply chain risk management: Tools for analysis*. Business Expert Press, New York.

Shannon, C. E., 1951, Prediction and entropy of printed English, *Bell System Technical Journal*, 30(1), pp. 50–64.

Stone, J. V., 2014, *Information Theory: A Tutorial Introduction*, University of Sheffield, Sheffield, UK.

Tang, O. and Musa, S. N., 2010, Identifying risk issues and research advancements in supply chain risk management, *International Journal of Production Economics*, 133(1), pp. 25–34.

Trenor, J., 2004, Weathering the influenza vaccine crisis, *New England Journal of Medicine*, 351(20).

WHO (World Health Organization), 2014, Recommended composition of influenza virus vaccine for use in the 2014–2015 northern hemisphere influenza season, Accessed November 29, 2014 at www.whoint/influenza/vaccines/virus/recommendations/2014 _02recommendation.pdf.

Appendix: List of Abbreviations

CLALIT the name of the health care service organization in Israel
DC distribution center
GAMS the name of a commercial software package
HCO health care organization
SC supply chain
VSC vaccination supply chain

Chapter 12

Sharing Knowledge or Just Sharing Data?

John S. Edwards

Contents

Summary

Advances in technology have made sharing data—even Big Data—very much easier, but does sharing data by itself achieve anything? There is a lack of research into exactly how using analytics pays off and into what needs to be taken into account in order to run an effective analytics program. This chapter examines some of the issues that have to be addressed if analytics and Big Data are to have a positive effect on organizational performance by reviewing the published literature and taking specific examples from the domain of oil and gas exploration and production. The message overall is that technology is not enough;

that knowledge needs to be shared as well as data; and that people, processes, structure, and technology together make up a whole that is much greater than the sum of its parts. Thus, the chapter acts in part as an antidote to the hype that is sometimes written, especially by software vendors, about analytics and Big Data.

12.1 Introduction

It is possible to spend a great deal of money on analytics and Big Data without seeing very much benefit from it, although organizations are naturally reluctant to admit publicly to having done this. In this chapter, we consider the issues that need to be addressed if analytics and Big Data are to have a positive effect on organizational performance.

We start from the position that analytics and Big Data represent evolutionary rather than revolutionary change. We look at where they have come from, why interest in them has grown so much lately, and what implications there are at the organizational level and from a business management perspective. Note that although we use the term *business*, the arguments in this chapter apply just as well to not-for-profit organizations.

The question we consider overall in this chapter is how can we share data, integrate data, and use analytics on that data more effectively so that we end up sharing knowledge not just sharing data?

Our preferred theoretical framework for thinking about this comes from knowledge management (KM) and identifies the three key elements in knowledge sharing—and indeed all of KM—as people, processes, and technology (Edwards 2015), supported by organizational structures:

■ The role of people: collaboration, culture, and change management in using analytics and Big Data
■ The role of processes: effective design, support tools, and workflows
■ The role of organizational and IT networks: enhancing knowledge-sharing capabilities

We cannot cover this entire field in one chapter, so we will be concentrating on the roles of technology and especially of people.

We will start the chapter with a couple of warnings about the big dangers of Big Data—what data and data scientists cannot do—then we will look at some relevant theory. Discussion of the issues follows with examples most often drawn from the domain of oil and gas exploration and production (E&P). The chapter ends with the reflection that future technological developments are unlikely to change the issues substantially.

12.2 The Big Dangers of Big Data

There's one big danger of Big Data analytics that is so obvious that it is often forgotten. The outputs of Big Data analytics can only be based on the data you have got. So you do a test drill and find oil/gas; then you've got the data on that, which is fine. You test drill and don't find any energy sources—not quite so fine as a business prospect, but you still have the data now and for use in the future. You may well be able to get hold of data on where others have found oil/gas and possibly even where they have searched and not found it. But have you got data on where someone should have drilled but no one did?

Nope.

So analytics will always be restricted to those data that someone already thought might be important enough to (a) collect and (b) retain in an accessible format.

The second big danger of Big Data is to regard it only as the concern of data scientists and not of those managing the business. But you do not have to be a data scientist to make sense of what's going on, and data scientists on their own cannot deliver improvements in organizational performance. We explain this in a bit more detail later in the chapter. Analytics and Big Data are all about understanding—making sense of—the target phenomena; whatever the domain is that the data are about. There are different types of understanding, and it isn't possible to substitute one for another. Spender (2015) identified that there are three complementary areas of understanding/knowledge:

- Data (generally objective)
- Meaning (subjective)
- Skilled practice (in the target domain, not in data science)

Analyzing Big Data to deliver an organizational improvement needs an integrated approach addressing all three areas.

12.3 Defining the Key Concepts

There does not seem to be an agreed-upon definition of Big Data. If we look at the evolution of some of the component parts of what is now called Big Data, we see that the term *business intelligence* was first used with its current meaning as long ago as the early 1970s. *Data mining* was a term first used in 1983, but it only really caught on at the start of the 1990s as software for mining data began to become commercially available, around which time the data warehouse had arrived as well. Looking at these dates makes it clear that the "big" in Big Data is a relative term: At the time of this writing, if you can crunch the numbers on your laptop, it isn't Big Data (unless you have a very special laptop). Big Data is often characterized in terms of high values of the three Vs—volume, velocity, and variety—but it still remains a relative term.

Analytics poses a more complex problem even though definitions are easier to find, for example, the commonly-seen split into descriptive, predictive, and prescriptive analytics (Lustig, Dietrich, Johnson and Dziekan 2010). It is not even possible to date the term *analytics* as it has always been used in certain fields (e.g., economics) for what those in other fields would call one particular type of quantitative analysis, and that is where the term came from. If we look at our example domain of oil and gas E&P, we see that analytics has been going on for several decades, although in this specific domain it was once called geostatistics—the analysis of seismic data (and in many E&P organizations, it still is).

Other domains may also have their own specific terms for analytics, but in our opinion, all these terms are really just the current buzzwords for management science as a comparison of definitions (which we do not have room for here) would demonstrate. Management science is an activity that has been going on in organizations since at least the 1930s, if not earlier. Analytics is just, at present, a better brand name for it. The only difference between now and the 1930s is that the scope of analytics is now much wider, in part because of Big Data and in part because of advances in information technology.

The difference Big Data makes is that it brings less structured data into the analytics orbit, adding to the structured, usually numerical data that has been analyzed by computers since the 1950s. This unstructured and semistructured data may include social media, messy text, speech, images, and sensor data. This may require a corresponding expansion in the range of analytics techniques used. Up to now, in E&P these have included causal, physics-based models; statistical models–regression, structural equation modeling; rule induction; machine learning by neural networks or genetic algorithms; and others. Social network analysis is one technique that may become more relevant with such types of data.

12.4 Getting Started with Analytics

Analytics, like any activity in business, except possibly research and development, is only likely to succeed if there is some form of strategy giving it direction—a guiding vision. The organization needs to consider this: What questions would you like answered (better) that you can't answer (well enough) now? To put this another way, "the first question a data-driven organization asks itself is not 'What do we think?' but 'What do we know?'" (McAfee and Brynjolfsson 2012).

Looking for previously published studies in our chosen domain of E&P, we find very few. For Big Data, published examples in the energy sector tend to be mostly further downstream than E&P, such as smart metering of electricity usage. One good example, however, is by Venkoparao, Hota, Rao and Gellaboina (2009), who used video analytics for petroleum flare monitoring. The size, shape, and color of the flame are used to deduce the composition of the gas being flared, and hence give an indication of aspects of the refinery's performance.

The position regarding analytics is similar: Published energy sector examples are again downstream, such as optimizing performance in regulated energy markets, or peripheral to the core business, such as monitoring oil spill effects and pollution. A good example here is that of Fernandes, Vicente and Neves (2009), who used rule induction (the Clementine® software package) to help control refinery waste products.

12.4.1 Knowledge and the Need to Share It

Let's turn our attention now to the wider issue of knowledge rather than analytics or Big Data per se. All organizations, whatever industry sector they are in, have to be concerned with knowledge. Some of those concerns will be general; others will be sector-specific. Characteristics of the E&P industry most relevant to knowledge and its management are the following:

- The need for coordination of many different professional specialists, often working for different organizations
- Coping with the uncertainty of an environment which no one has ever experienced before (such as full-scale drilling and extraction in the Arctic)
- Close public scrutiny

Figure 12.1 shows the knowledge life cycle: the activities that happen to items of knowledge in an organization. First they are either created (within the organization) or acquired (from outside it). Then they go into a cycle of store–use–refine. There are no arrows on that part of the figure as movement between activities may be in either direction. There may be a further final stage to forget or discard the knowledge, but we have omitted that for clarity.

At a more strategic level, another relevant distinction is that between knowledge exploration and knowledge exploitation: "The exploration of new possibilities … the exploitation of old certainties" (March 1991). This balancing of the future and radical change against the present and incremental change is a central concern of business. Fail to do the first one, and the business may have no future if demand for its current products or services declines. Fail to do the second, and it may be bankrupt before the great new ideas can be brought to market. Big Data is very much about exploration: It is concerned with knowledge creation rather than knowledge use. Analytics could be either exploration or exploitation, but is more likely to be exploitation, and then it is more concerned with knowledge use than knowledge creation. The literature on managing knowledge exploration and exploitation suggests that there is a considerable tension between the two (Andriopoulos and Lewis 2009). Interestingly, this is not reflected in the analytics and Big Data literature.

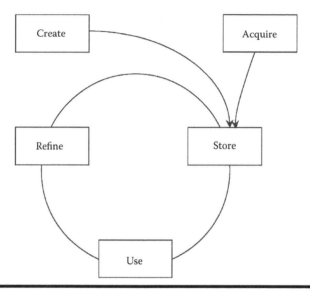

Figure 12.1 Knowledge life cycle. (Modified from J. S. Edwards, Artificial intelligence and knowledge management: How much difference can it really make? In *Proceedings of KMAC2000. Knowledge Management Beyond The Hype: Looking Towards The New Millennium*, Aston University, Birmingham, UK, pp. 136–147. Birmingham, UK: Operational Research Society, 2000.)

12.4.2 Knowledge Sharing: Easier Said Than Done

Most important to note is that knowledge sharing is not an activity in itself and so does not appear explicitly in Figure 12.1. Simply sharing knowledge with no specific purpose is the knowledge management equivalent of sending out junk mail, and it is not likely to deliver benefits to the organization. However, knowledge sharing can be, and usually is, a central element in any or all of knowledge creation, acquisition, use, and refinement and even of knowledge storage (when it is tacit knowledge stored in people's heads rather than explicit knowledge stored in documents, repositories, etc.).

For this reason, knowledge sharing is the most researched topic in knowledge management, both in the E&P industry and more generally. Unfortunately, many people still believe that technology is the answer to all problems of knowledge sharing despite the findings of this extensive research. For example, McDermott (1999) gave a lot of good advice more than 15 years ago summed up in his article's title, "Why Information Technology Inspired but Cannot Deliver Knowledge Management." So, why haven't business managers taken notice of what he (and others) have said? Because technology is *soooo* tempting: We all know people who must have the latest technological gadget as soon as it's on the market, and this behavior transfers over into their professional life, too.

KM researchers have known since at least 1996 that technology is not enough (Tenkasi and Boland 1996). The reason is that knowledge sharing always involves crossing some kind of boundary: There are limits to the use of technology as a boundary spanner whether it is bridging between people, departments, or even organizations. Even though technology is a moving target with ever-increasing capabilities, dialogue between people is an essential additional component in boundary spanning and thus in sharing knowledge. Don't underestimate how much of an obstacle these boundaries can be. Most readers will be familiar with criticisms of "silo-based" organizations. In Spender's terms, only people can add the meaning and skilled practice to whatever the data (even when analyzed) seems to be telling them. Remember, "it's good to talk" as a famous British TV advertisement used to say. As to what happens if people don't talk to each other, there is a classic management science study (Wedley and Ferrie 1978) showing large differences of opinion between analysts (data scientists as they might well now be called) and the managers for whom they worked even about something as fundamental as whether the recommendations of a study were actually implemented.

One issue on which the jury is still out concerns what sort of people the organization most needs to recruit in order to make the most of knowledge arising from Big Data and analytics: insiders (from their own industry sector) or outsiders? Some researchers, such as Waller and Fawcett (2013; "Data scientists need domain knowledge") advocate the insiders, and others favor outsiders ("Often someone coming from outside an industry can spot a better way to use big data than an insider, just because so many new, unexpected sources of data are available"; McAfee and Brynjolfsson 2012). Our experience from other KM initiatives suggests that outsiders may sometimes be helpful, especially for knowledge exploration. This is because they can bring meaning that is not constrained by existing thinking in the domain. However, skilled practice in a domain, by definition, requires insiders, especially if the main driver is knowledge exploitation. So we would expect that industry insiders will form the greater part of the demand. This is related to the question of the extent to which managers can "do it themselves" as far as analytics is concerned. The software is certainly becoming available, but it is debatable whether the average manager's ability to understand numerical data is up to the task even with the latest visualization techniques.

Whoever is involved, training will be needed, but the most effective training may not be what you might expect. Godfrey, Crick and Huang (2014) looked at training engineers to make use of Big Data. They found that an exercise involving the development of processes (systems architecture, if you prefer) was most effective in developing an awareness of the possibilities for Big Data. Remember, we mentioned the role of processes in the introduction? People, processes, and technology are all linked together (Edwards 2015).

So to summarize, knowledge sharing raises three related types of questions. The first is about knowledge: What to share? The second and largest group is about sharing: Who will share? When to share? Why share? Only then can the third type of question be tackled: How to share? Too much emphasis on technology means that the third type is certainly being answered before considering the second group and perhaps even before thinking about the first one!

12.5 Examples of Success and Failure in Knowledge Sharing

In the E&P domain, it took two attempts for the oil company Texaco to get it right as far as knowledge sharing was concerned. According to McDermott (1999), when they first installed IBM (then Lotus) Notes®, it was only used for e-mail despite the extensive document-sharing and other collaboration facilities the software included. "Not until they found an urgent need to collaborate and changed the way they worked together, did they use Notes effectively" (p. 104).

Vianello and Ahmed (2012) examined the sharing of drilling rig knowledge. They studied how the knowledge arising during the installation, commissioning, and operation of a drilling rig is transferred in a project involving building four rigs to the same design. They were particularly interested in the balance between the transfer of tacit knowledge, which is done by interactions between people, and that of explicit knowledge, codified into documents or repositories. Both the authors and the rig staff expected beforehand that knowledge transfer within one rig would turn out to be mainly explicit (thus codified) and transfer of knowledge across projects (e.g., to a different series of rigs) would be mainly face-to-face (thus personal). They found the opposite: much more personalization on the rig and codified documents used more for transfer across projects even though the documents did not distinguish well between the short-term local issues and the longer-term broader ones that those on other projects really needed to know about. This explained why the wider sharing tended to be ineffective as crucial elements of the context were being lost despite an apparent willingness to share both data and knowledge.

Schlumberger has been active in KM in oilfields for many years. This includes making extensive use of what we would now refer to as Big Data. However, Etkind, Bennaceur, Dmec and Luppens (2003) point out that connecting people to information, as they call this activity, is only one of many connections (including connecting to other people, to communities of practice, to knowledge, to learning) offered by Schlumberger's KM systems. The most crucial factor in the success of Schlumberger's KM, however, according to Etkind et al. (2003), has been the organization's knowledge-sharing culture.

12.6 Conclusions

Analytics can identify useful patterns and relationships, but they must be based on solid and reliable foundations: Garbage in, garbage out is as true in the era of Big

Data as it ever was. And only people can decide which relationships are truly useful to the business. Sharing data, even integrating data, will only help your business if the purpose for the sharing or integration is clear; it is not just a question of technology or algorithms.

The crucial need is for shared understanding, first of terminology, then of interpretation (the most difficult part of boundary spanning), then of action.

Big Data and analytics are undeniably useful, but their contribution has to be given meaning by people, all the way from setting a guiding vision through to understanding outputs. This then needs to be filtered through and incorporated into the skilled practice of the people and the organization. Thus, the understanding moves from terminology, to interpretation, then to action. Future technological developments in how to acquire, store, and analyze Big Data are most unlikely to affect any of these arguments. So they remain valid for the foreseeable future of analytics and Big Data.

We began with a question: How can we share data, integrate data, and use analytics on that data more effectively so that we end up sharing knowledge, not just sharing data? This could be rephrased as how to really make a difference with analytics. Our answer to both questions is simple to state, but not so simple to achieve: Knowledge sharing, not just data sharing, has to become part of your organization's core values and culture.

References

Andriopoulos, C. and Lewis, M. W., 2009, Exploitation-exploration tensions and organizational ambidexterity: Managing paradoxes of innovation. *Organization Science, 20*(4), pp. 696–717.

Edwards, J. S., 2000, Artificial intelligence and knowledge management: How much difference can it really make? In *Proceedings of KMAC2000. Knowledge Management Beyond The Hype: Looking Towards The New Millennium*, Aston University, Birmingham, UK, pp. 136–147. Birmingham, UK: Operational Research Society.

Edwards, J. S., 2015, Business processes and knowledge management. In M. Khosrow-Pour (Ed.), *Encyclopedia of information science and technology* (Third ed., pp. 4491–4498). Hershey, PA: Information Science Reference.

Etkind, J., Bennaceur, K., Dmec, M. and Luppens, C., 2003, Knowledge portals support widely distributed oilfield projects. In *Proceedings of IEEE International Professional Communication Conference*, Orlando, FL, pp. 189–200. New York: IEEE.

Fernandes, A. V., Vicente, H. and Neves, J., 2009, Solving challenging problems in the oil industry using artificial intelligence based tools. In *Proceedings of 7th Industrial Simulation Conference 2009*, Loughborough, UK, pp. 325–331. Ghent, Belgium: EUROSIS.

Godfrey, P., Crick, R. D. and Huang, S., 2014, Systems thinking, systems design and learning power in engineering education. *International Journal of Engineering Education, 30*(1), pp. 112–127.

Lustig, I., Dietrich, B., Johnson, C. and Dziekan, C., 2010, The analytics journey, *Analytics* (November/December), pp. 11–18.

March, J. G., 1991, Exploration and exploitation in organizational learning. *Organization Science, 2*(1), pp. 71–87.

McAfee, A. and Brynjolfsson, E., 2012, Big data: The management revolution. *Harvard Business Review, 90*(10), pp. 60–68.

McDermott, R., 1999, Why information technology inspired but cannot deliver knowledge management. *California Management Review, 41*(4), pp. 103–117.

Spender, J. C., 2015, Knowledge management: Origins, history, and development. In E. Bolisani and M. Handzic (Eds.), *Advances in knowledge management: Celebrating twenty years of research and practice* (pp. 3–23). Switzerland: Springer International Publishing.

Tenkasi, R. V. and Boland, R. J., 1996, Exploring knowledge diversity in knowledge intensive firms: A new role for information systems. *Journal of Organizational Change Management, 9*(1), pp. 79–91.

Venkoparao, V. G., Hota, R. N., Rao, V. S. and Gellaboina, M. K., 2009, Flare monitoring for petroleum refineries. In *Proceedings of ICIEA: 2009 4th IEEE Conference on Industrial Electronics and Applications*, Vols 1–6, Xian, P. R. China, pp. 3013–3018. New York: IEEE.

Vianello, G. and Ahmed, S., 2012, Transfer of knowledge from the service phase: A case study from the oil industry. *Research in Engineering Design, 23*(2), pp. 125–139.

Waller, M. A. and Fawcett, S. E., 2013, Data science, predictive analytics, and big data: A revolution that will transform supply chain design and management. *Journal of Business Logistics, 34*(2), pp. 77–84.

Wedley, W. C. and Ferrie, A. E. J., 1978, Perceptual differences and effects of managerial participation on project implementation. *Journal of the Operational Research Society, 29*(3), pp. 199–204.

Index

Page numbers followed by f and t indicate figures and tables, respectively.